Mistakable French

Mistakable French

Faux Amis and Key Words

Philip Thody & Howard Evans

HIPPOCRENE BOOKS
New York

First published in Great Britain 1985
by The Athlone Press Ltd
1 Park Drive, London NW11 7SG
and 165 First Avenue, Atlantic Highlands, NJ 07716
Copyright © Philip Thody and Howard Evans 1985
Paperback reprinted 1985, 1986, 1991, 1995
Hippocrene Books edition 1998
ISBN 0-7818-0649-6

Printed in the United States of America.

Contents

Introduction

'If you see two words that look the same in French and English, then watch out. They almost certainly mean different things.' Quite right: and such words are known as *faux amis*, 'false friends'. Thus *des coups de téléphone abusifs* doesn't mean telephone calls in which you insult people. It refers to excessive or improper use of the telephone, as when private calls are made from the office without paying. *Sa santé s'altère* isn't just that his/her health is changing. It means it is changing for the worse.

This phenomenon has not gone unnoticed, and the Selective Reading List on page 209 lists a number of books which have dealt with it from an essentially linguistic point of view. Our aim in this book is somewhat different, and can be summed up in Wittgenstein's famous *évidence* (see that entry) that the meaning of a word is its use. For usage is a result of the way people use a word in a particular social and historical context, and although *laïque* and lay are etymologically the same, the cultural resonances which each word has in its own language are very different. Because of the way French society developed in the nineteenth century, *laïque* means secular, especially when talking about schools, and does so in the slightly aggressive way in which the National Secular Society proclaims by its title that it has little time for the Church of England as by law established.

This difference of meaning cannot be fully grasped unless one knows something about the conflict between Republicanism and the Roman Catholic Church which led to the establishment in France, in 1881, of a wholly secular system of public education. Our aim is to provide such information by placing words such as *laïque* in their social and historical context, and we hope that comparable entries in other sections of this book will enable English-speaking readers to avoid the mistake of thinking that *le droit commun* is the same thing as Common Law, which is more accurately rendered as *le droit coutumier*, or of imagining that *une école libre* is one where you do not have to pay fees. As the entry for *libre* in Section IV points out, the meaning of the term *école libre* is quite the opposite. Because it used to mean a school free from State control, and therefore not financed by the taxpayer, you do in fact have to pay fees if you wish your children to attend it.

It is because we think that *faux amis* of this kind can be explained only by being placed in context that we have divided our book into sections. We naturally realize that some of our classifications might strike the alert reader as a shade arbitrary, and can see that *un avertissement* (a warning, not an advertisement, which is *une annonce publicitaire, une réclame* or *de la publicité*) could just have easily figured under Section III, which deals with Economics, Industry and Agriculture, rather than in Section II, with its title of History and Politics. We have also found it necessary to provide entries for some words (*action*, for example) in more than one section, and are acutely aware that none of our entries exhausts all the actual or potential meanings of the words under discussion. This book should therefore be used in combination with one of the dictionaries mentioned in the Selective Reading List.

Not even the best of dictionaries, however, is always an adequate guide when it comes to dealing with institutions such as *les Grandes Ecoles* or *la Cour des Comptes*, or with socio-professional categories such as *les artisans* or *les professions libérales*. While not *faux amis* in the strict sense of the word, terms such as these can lead to misunderstanding, and need to be looked at carefully by anyone trying to find out how French society works. The title of our book refers to such terms as 'key words', and readers will note that we have also included entries on a number of English and American words – degree, for example, in IV, or john, in VII – which occasionally cause problems for students of French. Neither will certain readers fail to notice that we have not included every single word which could be classified as a *faux ami*. A. list of all the words which are misleadingly or interestingly different in French and English would stretch from Dover to Calais and back again.

Our book also differs from the normal dictionary, as well as from other studies of *les faux amis*, by being occasionally subjective. Philip Thody (= P.T.) has not always tried to disguise the fascinated hate-love relationship which links him to that curious country where they call a dinner jacket *un smoking* and summon up terrifying but quite non-existent dangers in the countryside by describing a clay-pigeon shoot as *un ball-trap*. Howard Evans (= H.E.) is equally conscious of how a *Girondin* (see *jacobin* in II) suspicion of Paris has shaped some of his contributions, and we both realize that not everyone will share our presuppositions about French history and society.

For our vision of contemporary France has been shaped by our interest in a number of specific issues: the conflicts stemming from the secularization of France in the nineteenth century; the defeat of 1940 and the experience of occupation; the Algerian war and the establishment of the Fifth Republic; and France's place in the European

Community. A comparable study by a left-wing sympathizer would doubtless dwell more fully on the defeat of the *Commune* in 1871, the Popular Front of 1936–7 and the student rebellion of 1968. We nevertheless hope that our entries on words such as *Brumaire, gaullien* and *jacobin* – to say nothing of *ordre moral, républicain* and *patriote* – will be sufficiently neutral to satisfy, as the French would say, *ceux qui viennent de tous les horizons politiques et qui appartiennent à toutes les différentes familles spirituelles* – people of all political persuasions and ideological sympathies. We tried to keep Section I as short as possible, and to separate Administration and Law. Our failure is doubtless significant. Like Mr Dick's King Charles's Head, they were difficult to control.

We hope that the publication of this book will inspire one of our French colleagues to publish a companion volume (*un livre qui fera pendant à celui-ci*) in which she or he writes about those aspects of English-speaking society which we, as native speakers of English, have always regarded as so natural as to need no comment. What you most reveal in writing about a culture which is not your own, and which you therefore always see from the outside, is yourself. In spite of the apparent impersonality of most of the information it provides, this book is also a linguistic self-portrait. It is an account of what English-speaking culture has taught us to regard as natural. What we should most like to see now is a comparably innocent piece of self-description provided by a Frenchman writing about what General de Gaulle always used to call *les Anglo-Saxons*.

Philip Thody
Howard Evans

Acknowledgements

Our awareness of the need for a book such as this has become acute not only in our undergraduate teaching but also in the twice-yearly courses in Administrative, Legal and Technical French which the French Department of the University of Leeds has been running since 1973 for senior British Civil Servants involved in negotiations with the French authorities.

We are grateful to our many French friends and acquaintances who, over the years and often unwittingly, have provided us with the material for this book. Our special thanks are due to Jacques Magnet, *Conseiller référendaire à la Cour des Comptes,* for his help on several questions, and to Michelle Pépratx-Evans, *Agrégée de l'Université,* for her many comments on an earlier version of the typescript. The meticulous assistance generously given by Gwilym Rees, sometime Senior Lecturer in French at the University of Leeds, in the preparation of the final typescript and with the proof-reading has been invaluable. Lorraine Winter and Marie-France Mackie have typed the successive versions of this book with unfailing care and good humour.

However, in the time-honoured way, we accept full responsibility for the errors and shortcomings in this book.

How to use this book

Within each Section the entries have been arranged in alphabetical order of the head-words that introduce each of the entries. However, entries often contain explanations of other useful words and expressions related to the head-word; e.g. under *fermier* in Section III: *exploitant agricole, paysan, cultivateur* and *éleveur*.

An Index of Head-Words, giving the part of speech and the Section in which the corresponding entry will be found, e.g. conséquent, adj III, is provided on pp. 213–24.

Cross-references to head-words in other Sections are marked by an asterisk (*).

We have adopted the following conventional abbreviations:

adj.	– adjective
adv.	– adverb
fam.	– familiar
n.f.	– noun, feminine
n.f.p.	– noun, feminine, plural
n.m.	– noun, masculine
n.m.p.	– noun, masculine, plural
US	– American English

The vast majority of our head-words are French words or expressions. However, in a few cases (e.g. degree, old boy network, suspicious) we have felt it more appropriate, given the subject-based arrangement we have adopted, to place entries under English head-words in italics.

The translations of the passages used as illustrative material are our own, and since they aim at bringing out the meaning and usage of the word or expression under discussion are intentionally literal rather than elegant.

This book is intended to be used in conjunction with and not instead of a dictionary, and for all the meanings of the words we have included reference should be made to one of the standard dictionaries listed in the Selective Reading List on pp. 209–12.

I Administration, Law and the Armed Forces

abusif, adj. – not abusive (*injurieux*), but incorrect, illegal, unauthorized, excessive, as in *Le Chef de l'Etat interprète la Constitution de façon abusive, une extension abusive du concept de démocratie,* and *une hausse abusive des tarifs** (an excessive increase in public service charges). The verb *abuser de* and the noun *un abus* have similar meanings; thus, *abuser de ses droits* (make unauthorized use of one's rights), *abus de pouvoir* (by, say, a civil servant), *abus de langage* (distorting the meanings of words), and (in the Penal Code) *abus de confiance* (breach of trust, confidence trick). But note also the expression *si je ne m'abuse* (if I am not mistaken). See also ABUSIF in II.

acte, n.m. – note, in a legal context, the meaning of document, deed, certificate (*acte de vente, de décès,* etc.); an Act, as in an Act of Parliament, is not *un acte* but *une loi.* See also LECTURE in IV.

actuel, adj. – not actual (*réel, véritable*), but present-day, as in *les problèmes actuels. Les actualités* are the Radio or TV news. *Actuellement* thus means 'at the moment', 'right now', 'currently' or 'nowadays', and 'he's not actually here at the moment' may be rendered by *il n'est pas là en ce moment.*

adjudant, n.m. – not the Adjutant, in the sense of an officer in the British Army who assists the Commanding Officer in his administrative duties and is the general Unit dogsbody or drudge (*homme à tout faire, nègre, factotum*). The Adjutant is *le major* (see below, MAJOR). *L'adjudant* is the equivalent both in rank and mythology of the Sergeant-Major; in French slang he is called *le juteux* or *l'adjupète* (from *péter,* to fart).

administrer, v. – as in English, remembering Napoléon I's comment, *on ne gouverne bien que de loin, on n'administre bien que de près* (To govern properly, you need to be some distance away. To administer, you have to be close at hand) and his definition of the functions of the *préfet* (see below) as providing *tout ce qui tient à la fortune publique, à la prospérité nationale et au repos des administrés* – everything relating to the public weal, national prosperity and the tranquillity of those administered. The past participle *administrés* is properly untranslatable into English, and might also be seen as having unfortunate overtones in a democracy (see SUBJECT in II). One of Alphonse Daudet's *Lettres de mon moulin* describes *Le Sous-Préfet aux champs* as preparing a speech beginning *Messieurs et chers administrés,* and this phrase is still used by French *Préfets, Conseillers généraux* (see below, CONSEIL GÉNÉRAL) and *Maires** when addressing their flock. The avowed intention of successive French governments in recent years has been *d'associer les administrés à l'action administrative.* Boillot says that in French the word *administration, employé au sens absolu, a le sens de 'administration de l'Etat'.* The American 'the Reagan administration' is *le gouvernement Reagan.* See also below, POUVOIRS PUBLICS. But in business, *le Conseil d'administration* is the Board of Directors. 'To get a seat on the Board' is *entrer au conseil d'administration,* a member of the Board is *un administrateur. Il est administrateur de plusieurs sociétés* means he has a seat on a number of Boards of Directors. In Zola's *La Bête humaine* the parthenophilic Grandmorin, murdered by Roubaud in Chapter 3, is an *administrateur de société,* but not the Chairman and Managing Director, who is the *Président*-Directeur* *Général.* The head of a nationalized firm is *l'Administrateur Général.*

affecter, v., **affectation,** n.f. – in an administrative context, to assign or to post. *Il a obtenu l'affectation qu'il cherchait. Il est maintenant en poste à Bruxelles.* Also to allocate (funds). *Les crédits affectés à l'Education nationale sont nettement insuffisants* (grossly inadequate).

agenda, n.m. – not the agenda (*l'ordre du jour*), but a diary in the sense of what has to be done. A diary of things done or thoughts thought is *un journal.*

agent, n.m. – among its meanings note that of policeman (*agent de ville; agent de la circulation* – traffic policeman) and of public employee (*agent de l'Etat; agent des collectivités locales* – local authority employee).

agglomération, n.f. – an urban area, and also, especially in the context of the Highway Code, *Le Code de la Route,* a built-up area.

agréer, v., **agrément,** n.m. – not so much to agree (which is *être d'accord avec, approuver, donner son aval à,* as in *le comité a approuvé, a donné son aval aux projets formulés par le sous-comité* – the Committee gave formal approval to the proposals put forward by the Sub-Committee) as to give formal recognition to. *Un traducteur agréé par le tribunal* (see below, TRIBUNAL) is a translator recognized and accepted by the court. Also used in the formula for ending letters, *Je vous prie d'agréer, cher monsieur, l'expression de mes sentiments les plus distingués,* corresponding to Yours faithfully. There is no easy equivalent in French to the three levels (Dear Sir – Yours faithfully or truly; Dear Mr Jones – Yours sincerely; Dear Bill – Yours ever) which make letter-writing so simple in English. You don't write *Cher Monsieur Dupont* but *Monsieur* or *Cher monsieur.* When writing to someone very much above you – a Minister, say, or *le Conservateur* de la Bibliothèque Nationale* – you end *Je vous prie d'agréer, Monsieur le Ministre, Monsieur le Conservateur en chef, l'expression de ma haute considération.* To a less august superior, *l'expression de mes sentiments les plus respectueux* is best. If you are a gentleman, you can't go wrong with *mes sentiments les plus distingués,* but make sure you use *je vous prie* and not *veuillez* when writing to a lady: *Je vous prie d'agréer, chère madame, l'expression de mes sentiments les plus respectueux et de mes hommages les plus sincères.* A lady should not convey *hommages* to a gentleman or, in formal correspondence, the expression of her *sentiments. L'agrément* is formal authorization, but also pleasant, attractive features, as in *les agréments de la vie à la campagne,* the advantages of living in the country. *Un désagrément* is an unpleasant feature, annoyance, trouble, whereas a disagreement is *une différence d'opinion, une dispute, une querelle* or, in a legal or diplomatic context, *un différend.* I showed my disagreement, *Je lui ai montré que je n'étais pas d'accord.*

amiable, adj. – and in the expression *à l'amiable,* by mutual consent, without recourse to litigation or arbitration. Thus one has, in the context of the restructuring of French agriculture, *l'échange amiable des terres.* Note also *une vente aux enchères publiques et amiables,* a public auction. Amiable is *aimable* or *gentil.*

ancien, adj. – not only former, as in *l'Association des anciens combattants,* the French equivalent of the British Legion, but also senior. Hence *l'ancienneté,* seniority, and in the Civil Service (*la fonction publique* – see below, FONCTION), *l'avancement à l'ancienneté,* promotion by seniority, as distinct from *l'avancement au choix,* more rapid promotion based on the mark returned annually by one's superior (*la notation*). In the teaching profession *la notation* is based in part on the Inspector's report. See ACADÉMIE in IV.

application, n.f. – not what one submits when trying to get a job. The term for this is *poser sa candidature* or *formuler une demande d'emploi. Application* means diligence, attention to the task in hand. In the educational world, 'putting in an application for a job' is a less frequent activity than in Britain or the United States. In France, you do not apply for a specific post. You are appointed (*nommé*) to a school by the Ministry of Education or *le Recteur,* and this school may well be in an area where you do not want to live. See ACADÉMIE and DEGREE in IV.

apprécier, v. – can mean appreciate in the ordinary sense (*J'apprécie toutes ses qualités*) and in the financial one (*Le dollar s'est encore apprécié sur le marché des changes**, the dollar has gone up again), but its first meaning is to take account of or to pass an opinion on. In Camus's *L'Etranger,* the *procureur** who is acting for *Le Ministère Public* (see below, AVOCAT) in trying to prove Meursault's guilt and have him sentenced to death declares that *les jurés apprécieront* (will take due note of) the fact that the accused had drunk coffee in the presence of his mother's dead body. When François Mitterrand appeared on BBC television in September 1981, he replied to a question about the British Labour Party's policy on nuclear disarmament by saying *Je me garderai de toute appréciation de l'attitude de mes amis britanniques dans ce domaine.* The sub-titles correctly translated this as: 'I shall refrain from expressing an opinion on my British friends' attitude on this matter.' Thus note *c'est une question d'appréciation* or *préférer l'un à l'autre relève d'une appréciation personnelle* as meaning that it is a question of personal judgement. *Les hausses de prix ne doivent pas être appréciées sur un mois, mais sur l'année* is a claim that price increases must not be judged over a period of a month but over a whole year.

arabe, adj. – note the expression *le téléphone arabe* for the British English 'bush telegraph' or grapevine, the rapid dissemination of news, especially in a large organization, by techniques of communication mysterious to the outsider.

arguer, v., **argument,** n.m. – as in putting forward an argument but not as in a quarrel, *une dispute, une querelle. Une discussion* implies a degree of acrimony lacking in the English 'discussion'.

arrêt, n.m. – a judgement or legal ruling by a higher court. *Une maison d'arrêt* is a prison.

arrêté, n.m. – an administrative decision, *un arrêté ministériel, préfectoral, municipal.*

arrêter, v. – to stop, or arrest, but also, in an administrative context, to decide upon, to fix. *Arrêter les modalités d'un examen,* to make detailed arrangements for an examination. *Le gouvernement s'est réuni pour arrêter les nouvelles dispositions* (see below) *en matière de sécurité,* the government met to decide upon the new security measures.

assigner, v., **assignation,** n.f. – as well as to assign (more frequently *affecter* – see above – or *allouer*), means to summon someone to appear in court as defendant or witness. *Une assignation* is a summons. The words *citer* and *citation* are also sometimes used with this legal meaning. Note also the legal terms *assigner à résidence*, to oblige someone to live in a certain place, and *assigner en référé*, to seek an injunction against.

assistante sociale, n.f. – occasionally masculine, of course, but social workers tend to be women in France as well as in Britain. Recently, the term *travailleur social* has come to have this meaning.

assister, v., **assistance,** n.f. – although *la non-assistance à personne en danger* is a punishable offence in French law, *assister à* usually means to be present at, and *l'assistance* those present. *L'Assistance publique* (now *l'Aide sociale*) means Public Assistance (now Social Security and Welfare).

assumer, v. – not to assume in the sense of *supposer*. 'I assume you know that' is *je suppose, je présume, que vous savez que,* while *assumer ses responsabilités* is to take on one's responsibilities.

assurer, v. – as in English, and to insure, as when, in a wine-growing area, *une Compagnie d'Assurances* will offer you *une police* d'assurance contre la grêle*, a policy insuring you against the risks of hailstorms. Also means to provide, as in *le service d'autocars est assuré tous les jours ouvrables* (working days) *mais non pas les jours fériés* (public holidays).

auditeur, n.m. – a listener (*un auditeur libre* at university is a student who attends lectures but does not intend to sit the corresponding examinations) or a junior rank in *le Conseil d'Etat* (see below); but not an auditor, *un expert-comptable*.

audition, n.f. – as well as the meanings of audition and musical performance (*la première audition de la Symphonie Héroïque de Beethoven eut lieu en août 1804,* the first performance of Beethoven's Eroica Symphony took place in August 1804), note the expression *l'audition des témoins par le juge d'instruction,* the questioning of the witnesses by the examining magistrate. See below, AVOCAT, INSTRUCTION, MAGISTRAT.

avis, n.m. – in addition to its everyday meaning of view or position (*Quel est votre avis? A mon avis . . .*) this word means an official announcement (as in a newspaper, *des avis d'obsèques,* funeral announcements), as well as a formal opinion, as in *la Commission,* *consultée, a émis un avis favorable/défavorable,* the Commission has been consulted and has come out in favour/against. *Aviser* may be to inform, not to warn, which is *avertir.* Advice, to advise are perhaps more safely rendered by *un conseil, conseiller.*

avocat, n.m., **avoué,** n.m. – the important distinction in the French legal profession is between those who represent the interests of their clients and those who represent the State. Those who represent the State do so as judges, as prosecuting counsel/US attorneys or as custodians of the public interest in civil matters.

Thus an *avocat,* in a criminal case, unless he is representing *la partie civile* (see below) always appears for the defence. As a member of *une profession libérale*,* he receives fees (*des honoraires*) from his client unless the latter is entitled to legal aid (*l'aide judiciaire*). Until 1976, there were two separate professions, that of *avoué,* who prepared clients' cases before a trial (the role of the English solicitor) and that of *avocat,* who defended the clients' interests before the courts (the role of the English barrister). In 1976 the two professions were merged into the single profession of *avocat,* the only exception being in the Appeal Courts, where there are still *des avoués à la Cour d'appel,* who prepare appeals.

Unlike the English barrister, the *avocat* cannot be retained to represent the interests of the State. This is done by the *Procureur de la République,* Public Prosecutor, who is a salaried employee of the State and a member of the *Parquet* (see below), or *Ministère public,* the body of magistrates responsible for the observance of the law and the main-tenance of public order. The *Avocat Général* is the immediate subordin-ate of the *Procureur Général,* the chief Prosecuting Counsel for the State. However, in the *Cour de Justice de la Communauté Européenne,* the *Avocat Général* is the lawyer who represents the interests of the Community in general in advising the court as to which decisions it should take. In a criminal case, the *procureur* delivers *un réquisitoire,* in which he tries to prove the guilt of the accused while at the same time suggesting what sentence should be imposed. The *avocat* presents *une plaidoirie,* in which he seeks either to establish his client's innocence or to put forward extenuating circumstances, *des circonstances atténuantes.* Wit-nesses (*des témoins*) are called during *l'audition* (see above), and these may be *des témoins à charge* (witnesses for the prosecution) or *des témoins à décharge* (witnesses for the defence). The word *réquisitoire* is also used in a wider context to describe a detailed criticism of a person or policy, and the reply to such an attack is known as *un plaidoyer.* See also below, ÉVIDENCE, INSTRUCTION, MAGISTRAT, NOTAIRE.

bail, n.m. – not bail (*une caution*). See BAIL in III.

barge, n.f. – a flat-bottomed military landing-craft. A barge is *une péniche,* and a bargee *un batelier* or *un marinier.*

bombardement, n.m. – bombing as well as shelling.

box, n.m. – as in *le box des accusés,* the dock (also *le banc des accusés*). Note, however, that the witness-box is *la barre des témoins. Un box* also means a lock-up garage, but a box in the theatre is *une loge* or *une avant-scène.*

bribe, n.f. – not a bribe *(un pot-de-vin),* but a fragment (of music, of conversation).

brief – *un dossier.* To be well briefed, know one's brief, *avoir une bonne connaissance de ses dossiers.* See below, DOSSIER.

cabinet, n.m. – has a much wider meaning than in English. Thus *le cabinet du juge d'instruction* (the examining magistrate's office), *un cabinet de notaire* (lawyer's office), *de médecin* (doctor's surgery/US office), *d'agent immobilier* (estate agent's office). See also CABINET in II and LOO in VII.

calendrier, n.m. – not only a calendar but also a schedule of times by which certain things have to be done. In this usage *calendrier* is thus very close to *échéancier* (list of due dates), since the Roman settlement day was the calenda, or first day of each month, and *une échéance* is the date at which a loan, or an agreed interest payment on a loan, has to be repaid; *l'échéance des primes* d'assurance* is the date on which insurance premiums fall due. When a companion on a country walk drew Balzac's attention to the discrepancy between his view of humanity and the obviously happy family party on the front lawn of a *château,* Balzac replied: *Oui, sans doute*, ils sont heureux. Mais ils ont certainement des échéances à payer,* Yes, I suppose they are happy, but they certainly have bills to pay. If one is paying off e.g. a mortgage *(un prêt immobilier* or *une hypothèque* – see MORTGAGE in IX) by monthly payments, these are *des mensualités.* By extension, *une échéance* is a deadline, as in *c'est un bon journaliste; il respecte toujours les échéances.*

caractérisé, adj. – well marked, definite. *Une fraude* caractérisée* is a clear case of fraud.

carton, n.m. – cardboard or a cardboard box. Note especially *les cartons du Ministère,* the cardboard boxes in which documents are filed. *Le Petit Robert* actually gives the example *son dossier* (his file – see below) *dort dans les cartons du Ministère* (is comfortably asleep in the Ministry's cupboards) as a phrase so familiar that it cannot be attributed to any specific author.

casser, v. – as well as to break, means to quash, as in *casser pour vice de forme,* to quash on a technicality. The French equivalent of the British House of Lords is, from this point of view, *la Cour de Cassation,* which is the final court of appeal for both civil and criminal procedure. Note, however, that when *la Cour de Cassation* quashes a verdict, the case is not closed. A retrial is ordered in a different court (of equivalent standing) from that before which the original trial was held. The supreme court for administrative law is *le Conseil d'Etat* (see below).

cautionner, v. – not to caution (*prévenir* – see below – though French law seems to know no equivalent to the British 'I caution you that anything you may say', etc.) but to guarantee. To be let off with a caution is *s'en tirer avec une réprimande. Etre libéré sous caution or être remis en liberté provisoire* is to be let out on bail. See CAUTION in III.

centrale, n.f. – either an electricity-generating station or a national association of trade unions (see SYNDICAT in III) or one of the largest of the engineering *Grandes Ecoles**, the *Ecole centrale des Arts et Manufactures.* This institution is also known as *Piston* (from the piston of an engine), another opportunity for people to be *spirituels** since *avoir du piston,* or *se faire pistonner* means to have pull, in the sense of influence.

Chancellerie, n.f. – in addition to meaning the chancery, the administrative offices of an Embassy, is often used to designate the French Ministry of Justice. The Justice Minister, *le Ministre de la Justice,* also holds the title of *Garde des Sceaux* (literally, Keeper of the Seals).

charge, n.f. – occasionally has the English sense of accusation. But see also below, INCULPATION. Note *un témoin à charge,* a witness for the prosecution, *à décharge,* for the defence. Many other meanings, including *cinq enfants à charge,* five children to feed, *des personnes à charge,* dependants. See CHARGE in III.

chemise, n.f. – not only a shirt, also a folder for holding papers. A clip-board, *une planchette porte-papiers.* The file itself is *un dossier* (see below).

circulaire, n.f. – a circular, feminine because of *une lettre circulaire.*

collectif, adj. – frequently used where English has the term public, e.g. *les dépenses collectives*, public expenditure. As a noun, and in a budgetary context, it means supplementary estimates. *Une collectivité* is a group of people or a community (in the broad sense), and *les collectivités territoriales* are the units into which France is divided: *communes* – see MAIRE in II, *départements* – see below, and *régions*.

collégial, adj. – most frequently used not in an educational context but in a legal, administrative or religious one to indicate that decisions taken by a group of people are joint decisions for which responsibility is collective. Thus in the higher law courts in France, where several judges sit together, *la cour rend un jugement collégial;* in the Roman Catholic Church there is *le collège des cardinaux*, which makes *une élection collégiale* of the Pope. *La collégialité de la Commission de la Communauté européenne* is a famous phrase in Brussels to indicate a collective decision by the Commission.

commando, n.m. – not a soldier specially trained for dangerous operations, but a group or unit of such soldiers. The word is also used nowadays for groups of terrorists, as in *un commando de terroristes s'est emparé de l'ambassade*, a group of terrorists has occupied the embassy.

communal, adj. – not communal (*commun*) but belonging to the *commune*, the smallest unit of local government in France. Thus, the communal bathroom shared by the tenants of a house is *la salle de bains commune*, whereas *le lavoir communal* is the local authority wash-house where in the remoter country areas people may still be seen washing their clothes by hand.

compétence, n.f., **compétent**, adj. – not only competence and competent, but also having the authority to decide something. Thus *la répartition des compétences* is the distribution of responsibilities.

complaint – *une plainte* or *une réclamation*, but *Le Service des Réclamations* summons up a very different vision from the plaintive, semi-apologetic Complaints Department in Britain; the French evokes an overcrowded office full of indignant citizens, *fiers de leur bon droit* (knowing that they have right on their side). However, to make a complaint against, say, one's superior is *formuler une plainte,* and to complain in law (to the police or to *le Procureur de la République*) is *porter plainte*. If the author of the alleged offence is unknown, *on porte plainte contre X* (see below, 'X'). *Une complainte* is a lament, in poetry or music.

compléter, v. – to supplement, to make up (a collection, etc.), to finish off or put the finishing touches to a piece of work: to complete can usually be rendered more appropriate by *achever**. *Il faut des aides communautaires pour compléter les efforts nationaux dans le domaine de l'agriculture*, Community subsidies are necessary to supplement national efforts in the agriculture field. The adjective *complet* (for a bus, a hotel) means full.

Conseil constitutionnel, n.m. – the body responsible for ensuring the legality, *la régularité**, of elections, and for expressing an opinion (*émettre un avis*) as to whether Bills presented to Parliament do or do not conflict with the Constitution of France.

Conseil d'Etat, n.m. – the highest court for *le droit administratif*, administrative law. It deals with matters on which citizens consider that they have been victims of illegal action by the administrative services of the State, and with conflicts (*litiges*) between civil servants and their Ministry. It also has the task of giving advice on government Bills (*des projets de loi*) and Bills from Private Members (*des propositions de loi*) *pour les rendre plus conformes tant au droit préexistant qu'à la volonté réelle mais mal exprimée de leurs auteurs,* to bring them into line with the law as it already exists and with the real but imperfectly expressed intentions of their authors (*Les Cahiers Français*, 156–7, September–December 1973). There are a number of different sections. The Prime Minister is *le Président du Conseil d'Etat,* and *le Vice-Président* – who, since it is primarily a court of law, is a *magistrat* (see below) – is traditionally considered as *le plus haut fonctionnaire de l'Etat.* All the proceedings of *le Conseil d'Etat* are in written form.

Conseil général, n.m. – the elected local Council for *le département* (see below). Elections to *le Conseil général* are known as *les élections cantonales,* since each *canton* returns one councillor. Its main responsibilities are in the area of social services, some aspects of primary education, teacher training, planning and roads. With the Decentralization Act of 1982, its executive powers have been greatly increased.

constater, v. – not really a *faux ami,* but an essential word for any negotiator in France. *Je ne critique pas, je ne formule aucune louange, je ne fais que constater,* I am not criticizing or praising. I am merely noting. The corresponding noun is *une constatation.* If you are involved in a road accident in France and there is a dispute about whose fault it is (*Mais j'avais la priorité. Je venais de la droite* – 'But I had priority, since I was coming from the right'), you need to obtain *un constat d'huissier* (see below), a formal statement of the case made by an authorized officer of the courts. If the parties involved can agree on the circumstances of an accident, they fill in and sign *un constat amiable* (agreed accident statement). For AMIABLE, see above.

contrôle, n.m., **contrôler,** v. – originally, *contrôler* simply meant to check. This usage survives in *un contrôleur d'autobus, des chemins de fer,* a ticket inspector, *le contrôle au théâtre,* the place where you go to check that the ticket you have bought in an agency is actually valid (*valable*) for the performance in question, and *appellation contrôlée,* a term indicating that a wine calling itself 'Médoc' or 'Meursault' has been made from grapes grown in a vineyard (*vignoble*) which the *Office National du Vin* has checked (*contrôlé*) and officially declared as producing that wine. Many French ministries have a *Corps de Contrôleurs,* with unrestricted access to all the services for which that Ministry is responsible and direct access to the Minister (even bypassing his *cabinet**). *La Cour des Comptes* has the specific and limited function of being a *corps de contrôle,* a body which simply checks whether or not the money allocated (*affecté* – see above) to a particular undertaking or for a specific purpose has been correctly used. But it does not have the right to control, in the English sense of *limiter,* the amount of money spent. One can also have a preliminary check as to whether something ought or ought not to be done at the moment, *un contrôle d'opportunité**. See also below, TUTELLE; CONTRIBUTIONS in III; CONTRÔLÉ in VIII.

However, under the influence of English, *contrôle* has now taken on many of the meanings of 'control'. Even *Le Petit Robert* gives *le contrôle de soi* for self-control, although *savoir se maîtriser* is regarded as more Gallic, and *le contrôle des naissances* for birth control, when it would be less ambiguous to talk about *la limitation des naissances.* One also frequently sees *les contrôleurs aériens* (who work in *une tour de contrôle*) when a purist might prefer the more poetic *les aiguilleurs du ciel. Perdre le contrôle de son véhicule* is perfectly acceptable linguistically, but very dangerous at a practical level.

In a legal and administrative context, *contrôle* can create problems. Sometimes, as in *le contrôle parlementaire de l'exécutif,* it is obviously used in the stronger, Anglo-Saxon sense of parliamentary control. But *le contrôle des dépenses publiques* (or *collectives* – see above, COLLECTIF) could be either what *la Cour des Comptes* actually does or the limitation of public expenditure. However, the remark on p. 168 of Ross Steele, *La France des Français* (1972) that the *écoles confessionnelles* (which constitute *l'enseignement libre**) *reçoivent une aide financière de l'état et sont contrôlées par lui* merely means that they are open to regular inspection by the *inspecteurs.* In *le contrôle continu des connaissances* for continuous assessment, the more limited meaning is nevertheless as obvious as in *les contrôles d'identité,* the activities which enable the French police to examine their compatriots' *carte d'identité nationale.*

convention, n.f. – in addition to the meanings of the English convention, note that of a binding agreement, *un accord contraignant*. *Une convention collective* is an agreement between the two sides of industry covering wages, conditions of work, productivity, etc. *Des prix conventionnés* are prices agreed between the government and the retailers' associations, *les associations de détaillants*, and *un médecin conventionné* is a doctor who has agreed to charge his patients the fees laid down by *la Sécurité sociale*. See DROGUERIE in VII.

Cour des Comptes, n.f. – one of the *Grands Corps de l'Etat* (see below). Its functions are similar to those of the British Controller and Auditor General in that it has the responsibility for *la bonne garde des deniers publics*, that is to say of checking the accounts of all bodies (including local authorities and nationalized firms) which spend public money. It presents an annual report to the President of the Republic, which is published and often summarized in the more serious press. It is an independent court of law and sits as such. Its members are therefore *magistrats* who are *inamovibles* (see below for both terms). However, like other *hauts fonctionnaires*, they are frequently *détachés en mission* (see below) and entrusted with responsibilities in other State organizations; the post of *Directeur Général de la Sécurité Sociale*, for example, is traditionally occupied by a senior member of *la Cour des Comptes*. They can also obtain a *détachement* which enables them to enter a *cabinet* ministériel*. If subsequently they wish to pursue an independent political career, they apply for a *mise en disponibilité*. Jacques Chirac, the first person to be elected as Mayor of Paris, in 1977, and the principal right-wing rival of Giscard d'Estaing, is a member of *la Cour des Comptes*. Should a member find politics ultimately unsatisfying, he can *réintégrer son corps d'origine* – go back to being a member, at the appropriate rank. The majority of its members, like Chirac himself, are *anciens élèves de l'Ecole Nationale d'Administration* (see below).

décliner, v. – in addition to its uses as in *décliner une invitation, décliner un verbe*, note the expression *décliner son identité*, to state who you are.

décomposer, v. – to break down, say, a problem, a difficulty, into its different parts. See also below, VENTILER.

défendre, v. – to defend or to forbid, according to the context.

déférer, v. – to refer a suspect to *le parquet* (see below) for trial. To defer is *différer*. To differ is *ne pas être d'accord* or *être différent*, according to the context.

délai, n.m., **délayer,** v. – except in expressions such as *sans délai*, which does mean immediately, not so much a delay, which is *un retard*, as a period within which one has to do something. *Il faut faire sa déclaration d'impôts dans un délai de trente jours* means 'You have to make your income tax return within thirty days'. When Brussels airport is closed by fog, a notice in English appears promising to get travellers to their destination 'in the best delays' (*dans les meilleurs délais*, i.e. as soon as possible). When you manage to do something *dans les délais voulus*, it means you meet the deadline, and *le délai d'exécution des travaux* (see EXÉCUTER in III) is the time allowed for completing a programme of work.

Note also that *délayer* is not to delay (*retarder*) but to thin (paint) or, in cooking, to mix (flour with water, etc.).

délibération, n.f. – not so much the discussion in a local council, but the final decision taken by it. See also DÉLIBÉRATION in II.

département, n.m. – a unit of local government and decentralized administration, established at the time of the French Revolution, when France was divided into 83 *départements*. There are now 95 in metropolitan France. Until the Socialist Decentralization Law of 1982, the local government executive functions at this level were entrusted to the *préfet*, appointed by the central government. These functions have now been transferred to the Chairman of the elected council, *le Président du Conseil général*. See above, CONSEIL GÉNÉRAL and below, PRÉFET.

déposer, v. – to depose (a king, etc.) but also to give written evidence. *Faire une déposition*, to make a statement. See below, ÉVIDENCE.

député, n.m. – not a deputy but the equivalent of a Member of Parliament or a Congressman. A deputy is *un délégué;* an assistant, *un adjoint*. Thus, *le maire* et ses adjoints* means the mayor and his assistants, and *le Député-maire*, a *député* who is at the same time the *maire* of a *commune*. See MANDAT in II.

désigner, v. – to appoint, as in *un avocat désigné d'office pour défendre un accusé*, a lawyer appointed by the court to defend an accused person, *le mode de désignation du Premier Ministre*, the method by which the Prime Minister is appointed. See below, NOMMER. To design in the sense of drawing is *dessiner*. Note the difference between *un dessin*, a drawing, sketch, and *un dessein*, a project, plan.

desservir, v. – can mean to do someone a disservice, or to clear the table (more commonly *débarrasser*), but more generally has the sense of to service. *C'est une ville bien desservie par tous les moyens de transports en commun* means that it is a town with a good public transport system. *Le Capitole, train rapide, relie Paris à Toulouse, après avoir desservi Limoges, Brive, Cahors et Montauban,* The express *Le Capitole* links Paris to Toulouse, stopping at Limoges, etc.

destitution, n.f. – dismissal. See below, RÉVOQUER. Destitution, *la misère, le dénuement.*

dilatoire, adj. – note particularly *des mesures dilatoires* in the sense of delaying tactics.

disposer, v. – not to dispose of, which is *se débarrasser de* (though to dispose of somebody is *exécuter* quelqu'un* or even *le supprimer*), but to have at one's disposal. Thus, *vous disposez maintenant de tous les éléments nécessaires pour résoudre le problème,* you now have all the elements necessary for solving the problem. Note the expression *Vous pouvez disposer,* You may leave. See also below, DISPOSITIF and DISPOSITION.

dispositif, n.m. – in a technical context, a device, *un dispositif de sécurité* being a safety device. In administrative language, however, the word means machinery, as in *le dispositif de protection de l'enfance,* the measures available for the protection of children.

disposition, n.f. – in administrative parlance, provisions, as in *des dispositions spéciales devront être prévues,* special provisions will have to be made. See PROVISION in III.

domaine, n.m. – as in English, but note the expression used when speaking of a book or piece of music, *tomber dans le domaine public,* to come out of copyright.

dossier, n.m. – not only a file but, more generally, in an administrative context, a question or issue. *Le Conseil des Ministres des 10 a consacré* toute la séance au dossier agricole,* The Council of Ministers of the 10 devoted the whole meeting to the agricultural question.

droit commun, n.m. – not Common Law, in the sense of a legal system based on precedent and the interpretation of Acts of Parliament by the courts, which is *le droit coutumier. Le droit commun* is the legal rule which is normally applied, and is thus best defined by its opposite: *le droit d'exception.* Thus when Jean-François Deniau writes in *Le Marché Commun* (1971, p. 67) that *c'est la majorité qualifiée qui est le droit commun du Traité* he means that what should and does normally happen is that a decision is taken by a 'qualified majority' agreed in advance, e.g. two thirds of those entitled to vote (see below, PON-DÉRER). In the same way, the regionalization decrees of 1964 state: *Le département* (see above) *est et demeure l'unité administrative de droit commun. Un criminel de droit commun* is a 'common criminal', one sentenced for an ordinary crime, such as bigamy or burglary, and not one condemned for political reasons by a special court, *un tribunal* (see below) *d'exception.* The prisoners whom Solzhenitsyn's French translators describe as *les droits communs* often enjoy privileges denied to political dissidents. As the inmates of the Maze Prison in Northern Ireland know, everyone sentenced in a British court is officially *un condamné de droit commun.* One of the first acts of the new Socialist government in France in 1981 was to abolish the *Cour de Sûreté de l'Etat,* which since 1958 could pass sentences for political crimes, so that France too now has only *des condamnés de droit commun.*

Readers should note that 'law' is translated either by *la loi* or by *le droit. La loi* is a specific piece of legislation – *nul n'est censé ignorer* la loi,* ignorance of the law is no excuse. *Le droit* is either the academic discipline (*Faculté de Droit, étudiant en droit*) or the whole corpus of legislation and case law in a given field, e.g. *le droit administratif, le droit commercial, le droit communautaire* (Common Market Law). See below, JURISPRUDENCE.

Les droits are rights, as in the 1789 *Déclaration des droits de l'homme,* and *les droits acquis* are as much an obstacle to progress and change in France as vested interests are in the English-speaking world. Just as there is no exact French equivalent of 'vested interests', there is no convenient English term for *les droits acquis.*

Un membre de droit (d'une Commission, etc.) is an *ex officio* member (by virtue of the position he or she holds).

Ecole Nationale d'Administration (ENA), n.f. – the post-graduate school, now in the Rue de l'Université, Paris VIᵉ, which trains French higher civil servants. It is generally referred to as *l'ENA,* and its products as *énarques.* In 1967, this inspired the pseudonymous Jacques Mandrin to write an amusingly entitled little book, *L'Enarchie, ou les Mandarins de la société bourgeoise.* Competition is intense for the 150 or so places in each year, and there is also *un concours* de sortie* which enables the top twenty members of each *promotion* (see below) to choose which of *les Grands Corps de l'Etat* they are going to enter. Most of the others join *le Corps des administrateurs civils* or *le Corps préfectoral* and have fewer opportunities to obtain a *détachement* which will enable them to join *un cabinet* ministériel* and move on, if they wish, to a political career of their own. *Enarques* currently prominent in French political life include Jacques Chirac, Valéry Giscard d'Estaing, Alain Peyrefitte,

Michel Jobert, Jean-Pierre Chevènement and Michel Rocard, which is an indication that the school produces socialists as well as conservatives. Should any of these *énarques* find the going too tough, they can *réintégrer leur corps d'origine* – i.e. go back, as Giscard d'Estaing could if he so wished, to *l'Inspection des Finances*, or Jacques Chirac to *la Cour des Comptes*. This is not a possibility open to those who choose to work for private industry, *d'aller pantoufler dans le privé*. If they have not already done ten years in the Civil Service, they have to repay the cost of the training and salary they received while at *l'ENA*, and it is this action of repayment which is expressed by the term *acheter sa pantoufle*. Since its establishment, *depuis sa création*, in 1945, the school has trained some 2700 higher civil servants, *hauts fonctionnaires, grands commis de l'Etat*, just over a third of those currently holding senior posts in the French Civil Service.

There are three methods of entry to *l'ENA: le concours* externe* (in 1983, about half the available places) for students, most of whom have degrees in law or political science or are graduates of one of the other *Grandes Ecoles**; *le concours interne* (the number of places available has been increased since the Socialists came to power) for serving civil servants; and, since 1983, *une troisième voie d'accès*, a third mode of entry, reserved for trade-union officials, local government councillors and officials of non-profit-making voluntary organizations.

The training (*la formation**) which *l'ENA* provides takes the form of *un stage**, a period of work experience, in a government department or in a *Préfecture*, followed by fifteen months at the school, where most of the teaching is provided by serving civil servants. *L'ENA* has sometimes been criticized for giving too many rewards to those who have chosen to be born to parents well established either in *les professions libérales** or in *la haute fonction publique* itself, and – since the best preparation for the entrance examination is provided at *l'Institut des Sciences Politiques* ('*Sciences Po*') – who also happen to live in Paris. Since the training of higher civil servants is too important a matter to be entrusted to the Minister of Education, *l'ENA* is described in the *Bottin Administratif* as being the administrative preserve of the Prime Minister, *elle relève du Premier Ministre*.

enquête, n.f. – much broader in meaning than the English inquest, for which the equivalent might be *enquête judiciaire pour cause de mort subite*. *Une enquête* is an inquiry or investigation, as in *la gendarmerie a ouvert une enquête*. A public inquiry before major public works are undertaken is *une enquête d'utilité publique*, and the government inspector, *le commissaire-enquêteur*.

établissement public, n.m. – roughly equivalent to a British Public

Corporation. See also ÉTABLISSEMENT in IV. The French use the English term *l'Establishment* to evoke the conspiracy theory of power.

état civil, n.m. – one's official identity, 'civil status' as given on one's *fiche d'état civil*, which a French citizen may obtain from the *mairie* of the locality where he or she was born, and indicating *nom* (name), *prénoms* (forenames, first names), *date et lieu de naissance* (date and place of birth), *nom et prénoms des parents**, *situation de famille* (marital status). Balzac's proclaimed ambition, in the *Avant-Propos* to *La Comédie humaine*, in 1834, was to *faire concurrence à* (compete with) *l'état civil*, that is, to create a world with its own parish registers. Like other European, and especially Latin, people, the French often strike the critically-minded Anglo-Saxon observer such as P.T. as afflicted with a worry about who they are. It is for this reason, some may feel, that they carry around with them a small oblong piece of reassuring cardboard, *leur carte d'identité nationale*, which has the additional advantage of having their photograph on it. However, the real reasons may be the frequency of *des contrôles d'identité*, in which you have to prove who you are to a policeman, *un agent de police* (you call him *Monsieur l'agent*); *une certaine méfiance instinctive d'autrui*, a certain instinctive mistrust of other people, which characterizes French life (see SUSPICIOUS in V, ALSACIEN in IX); the experience of occupation (1940–1944) and of near civil war, *la guerre civile larvée*, in 1960–1962, at the time of the Algerian conflict; *la tradition césarienne**, *gaulliste**, *jacobine** of encouraging the State to play a substantial part in the life of its citizens or *administrés* (see above, ADMINISTRER). On the other hand, H.E. argues that the *carte d'identité nationale* is an easily recognizable and a generally accepted means of identification, which replaces a passport when travelling to neighbouring countries, and is useful when withdrawing cash from a bank where one is not known or collecting a registered letter, *une lettre recommandée*, from the Post Office.

Also important for the French citizen's 'official' existence are *le livret de famille* and *le casier judiciaire*. The former is given to each couple when they are married, contains the *état civil* of each partner and the names of the parents, and is brought up to date for each event affecting the family. The latter, obtainable from *le commissariat de police*, is one's criminal record. When applying for an official job, or before sitting one of the *concours**, it is necessary to provide *un casier judiciaire vierge*, proving that one has no criminal convictions.

One of the functions of the *maire** is that of *officier d'état civil*, the equivalent of the British Registrar of Births, Marriages and Deaths; the term *l'Etat civil* is consequently also used for the department in *la mairie*, town hall, that deals with such matters.

évidence, n.f. – not evidence, which is *une preuve, un témoignage, une déposition* (see above, DÉPOSER) or (in the sense of an exhibit) *une pièce à conviction,* but that which is self-evident or goes without saying, as in *C'est l'évidence même* or *Inutile de nier une regrettable évidence,* Why deny such a self-evident, although unfortunate, fact? Cf. the remark in the Introduction about Wittgenstein's 'The meaning of a word is its use'. What else could it possibly be?

For a characteristic example of the use of the word *évidence,* note the remark in *Le Monde* of 15 May 1982 on the Falklands crisis, *l'affaire* des Iles Malouines,* and the European Community: *Mme Thatcher aurait beaucoup gagné à reconnaître cette évidence: les intérêts des millions d'agriculteurs européens valent bien ceux de quelques éleveurs de moutons des Antipodes.* (It would have been very much to Mrs Thatcher's advantage if she had recognized the obvious fact that the interests of millions of European farmers are just as important as those of a few sheep-breeders in the Antipodes.) *Les Iles Malouines* are so called because they were discovered by French sailors from Saint-Malo. See also the comment of the conservative-minded *Le Point* on 1 February 1982 on the attitude which certain members of the editorial board, *le Comité de rédaction,* of *Les Temps Modernes,* the left-wing monthly review founded by Sartre in 1945, had towards the imposition of martial law in Poland (see BRUMAIRE in II). Left-wing intellectuals, observed *Le Point, se heurtent à cette intolérable évidence; le socialisme démocratique n'existe plus, et la doctrine marxiste-léniniste conduit inévitablement à l'oppression et à la dictature* (come up against the obvious fact which they cannot accept, namely that democratic socialism has ceased to exist, and that Marxism-Leninism leads inevitably to oppression and dictatorship).

exercice, n.m. – note the following expressions: *l'exercice financier,* the financial year (in France, 1 January–31 December), and *le Président* en exercice,* the current Chairman/President.

expertise, n.f. – especially, a valuation by an expert assessor for purposes of sale or insurance. Expertise is best rendered by *des connaissances techniques.*

exploit, n.m. – note the expression *un exploit d'huissier,* the legal document, *l'acte,* drawn up and delivered by *l'huissier* (see below). An exploit in the sense of an outstanding achievement is *une prouesse* or *un haut fait,* as in *les hauts faits des chevaliers du Moyen Age,* the exploits of the knights of the Middle Ages. In a less literary context, it can be *une performance,* or indeed *un exploit,* as in *un exploit sportif, oratoire,* etc. See EXPLOITER in III.

flagrant, adj. – note the phrase *pris en flagrant délit,* caught in the act, red-handed. *Un tribunal* (see below) *des flagrants délits* is a court that deals summarily with minor offences.

flexible, adj. – although one does see 'flexitime' translated as *des horaires flexibles*, purists prefer *des horaires souples*. See below, SOUPLE. The expression *le temps choisi* is now sometimes used with the same meaning.

fonction, n.f. – note *un appartement de fonction* in the British English sense of a 'tied cottage', a house or apartment you live in because it goes with the job. Agricultural labourers (see LABOURER in III) in England are still sometimes forced to live in a house provided by the farmer (see FERMIER in III) employing them. *Une voiture de fonction,* a car that goes with the job, is another *avantage en nature,* which makes you more vulnerable to the whims of your employer, since it means that you are suddenly immobile if you lose your job, *si vous perdez votre emploi, ou si vous devenez licencié économique.*

La Fonction Publique is also the Civil Service, a more prestigious entity in France than in England, and one that plays a much more important role in people's lives than any comparable organization in the United States. Since only French citizens (*des ressortissants français,* see SUBJECT in II) can be French civil servants, it follows that only they can hold a permanent teaching post (*être régulièrement titularisés,* see below, TITULAIRE) in a State school. The aim of the Treaty of Rome to establish *la libre circulation des travailleurs,* the free movement of workers, throughout the European Community thus works only in one direction, *à sens unique,* in the educational field. A civil servant is *un fonctionnaire* or *un agent de l'Etat,* also known by the slang term of *un rond de cuir* from the leather cushion which used to be put on his chair in the office. But note also *les prêts sont fonction de vos revenus,* the amount you can borrow depends on how much you earn.

forfait, n.m., **forfaitaire,** adj. – not a forfeit in a game, which is *un gage**, or a fine for non-fulfilment of contract, which is *une amende,* but an inclusive contract. Hence the expression *un voyage à prix forfaitaire* for a package tour, where you pay a lump sum in advance and hope to have no further expenses (also, *un forfait-ski, un forfait hôtelier*). When a civil servant puts in a claim for expenses incurred while living away from home, *une indemnité de séjour,* he receives *une somme forfaitaire,* a lump sum, which saves him the trouble of enumerating what he has spent on what (*une analyse détaillée des dépenses par postes séparés*) and spares the accountant (*le comptable responsable du contrôle financier*) the time needed to check, *contrôler* (see above) *sa feuille de dépenses,* his expenses form. Note also, in a Social Security context, *une allocation* *forfaitaire* to indicate a flat-rate allowance, i.e. one that does not depend on the particular circumstances of the payee, *l'allocataire.* For sportsmen, in particular, *déclarer forfait* is to withdraw from a competition. But *un forfait* is also a crime, as in *avouer, maquiller son forfait,* confess, cover up one's crime.

formaliser, v. – Not really to formalize, in the sense of make official. *Régulariser une situation* would be current usage in the sense of 'to formalize your position', as when a couple who have been living together decide to get married. Soon after coming to power in 1981, the Left obtained parliamentary approval for a Bill enabling *les immigrés clandestins,* immigrants who had entered France illegally, to *régulariser leur situation* and thus obtain *une carte de séjour,* a residence permit, and *une carte de travail,* a work permit. *Se formaliser* means to take offence: *Ne vous formalisez pas, ce règlement s'applique à tout le monde,* Don't get so upset, this regulation applies to everybody.

formel, adj., **formellement,** adv. – strict(ly), categorical(ly), as in *La législation française interdit formellement aux cambistes de jouer contre le franc,* French law strictly forbids exchange brokers speculating against the franc. Note also *il a été formel,* he was quite definite about it. However, occasionally these two words can mean 'from a formal point of view': *La démocratie peut d'abord se définir, formellement, par son origine* (Democracy can first of all be defined, from a formal point of view, by its origin) (Jean-Marie Pontier, *L'Etat et les Collectivités locales – la répartition des compétences,* 1978, p. 27).

formidable, adj. – the French word has completely lost the original meaning of awe-inspiring which its English counterpart has retained, and now, used especially by adolescents, means only wonderful, smashing, super. Thus, one would have to render a formidable weapons system by *un système d'armes redoutable.*

formulaire, n.m. – a form to fill in (*remplir un formulaire*), usually at least in triplicate, *en trois exemplaires.*

gracier, v. – to pardon. *Le droit de grâce,* the right of pardon, one of the traditional attributes of the President of the French Republic. See also GRÂCE in V.

Grands Corps de l'Etat, n.m.p. – a generic term for which there is no equivalent in English and which designates *Le Conseil d'Etat* (see above), *La Cour des Comptes* (see above), *L'Inspection des Finances* (see below) and, incorrectly in some people's view, *Le Corps Diplomatique.*

What often seems to matter most to a higher civil servant in France is less the rank which he holds than the *corps* to which he belongs. The various *corps techniques (Le Corps des Ingénieurs des Ponts et Chaussées, Le Corps des Ingénieurs des Mines)* are like the *Grands Corps* in the sense that once admitted (after *le concours de sortie* from your *Grande Ecole* – see IV) you remain a member for life. You thus do not need even to resign from your *corps* when elected as a *député* or on becoming a Minister, you merely apply for *une mise en disponibilité,* and this might strike the Anglo-Saxon observer as difficult to reconcile with the principle of *la séparation des pouvoirs,* especially between the legislative and executive, which officially characterizes the Fifth Republic. Members of the *corps* are untroubled by such suggestions, pointing out that *les Grands Corps* stand apart from – as well as above – all other entities in the State.

The ability of the members of the *Grands Corps de l'Etat* – and of the other *corps* – to alternate between their official duties and the more prestigious functions which they fulfil when *en détachement* or *en disponibilité* is clearly one of the more dramatic differences between the French and the United Kingdom Civil Service. However, it does not affect more than about 7 per cent of the *anciens élèves de l'ENA,* and even fewer of the *anciens élèves de Polytechnique*, de Centrale* (see above) *ou des Mines.* The promotion pattern for career members of the *corps des administrateurs civils* is from *Administrateur de bureau* to *Chef de bureau,* to *Sous-directeur,* to *Directeur général adjoint* or *Chef de Service,* to *Directeur général,* or *Directeur,* and perhaps even to *Secrétaire général.* Some top civil servants (*les grands fonctionnaires, les grands commis de l'Etat*) are placed *hors échelle,* above the normal incremental scale, in order to dissuade them from going off to *pantoufler dans le privé,* resign from the Civil Service in order to work for a private company. In the *Cour des Comptes* most members will follow the normal progression from *Auditeur 2e classe* to *Auditeur 1ère classe* to *Conseiller référendaire (2e and 1ère classe),* and to *Conseiller-maître.* The next stages, obviously more difficult to reach, are *Président de Chambre, Procureur général* and *Premier Président.* In the *Conseil d'Etat,* one goes from *Auditeur (2e and 1ère classe)* to *Maître des requêtes* to *Conseiller d'Etat* to *President de section* and to *Vice-président.* In most cases, *l'avancement est par ancienneté,* promotion is by seniority.

greffe, n.m. – do not confuse *une greffe,* a graft, as carried out by a gardener, or a transplant, as carried out by a surgeon, with *un greffe,* the Clerk's Office in a court of law. *Le greffier* is the Clerk to the Court.

habiliter, v., **habilitation,** n.f. – to give official authorization. Thus, *le comptable est seul habilité à signer des chèques,* only the accountant is authorized to sign cheques. Also ministerial validation of university degrees (see DEGREE in IV).

habitation, n.f. – more frequently used than the English term, especially in *habitation à loyer modéré* (HLM), publicly provided low-rent accommodation. A general word for housing is *l'habitat*, and there is also the term *le parc immobilier* for housing stock.

honoraire, adj. – not honorary in the sense of unpaid, which is *bénévole**, but in the sense of emeritus, having retired but authorized to retain a title. Thus an Emeritus Professor is *un professeur honoraire*. Note, however, that *honoraire* is used much more widely than is English emeritus, which is restricted to Professors. It occurs not only in education but is also applied to high-ranking officials of certain other Ministries, thus giving *préfet honoraire* as well as *directeur d'école honoraire, instituteur honoraire. Un professeur honoraire* could thus be a retired secondary-school teacher. Note that the Honorary President of a charitable or cultural organization is *le Président d'honneur*, whereas *le Président* is the Chairman, who does all the work.

The adjective *émérite* is also a 'false friend', indicating as it does someone of outstanding ability, even before retirement. Thus, in *La Peau de Chagrin*, Balzac talks about *ces professeurs émérites de vices et d'infamie*, these outstanding teachers of vices and infamy.

huissier, n.m. – usher, but also a court official responsible for delivering a summons, *une assignation à comparaître*, and ensuring that the court's decisions are carried out.

impression, n.f. – as in English, except that *une faute d'impression* is a printing error, otherwise known as *une coquille*. When wishing in a Committee to prolong the discussion until adjourning for tea, *on peut toujours partir à la recherche de coquilles*, you can always start looking for printing errors. When marking printer's proofs in France (*les épreuves*, les placards)* you have to give the *bon à tirer* (authorization to print) to show that you are satisfied (generally at the stage of page proof, *seconde épreuve*) and to *dégager la responsabilité de l'imprimeur*, indicate that you as author now accept responsibility for the text.

inamovible, adj. – immovable in a legal rather than a physical sense. *L'inamovibilité des juges du siège* is the concept that judges cannot be moved to another post by an administrative decision of the executive, except by a highly complex disciplinary procedure. A *procureur* or his *substitut*, members of *la magistrature debout*, is quite frequently *et tout à fait régulièrement* (and in full accordance with the rules) – see below, RÉGULIÈREMENT – moved from one town to another. Immovable in a physical sense would be *fixe, impossible à déplacer*, but immovable property such as land or buildings is *des biens immobiliers* as opposed to *des biens mobiliers* (stocks, shares, etc.). See FUTILE in II.

inculper, v. – to bring a formal charge against. A charge is *une inculpation.*

information, n.f. – a piece of news, as in *les informations,* the news bulletin. A piece of information is *un renseignement,* and the Information Office, *le Bureau des Renseignements.* But note *ouvrir une information,* to open an official legal enquiry. See below, INSTRUCTION.

injure, n.f. – not an injury, *une blessure,* but an insult; *injurier quelqu'un* is to insult someone, not to wound him, *le blesser.*

Inspection des Finances, n.f. – one of the *Grands Corps de l'Etat,* the smallest in number (just over one hundred strong, as against just over two hundred each for *Le Conseil d'Etat* and *La Cour des Comptes)* but perhaps the most influential. Although not a court of law (see above, COUR DES COMPTES), it has the responsibility for checking – *de contrôler, de vérifier* – the way in which public money is spent, as well as for giving advice on economic and financial matters to the various Ministries. It is itself part of *le Ministère de l'Economie et du Budget,* and its members are frequently entrusted with special missions elsewhere in the public services. The *Inspecteurs des Finances* are also very frequently *détachés de leur corps d'origine* to work either in *des cabinets ministériels* (see CABINET in II) or in public enterprises.

instamment, adv. – not instantly, *tout de suite,* but urgently, as in *Vous êtes instamment prié de payer les sommes dues,* You are urged to pay the money owing.

instance, n.f. – a legal term, as in English, but also an official body exercising authority. *Les principales instances communautaires (de la CEE) sont la Commission, le Conseil des Ministres, le Parlement européen, la Cour de Justice et la Cour des Comptes. Il a siégé au sein de l'instance dirigeante de son Parti jusqu'en 1979,* He sat on his Party's central committee until 1979. And note this fitting metaphor in *Le Monde,* 4 September 1981: *'Le tennis administratif' qui consiste à se renvoyer une affaire* d'une instance à une autre,* the game of 'administrative tennis' which consists in sending a question back and forth from one Department to another. See also below, TRIBUNAL.

instruction, n.f. – note particularly the earlier meaning of education in *le Ministère de l'Instruction publique,* the title for the Ministry of Education until 1932, as well as the administrative and legal meanings associated with *instruire* – to prepare all the elements of a question before a full discussion or debate, or to draw up a case. Thus when a crime has been committed or is suspected, and the *procureur* (see above, AVOCAT) is not satisfied that the evidence available is sufficient to bring an immediate case in open court, *il ouvre une instruction et confie l'enquête au juge d'instruction,* he hands the case over to the examining magistrate. The latter then proceeds to make his enquiry, and has the power to summon and question witnesses, *de convoquer et d'interroger des témoins,* to sign arrest warrants and search warrants, *des mandats* d'amener et des mandats de perquisition,* to free the accused on bail, *mettre l'inculpé en liberté provisoire, sous caution,* to remand him in custody, *en détention préventive,* to order the police or other judicial authorities to take evidence (*une commission rogatoire*). If he considers the evidence inadequate, he can *relaxer l'inculpé,* dismiss all charges (see below, RELAXER) and *délivrer une ordonnance de non-lieu,* say that there is no case to answer at the moment (see below, ORDONNANCE). This is what happens to the eponymous heroine of Mauriac's novel *Thérèse Desqueyroux* (1927), and explains her vulnerability in the rest of the novel: a *non-lieu* leaves the possibility of the case being reopened if further evidence emerges. If the magistrate thinks the evidence adequate, the case then goes back to the *procureur,* and is in due course brought in open court. In very exceptional cases – such as at the end of the Second World War, for *des crimes de collaboration,* and during the Algerian war, for *des actes de terrorisme* – when the accused is known but cannot be found, he may be tried and sentenced in his absence, *jugé et condamné par contumace.*

In France a suspect does not have to be presented in open court as soon as possible after his arrest. The period of several days during which he may be held by the police before being presented to the *parquet* (see below) and charged, *inculpé,* is known as *la garde à vue.* Foreigners therefore often believe that you are considered guilty in France until you prove your innocence. This is definitely not the case, and the contrary principle is set forth in Article IX of *La Déclaration des Droits de l'Homme et du Citoyen* (1789), to which the Preamble to the 1958 Constitution proclaims the attachment of the French people. However, widespread disregard for *le secret de l'instruction,* the secrecy of the judicial enquiry, leads to the situation where the euphemistic British 'A man is helping the police with their enquiries' becomes, in many French newspapers, and even on the French radio, *L'abominable assassin est déjà sous les verrous,* 'the monstrous murderer is already behind bars'. Anyone who violates *le secret de l'instruction* can be prosecuted for *outrage à magistrat,* the nearest equivalent of contempt of court.

intention, n.f. – note particularly the expression *un procès d'intention,* an accusation of bad faith (see below, PROCÈS). Thus *Le Nouvel*

Observateur wrote in 1981: *Ce n'est pas encore la guerre entre le libéralisme* et le dirigisme, mais les procès d'intention vont bon train,* There is not yet a state of war between private enterprise and the planned economy, but accusations of bad faith are flying back and forth. As regards the adjective *intentionnel,* and in addition to the sense of intentional, deliberate (*un délit intentionnel,* a deliberate offence, as opposed to one committed through carelessness, *par imprudence*), note the following: *N'ayant pas de valeur réglementaire, ces documents ne constituent que des documents intentionnels,* These documents do not constitute regulations but only set forth intentions. In many general contexts, intentional may be rendered by *voulu.*

intéresser, v. – not only to interest but also to concern. Hence *les parties intéressées,* those concerned. Also self-interested: *je ne lui demanderai pas son avis, il est intéressé,* I won't ask him for his opinion, he has a vested interest in the question.

interpeller, v., **interpellation,** n.f. – *un suspect interpellé par la police,* a suspect stopped by the police, asked for his papers, etc.

interroger, v. – even in a judicial context, does not always have the associations of the English to interrogate, and may often be better rendered by to question. Note, however, that questioning or interrogation is *un interrogatoire,* whereas *une interrogation* is a test or examination at school or university (see DEGREE in IV).

inutile, adj. – unnecessary as well as useless. *Inutile de vous dire que,* I don't need to tell you that . . . *Rayer les mentions inutiles,* cross out the sections/entries which do not apply (on a form or questionnaire). For another meaning of *mention,* see DEGREE in IV.

item, adv. – is used in French especially in speech, when ironically enumerating individual matters, and often in legal documents or invoices, but is much less frequent than item in English. 'The various items on the agenda' (see above, AGENDA), *les différentes questions à l'ordre du jour.*

jurisprudence, n.f. – case law.

libeller, v. – not to libel, which is *diffamer,* but to make out a cheque, to word or draw up a document, especially in formal language; hence *le libellé,* the way a document is drafted or a cheque made out. *Un libelle* is a lampoon or satire.

licence, n.f., **licencier,** v. – *une licence* is not a driving licence, which is *un permis de conduire,* but either a university degree (*licence d'anglais,* etc.), an import licence (*licence d'importation*), membership of a sports federation, or licence as in licentious, *licencieux.* The television licence is *la redevance de télévision.* The road tax disc is *la vignette auto,* calculated in France according to *l'importance* du cylindrage,* the power of the engine.

Licencier does not mean to license, which is *autoriser* or *accorder un permis.* A licensed jester is *le fou du roi. Une indemnité* de licenciement* is redundancy payment, since *licencier* means to dismiss, to sack, and *licencier pour cause économique,* to make redundant. Again, in a sporting context *un concours* de tennis réservé aux licenciés* does not mean that the competition is solely for university graduates or for people who have just lost their jobs, but for members of the Tennis Federation.

liquider, v. – note the expression *liquider une pension,* to determine, when someone retires, how much pension he is entitled to; also *la liquidation judiciaire,* winding-up (of a firm), as after bankruptcy.

litige, n.m. – legal dispute, hence *litigieux,* litigious, contentious.

local, n.m. – premises, as in *les locaux administratifs,* administrative offices, *les locaux scolaires,* school buildings, etc.

magistrat, n.m. – a generic term, much more widely used than magistrate in English. Thus *Le Président de la République est le premier magistrat de France.* There are no unpaid, voluntary magistrates, *des magistrats bénévoles*,* in France, and the functions of the British Justices of the Peace, in the lowest courts, are fulfilled in France by professional *juges de première instance,* formerly called *juges de paix.*

Since its establishment in 1970, the *Ecole Nationale de la Magistrature* in Bordeaux trains all lawyers who wish to be employed by the State, whether as *juges* – in which case they belong to *la magistrature assise* – or as members of *la magistrature debout.* It is the officers of *la magistrature debout* who constitute *le ministère public,* defined in *Le Petit Robert* as *le corps des magistrats établis près des tribunaux avec la mission de défendre les intérêts de la société, de veiller à l'exécution des lois et des décisions judiciaires* (the body of magistrates appointed to the courts with the duty of defending the interests of society and of ensuring that the law and judicial decisions are enforced). *Le ministère public* is also known as *le parquet,* and in a criminal case is represented in court by *le procureur.* Like the Procurator-Fiscal in Scotland, he is responsible for prosecution. *Des substituts* are appointed to help him, and the central character in Anouilh's play *Pauvre Bitos* (1956) is very conscious of the fact of being *nommé* (see below, NOMMER) *substitut* and therefore having the dignity – and physical inviolability – of a *magistrat*. In a civil case, *le ministère public* presents an opinion reflecting the interests of society. While members of *la magistrature assise* are theoretically *inamovibles* (see above) in the very strict sense of not being movable to another court by an administrative decision of the State, *la magistrature debout* does not enjoy this privilege. The term *magistrat* also designates members of the two main *organes de contrôle* (see above) in France: *Le Conseil d'Etat* (see above) and *La Cour des Comptes* (see above). See also above, AVOCAT, INSTRUIRE, and below, TRIBUNAL.

major, n.m. – except in the Belgian Army, not a Major, *un commandant,* but an army medical officer, addressed as *Monsieur le major.* The word can also mean the regimental adjutant; the vice-chief of naval staff; the rear-admiral, *le contre-amiral,* in charge of a naval dockyard. When addressing an officer in the French Army, *l'Armée de Terre,* or Air Force, *l'Armée de l'Air,* a man precedes the rank with '*Mon*' (*mon lieutenant, mon capitaine,* etc.). This is not a possessive adjective but an abbreviation for *Monsieur le.* Ladies do not use '*Mon*'. In the Navy, *la Marine nationale,* '*Mon*' is not used; while on shore, officers are addressed by their rank (*lieutenant, capitaine,* etc.), but at sea a ship's captain, whatever his rank, is always referred to as *commandant.*

The term *major* also designates the student who comes out top in *le concours de sortie d'une Grande Ecole* (see IV).

médiateur, n.m. – the equivalent of the British Ombudsman.

milieu, n.m. – used absolutely, means the (criminal) underworld.

ministère, n.m. – in addition to Ministry (*le Ministère de l'Education Nationale)* and *le ministère public* (see above, AVOCAT, MAGISTRAT), also has the important sense of government, as in *La séparation de l'Eglise et de l'Etat eut lieu en 1905, sous le ministère Combes.* Both the Third Republic (1870–1940) and the Fourth (1946–58) were characterized by *l'instabilité ministérielle;* de Gaulle notes in the first volume of his *Mémoires de Guerre* that between 1932 and 1937, when he was *affecté* (see above) *au secrétariat général de la Défense nationale,* he served *sous quatorze ministères.* Since 1958 the habit has grown of referring to governments as *des gouvernements.* See CABINET in II.

minute, n.f. – a minute, and also the copy of a legal document. But the minutes of the meeting are *le procès-verbal de la réunion* or *le compte-rendu de la réunion.* To minute a discussion is *prendre note d'une discussion,* whereas to note the remarks made in a discussion is *prendre acte des observations formulées au cours de la discussion.*

mission, n.f. – used more frequently in an administrative context than its English counterpart. Thus, a civil servant who is sent on official business away from his normal place of work is *envoyé en mission*, and in the late forties the precursors of today's *Préfets régionaux* (see below) rejoiced in the eminently acronymic title, *Inspecteurs généraux de l'administration en mission extraordinaire* (IGAME).

moral, adj. – see the entry in V, but also note that *une personne morale* (contrasted in law with *une personne physique*, a specific individual) has the sense of a legal, corporate entity, able to own property, to buy and sell, to receive gifts and legacies (*des legs*), to be prosecuted, and to initiate civil proceedings in the courts (*ester en justice*).

motif, n.m. – in addition to meaning a recurring pattern, also means a motive, as in *l'exposé des motifs*, setting out at the beginning of a parliamentary Bill the reasons for introducing the new legislation. In more general contexts, a motive may also be rendered by *un mobile*.

mutation, n.f. – not only biological and sociological, but also administrative, as in the remark that *Pendant la guerre d'Algérie, les mutations d'enseignants étaient de véritables sanctions* (see below). *Si on signait une pétition contre la torture, on risquait de se trouver muté de Paris à Alès ou d'Aix-en-Provence à Roubaix.* (During the Algerian war, the transfer of teachers from one post to another was used as a form of punishment. If you signed a petition against torture, you ran the risk of being transferred from Paris to Alès or from Aix-en-Provence to Roubaix.) In this sense *la mutation*, transfer to another post, might be: *sur la demande de l'intéressé(e), pour raisons de convenance personnelle* (at the request of the person concerned, for reasons of personal convenience); *pour raisons de service* (for reasons of managerial interest) – unusual in the teaching profession, more frequent in the Administrative Civil Service; or *la mutation d'office*, a severe and relatively rare administrative *sanction* (see below, OFFICE). See also above, INAMOVIBLE and below, RÉVOQUER, TITULAIRE. See also DEGREE in IV.

nommer, v. – the sense of to appoint as well as to name goes back a long way. In Racine's *Britannicus* (1669) Burrhus evokes the idyllic atmosphere characterizing Néron's early reign by saying *Le peuple au Champ de Mars nomme ses magistrats* (Act I, Scene 2). In the Constitution of the Fifth Republic, *le Président de la République nomme le Premier Ministre*, appoints the Prime Minister. *Désigner* is also often used in this sense. The corresponding nouns are *une nomination* and *une désignation*. *Les appointements* exists only in the plural, and has the sense of salary. See SALAIRE in III.

notaire, n.m. – the member of the legal profession who deals with the legal aspects of his clients' personal affairs: purchase and sale of property, marriage contracts, wills. In France this function is distinct from that of the *avocat* (see above), who assists his clients in litigation.

notamment, adv. – in particular, especially.

nuisance, n.f. – used only in a legal context, having the same sense as in the English 'Commit no nuisance'. *Les nuisances provoquées* (see below) *par les effluves toxiques,* the environmental hazards caused by poisonous discharges. In France you can be prosecuted for making too much noise after ten o'clock at night, an offence known as *le tapage nocturne* and falling into the general category of *les nuisances sonores.*

occurrence, n.f. – not occurrence, which is *un événement* ('it's a regular occurrence', *cela arrive régulièrement)*, but instance, case, especially in the expression *en l'occurrence,* in this particular case.

office, n.m. – a quasi-autonomous official organization established at national or local level for a specific task: *l'Office du Tourisme,* tourist board, *l'Office des Forêts,* responsible for managing France's woodlands, *l'Office du Blé,* for organizing the production and marketing of wheat, *l'Office national des Ecoles et des Universités,* for arranging student exchanges, etc. In this case gender is important since *une office* is a pantry, and *dîner à l'office* is to eat with the servants. Note also *nommer quelqu'un d'office,* to appoint someone by virtue of the powers you have, *un avocat désigné d'office,* a lawyer appointed by the court to defend an accused person who has not chosen his own lawyer. Thus, *d'office* is not 'ex officio', which is *de droit.* Also *faire office de,* carry out a function which is not one's normal function: *Lors de la soirée offerte aux personnes du troisième âge, c'est Monsieur le Maire qui a fait office de présentateur,* At the pensioners' party the Mayor acted as compère.

officiel, adj. – official, and *de source officielle,* from an authorized source. *Officieux* used to mean useful, obliging, as in Racine, *Britannicus,* Act IV, Scene 4, *Seigneur, j'ai tout prévu pour une mort si juste:/ Le poison est tout prêt. La fameuse Locuste/A redoublé pour moi ses soins officieux/ Elle a fait expirer un esclave à mes yeux* . . . (All is ready, my lord, for so deserved a death. The famous Locusta has obliged me with redoubled zeal. She put a slave to death before my very eyes . . . but now usually means unofficial: *Officieusement, je peux vous le faire savoir,* I can tell you unofficially.

old boy network – is evoked by the title of Robert de Jouvenel's diatribe against the political habits of the Third Republic: *La Républi-que des camarades* (1914), but exists more effectively in the publication of *L'Annuaire des anciens élèves de l'Ecole Nationale d'Administration* (see above). This directory gives telephone numbers as well as current responsibilities. However, it is not a peculiarity of *l'ENA*. Certain other *Grandes Ecoles*, especially *l'Ecole polytechnique*, do it as well. *La mafia* is often jocularly used in this context. See also below, RÉPER-TOIRE.

ordonnance, n.f. – much wider than ordinance ('This Degree Cere-mony is held according to the Ordinances and Statutes of the University of Leeds'), though it also has the sense of the English 'ordonnance' (systematic arrangement of a literary work). Thus *gouverner par ordonnance*, to rule by decree; the statement *L'Ecole Nationale d'Administration, fondée par l'ordonnance N° 45–2283 du 9 octobre 1945* indicates that it was an executive decision taken by the govern-ment, not part of its legislative programme needing parliamentary approval. Under the Constitution of the Fifth Republic a clear distinction is made between those government actions needing par-liamentary approval (*du domaine législatif*) and those not needing such approval (*du domaine réglementaire, des arrêtés, des décrets*). The term *ordonnance* is used in this context for government measures which normally need specific parliamentary approval, but for which, for reasons of urgency, blanket parliamentary approval has been given. Recourse to this procedure, used by both de Gaulle and Mitterrand, is hotly disputed, *controversé*. Also a ruling by a single judge – *le juge d'instruction a rendu une ordonnance de non-lieu* (see above, INSTRUCTION) – as distinct from *un jugement* or *un arrêt collégial*, made when several judges sit together (see above, ARRÊT and COLLÉGIAL).

Une ordonnance is also a doctor's prescription (for drugs). *Une prescription* is used for a prescription for medical appliances. See DROGUERIE in VII.

organe, n.m. – note the sense of an administrative body with a specific responsibility, as in the expression *les organes de la Communauté Economique Européenne*, the governing bodies of the EEC. See also ORGANE in X. Related terms are *un organisme* and *une organisation*, the former being narrower and less abstract in meaning than the latter, and implying that the body has been established to fulfil a limited task. *Un organigramme* is a flow chart, or an organizational chart.

outrage, n.m. – insult; thus *outrage à agent,* insulting behaviour to a policeman; *outrage à magistrat,* contempt of court; *outrage aux bonnes mœurs,* offence against public decency. An outrage is *une atrocité* and a bomb outrage *un attentat à la bombe.*

parallèle, adj. – note the expression *les polices parallèles* for semi-secret police forces established to supplement the activities of the official and more public organizations. See INDIFFÉREMMENT in V.

parole – in the sense of a prisoner being released on parole is *la liberté conditionnelle.*

parquet, n.m. – not only a parquet floor, but the place in a law court reserved for the representatives of *le ministère public* (see above, MAGIS-TRAT) and hence *le ministère public* itself. Thus *le parquet a été saisi* means that the Public Prosecutor has been officially informed (that a crime has been committed); and, normally only by a mind-boggling flight of the imagination, that somebody has stolen the floorboards. However, the guide at the Abbaye de Bec-Hellouin, in Normandy, the Mother House of the Church of England, explaining to visitors on 7 August 1983 just how badly the Monastery had been treated during and immediately after the Second World War, added as evidence the fact that the local vandals *'avaient même saisi le parquet'* – had stolen the floorboards.

partie, n.f. – note especially the legal expression *se constituer partie civile,* to link one's claim for damages to those of *le ministère public* acting on behalf of the State in a criminal case. The two cases are thus heard at one and the same time, and it is only when he is acting for *la partie civile* that an *avocat* (see above) appears for the prosecution. Thus Louis says of himself in Mauriac's *Le Nœud de Vipères* (1933): *Je fixai sur lui mes yeux tant redoutés au Palais par l'adversaire, et qui, lorsque j'étais l'avocat de la partie civile, ne quittaient jamais ma victime avant qu'elle ne se fût effondrée, dans le box* (see above), *entre les bras du gendarme.* (I fastened my eyes on him, eyes that were dreaded by my adversaries in court and which, when I was representing a claimant, never left my victim until he had collapsed in the dock in the arms of the gendarme.)

passible, adj. – liable to, for (in law), as in *passible d'une amende de 300 francs,* liable to a fine of 300 francs. The English passable is either *passable* (of the standard of a piece of work) or *praticable* (of a road, etc.).

peine, n.f. – not pain, *la douleur,* but sadness, as in *j'ai de la peine pour lui,* and, in a legal context, sentence: *condamné à une peine de six mois de prison,* sentenced to six months' imprisonment. *Une peine de prison peut être soit ferme soit avec sursis,* a prison sentence may either be unconditional or suspended. *Une remise de peine* is a reduction in the sentence.

permission, n.f. – sometimes permission, as in *avec votre permission,* but usually leave (of absence) in the Army, etc. Permission is normally *l'autorisation.*

personnalité, n.f. – all the English meanings, plus that of somebody well known to the public because of the official position he holds: *Les personnalités civiles, ecclésiastiques et militaires* are official representatives of the State, Church and Armed Forces. See also NOTABLE in II.

pièce, n.f. – the general word for room (see PIÈCE in X) and also (in addition to a coin, a tip, a play or a piece) a document. Thus *une pièce d'identité* can be an identity card, a passport, a driving licence or a club membership card. *Une pièce à conviction* is a physical piece of evidence (forged letter, bloodstained hammer) proving the guilt of *l'accusé.*

planning, n.m. – a detailed work programme. Also, especially for hotels or camp sites (*des campings*), *un planning de réservation.* Economic planning is *la planification,* and family planning, *la limitation des naissances.* See ALLOCATION, FERTILITY in VI.

policé, adj. – civilized, refined.

polyvalent, adj. – note especially the use of the noun *les polyvalents,* the tax inspectors empowered to look at all aspects of the book-keeping, *la comptabilité,* of small shopkeepers. In the 1950s, they excited the fury of Pierre Poujade (born in 1920) and in the 1970s that of Gérard Nicoud (born in 1947). Both men sought to defend *les travailleurs indépendants* (self-employed workers), especially *les artisans* et petits commerçants* (small shopkeepers), against what they termed *les enquêtes abusives* (see above, ABUSIF) *du fisc,* symbolized by *les polyvalents.* See also POU-JADISME in II. *Un lycée polyvalent* is a high school providing classical, modern and technical streams (see COLLÈGE in IV).

pondérer, v. – not to ponder, *méditer,* but to balance or to weigh. Hence the expression *une majorité pondérée,* a weighted majority, as in the European Community. *La pondération* also means careful thought before expressing an opinion, as in the polite way of saying that someone had made some very hasty judgements: *on nous avait accoutumés à plus de pondération,* we had grown accustomed to having matters more carefully considered.

pouvoirs publics, n.m.p. – a frequently used general term, the equivalent of the British 'the authorities'.

préfet, n.m. – a senior civil servant, seen in the past by many as symbolizing administrative centralization at the level of *le département* (see above, ADMINISTRER). The first *préfets* were appointed by Napoléon, although Louis XIV's *intendants de justice, de police, des finances* may be seen as precursors. Many are *énarques* (see above, ECOLE NATIONALE D'ADMINISTRATION) or graduates, *anciens élèves*, of another *Grande Ecole**. Appointed by the *Conseil des Ministres*, the Cabinet, they are regularly moved from one post to another; either, occasionally, as a disciplinary measure, or so that they should not identify themselves too closely with their *département*, or, as happened in some cases after May 1981, as a result of a change in the political complexion of the government. They are thus far from being *inamovibles* (see above). Until 1982 the *préfet* – assisted by a *sous-préfet* in each *arrondissement* – represented the interests of the State in his *département*, and his wide-ranging functions included supervision of all government services in the *département* (significantly called *les services extérieurs*), economic development, keeping the government informed of the state of public opinion, law and order, and, traditionally, the executive functions now entrusted to the *Conseil général* (see above). He used also to be responsible for administrative supervision of local authorities (*la tutelle*, see below; see also OPPORTUNITÉ in II). In one of the first legislative measures when the Socialists came to power in 1981, a Decentralization Act, the *préfet* was stripped of the last two functions, the executive powers of the *Conseil général* were transferred to its *président*, and local authority decisions were immediately applicable, *exécutoires de plein droit*, and no longer subject to his *tutelle*. At the same time, while he retained his other functions, his title was changed to *Commissaire de la République* (with its obvious Revolutionary overtones) and his headquarters was no longer to be called *la préfecture* but *l'hôtel départemental*.

In Paris and several large towns there is also *un Préfet de Police*, also appointed by the government, and since the 1960s *un Préfet de Région* in each of France's 22 regions.

préjudice, n.m. – legally, a tort, and in ordinary language, damage, as in *faire quelque chose au préjudice de quelqu'un, porter préjudice à*, do something to another person's disadvantage. Prejudice is *un préjugé* or *un parti pris;* 'to look at something with an unprejudiced eye' is *examiner quelque chose sans parti pris. Une question préjudicielle* or *un jugement préjudiciel* is an interlocutory question, judgement, as when a national court asks the European Court of Justice to make a ruling, *statuer*, as to whether the Treaty of Rome is applicable in a particular case. This is because Community law takes precedence over national law, *car en effet le droit communautaire prévaut sur le droit national, prime le droit national.*

présentement, adv. – at the present time, now. Presently, as in 'I'll do it presently', is *tout à l'heure*.

prévarication, n.f. – not refusal to give a direct answer (*tergiverser;* and 'Don't prevaricate!' is *Alors? C'est oui ou non?*), but maladministration, especially in the sense of fiddling the books. *Prévariquer*, to fail in one's duties. See also below, RÉFORMER.

prévenir, v. – a confusing word in that it can mean to warn, as in *il faut prévenir la police*, and to prevent, in the sense of avoiding, averting, forestalling, as in *comment prévenir le terrorisme?* and *mieux vaut prévenir que guérir*, prevention is better than cure. To prevent in a more positive sense is *empêcher*. The adjective *prévenant* means thoughtful, considerate, and *un prévenu* is an accused person, a defendant (in law); (see below, TRIBUNAL). *La prévention* can mean prevention, of crimes, or accidents, as in *la prévention routière*, road safety. It also means prejudice, as in *combien de préventions à dissiper dans ce domaine*, in this area how many prejudices have to be overcome. *La détention préventive*, remand in custody (awaiting trial).

primer, v. – not to prime, which is *amorcer*, as in *amorcer une pompe*, to prime a pump. Neither does it mean *faire boire*, as in to prime with drink, or *mettre au courant*, as in to arrive at a meeting well primed. What it does mean is take precedence over, as in such expressions as *le droit communautaire prime le droit national*, Community law takes precedence over national law.

procès, n.m. – a trial. A process is *un procédé* (if a simple operation) or *un processus* (if a complex operation).

projet, n.m. – project, but also draft as in *projet de lettre* (*un avant-projet* is a first draft). *Un projet de loi* is a government Bill/US Bill before Congress. See below, PROPOSITION.

promotion, n.f. – can mean promotion, especially to a higher rank in an order: *on vient de fêter sa promotion au grade d'Officier dans l'Ordre des Palmes académiques*, we have just celebrated his promotion to the rank of *Officier* in the *Ordre des Palmes académiques* (*Les Palmes académiques* are a distinction awarded to those who have rendered outstanding service to French education, culture and science). The more usual word for promotion is *l'avancement*. *Une promotion* has the particular meaning of one's year, in the sense of all the people who entered a course of study at the same time, as in *il appartenait à la même promotion que moi*, he was in my year. Note also *la promotion sociale*, upward social mobility of the working class, social advancement. See also PROMOTION in III.

proposition, n.f. – proposition but also proposal; *une proposition de loi* is a Private Member's Bill in Parliament.

provoquer, v. – to cause, as well as provoke, as in *provoquer un accident,* or *l'accident a provoqué un immense embouteillage,* the accident caused a huge bottleneck.

purger, v. – note the expression *purger sa peine,* to serve one's sentence (see above, PEINE).

reconnaissance, n.f. – as the English (military) reconnaissance, but also recognition, as in *la reconnaissance d'un nouveau régime,* and gratitude.

récupérer, v. – to recover, in the sense of *récupérer un prêt,* to get back a loan. Also to salvage for recycling, to reuse. P.T. was once told that pig-swill was *un bouillon de récupération* (the normal meaning of *bouillon* is broth). Also to recuperate, recover one's strength after an effort, but not after illness, which is *se remettre, se rétablir;* though presumably not, if P.T.'s informant was right, *avec du bouillon de récupération.*

réformer, v. – not only to improve by change, but also to exempt someone from National Service, *le service militaire,* on health grounds or to discharge a man from the Army for ill-health: *il a été réformé pour invalidité,* disablement. Hence, *Réformé, mon cher! Cassé pour prévarication* (see above) – 'Discharged, old chap! Cashiered for fiddling the books.' In this context, the Board that decides whether a young Frenchman is fit for military service, *apte* pour le service,* is known as *le conseil de révision.*

régime, n.m. – more meanings than régime has in English, including a diet, a hand of bananas, and a scheme, as in *le régime général de la Sécurité Sociale.*

régulier, adj., **régulièrement,** adv. – note the meaning of 'quite legally': *Notre équipe l'a emporté tout à fait régulièrement,* our team won quite fairly; *des députés régulièrement élus,* Members of Parliament elected under the normal rules. Note also de Gaulle's assessment of Pétain's attitude in 1940: *Ce vieux soldat, qui avait revêtu le harnois au lendemain de 1870, était porté à ne considérer la lutte que comme une nouvelle guerre franco-allemande. Vaincus dans la première, nous avions gagné la deuxième . . . nous perdions maintenant la troisième. C'était cruel, mais régulier.* (This old soldier, who had put on uniform immediately after 1870, was inclined to consider the struggle as no more than another

Franco-German War. Beaten in the first, we had won the second . . . we were now losing the third. It was cruel, but quite above board.) A regular soldier is *un militaire de carrière* as opposed to *un appelé, un militaire du contingent**.

relaxer, v. – to acquit, discharge (an accused person), whereas *relâcher* is to release (a prisoner). *La relaxe* is acquittal. The very fashionable adjective *relax* or *relaxe*, to be relaxed, and the verb *se relaxer*, to relax, are still frowned upon by many French people who prefer *détendu* and *se détendre*. *Il est très relax*, He's really laid-back (adolescent English, 1983).

relevant, present participle – not relevant, which is hard to translate. A relevant question is *une question pertinente*, but 'That's quite irrelevant' has to be something like *Cela n'a rien à voir avec la question*. Irrelevant issues are *des problèmes, des considérations, tout à fait hors de propos*. *Relevant* is the present participle of *relever*. *Relever de* means 'to be the responsibility of'. The large number of expressions involving *relever* and its derivatives shows how necessary it is to use this book in conjunction with a dictionary.

repaire, n.m. – not repair, which is *une réparation*, but den or hide-out: *La France s'efforce de ne pas être le repaire et le sanctuaire du terrorisme international*, France is making every effort not to be the hide-out and sanctuary of international terrorists.

répertoire, n.m. – in addition to repertory and repertoire, means an alphabetical list (of names and addresses, legal decisions, etc.).

répréhensible, adj. – as well as having the same moral association as the English word, can also mean liable to be punished by law.

répression, n.f. – from the verb *réprimer*. Has the meaning of the English word repression (*Aussi la répression en Pologne a-t-elle été vue par le Kremlin comme un épisode de cette guerre permanente et non comme une atteinte aux libertés fondamentales*, Thus repression in Poland was seen by the Kremlin as an episode in this continuous war and not as an attack on the basic freedoms; Jean-François Revel, *Comment les démocraties finissent*, 1983, p. 142). But also, in legal parlance, a neutral word for curbing, suppression: *répression de la fraude** *fiscale* (tax evasion) and, in notices displayed in some French cafés, *répression de l'ivresse* (drunkenness).

requête, n.f. – not a request, *une demande* (see DEMANDER in III) but a legal petition: *pour demander le divorce, l'époux demandeur doit présenter, par l'intermédiaire d'un avocat* (see above, AVOCAT), *une requête au juge aux affaires* matrimoniales* (the judge responsible for matrimonial cases).

révoquer, v. – to dismiss, especially a civil servant. On being warned in 1935 by her *inspecteur d'académie** of the possible consequences for her teaching career of her extreme left-wing political activities, the philosopher Simone Weil replied: *J'ai toujours considéré la révocation comme le couronnement de ma carrière* (Simone Pétrement, *La Vie de Simone Weil*, 1973, vol. 1, p. 227), I have always thought that to be dismissed would be the crowning point of my career (she was not *révoquée*). To revoke at bridge is *faire une fausse renonce*. To bid is *annoncer*; to double, *contrer;* to go down, *chuter;* three down, doubled, redoubled and vulnerable, *trois de chute, contrés, surcontrés et vulnérables*. Why include this information, *ces renseignements? Tout honnête* homme devrait pouvoir faire un quatrième au bridge*, should be able to make up a fourth at bridge.

rude, adj. – not rude like minor functionaries (*grossiers, peu polis*) or as in a rude story (*une histoire triviale*, une histoire grivoise, une gauloiserie*). *Rude* means coarse, as in *c'est un personnage un peu rude* (he's a bit uncouth); and harsh. When Robert Damiens (1715–57), a servant who tried to stab Louis XV with a penknife, learned that he was to have his right hand burned off, boiling pitch poured into his wounds, and be torn apart by horses, he commented – to the horrified admiration of Diderot – *la journée sera rude*, it's going to be a hard day (letter 194, to Sophie Volland, 14/15 October 1760). More recently (1 February 1982), discussing the difficulties encountered by left-wing intellectuals with the Left in power, *Le Point* wrote: *Ils font, en cette rude année du changement, cure* de modestie* – In this harsh year of change, they are having a course of treatment in modesty.

saisir, v. – to seize physically (*il m'a saisi le bras*) but also officially to inform or refer to, as in *il existe pour les pays indépendants la possibilité de saisir l'ONU* (UNO), and, when a crime has been committed, *le parquet* (see above) *en est saisi*, the public prosecutor's office is informed, as in the very technical 'The court is seized of the matter'. *Une saisie* is seizure (by a court), distraint, whereas *une saisine* is a decision to refer a matter to a court or administrative body.

sanctionner, v. – to punish a person or a fault, as in *tout délit* (see below, TRIBUNAL) *doit être sanctionné par la loi*. But also to approve, to confirm official recognition upon, as when Roland Barthes commented, in defence of his structuralist approach to Racine in 1965 against the criticism by Raymond Picard, *Picard prétend* que la critique* *universitaire n'existe pas. A tort, car l'Université est une institution. Elle a son langage, son système de valeurs, qui sont sanctionnés par les examens.* (Picard claims that University [academic*] criticism does not exist. He's wrong, since the University is an institution. It has its language, its value-system, on which official approval is bestowed through examinations.) To the non-native speaker (*à celui dont le français n'est pas la langue maternelle*), *sanctionner* can also occasionally seem ambiguous, as when *Le Monde* wrote on 15 May 1982, when talking about the Argentinian invasion of *Les Malouines*, the Falklands: *Même ceux à qui de telles mesures répugnent, comme l'Irlande et l'Italie, ont sanctionné le coup de force militaire* (Even those countries that find such measures repugnant, such as Ireland and Italy, have approved sanctions against the armed attack); or when the same newspaper on 4 September 1981 quoted the Economy Minister, Jacques Delors, as saying: *La démocratie veut qu'après la discussion, il faut savoir sanctionner* (In a democracy, after discussion, one must be able to impose sanctions). A similar ambiguity may be noted for the corresponding noun, *une sanction.*

schéma, n.m. – not a scheme (*un projet* or *un régime* – see both terms above) but a diagram, a sketch or an outline plan; *un schéma directeur* is a master-plan for a town, a region.

seconder, v. – to help, assist, not to second (a motion, a proposal), which is *appuyer (une motion, une proposition)*. A civil servant who is seconded is *détaché* (see above, GRANDS CORPS DE L'ETAT).

souple, adj., **souplesse**, n.f. – flexible, flexibility, especially in the context of negotiations, *des négociations, des pourparlers, des tractations.* According to popular French mythology, this is not a quality for which the UK negotiators in Brussels are noted. Likewise, the UK is criticized for its unwillingness to recognize *le principe du donnant-donnant*, give-and-take, officially known as *la solidarité communautaire.* Thus, in return for support over the Falklands issue, the UK should have been more flexible, *souple,* over agricultural prices and budget contributions.

supporter, v. – although *supporter* is usually to stand, bear, put up with, and not to support, which is *appuyer* or *soutenir* (see II), note that *un support* is a support both physically and in an administrative context, as in *la région comme support de la planification décentralisée,* the region as the basis for decentralized planning. *Un supporter* is, however, used in a sporting context for a supporter.

terme, n.m. – care is needed with this word, since it can mean either term or conclusion, ending. Thus there is a difference between *aux termes de l'accord* (according to the terms of the agreement) and *au terme des négociations* (at the end of the negotiations). *A terme* means in the long term, as in *à long terme, à moyen terme, à court terme*. See also TERME in III.

territorial, adj. – as in English, when talking about *les eaux territoriales,* but note that *les territoriaux* are not the Territorials (in the Army, who are *les volontaires)* but the oldest troops.

titulaire, adj., **titulariser,** v. – whereas titular suggests ownership only in name, *titulaire* denotes effective ownership as by right: *un professeur d'université est titulaire de sa chaire,* cannot be removed from his Chair. In the *Ancien Régime,* before 1789, all legal officers (*tous les hommes de loi, les juges, aussi bien que les notaires et avocats*) were *titulaires de leur charge,* owned their practices. *Notaires* (see above) still do (see below, VÉNAL). To possess a driving licence is to be *titulaire d'un permis de conduire.* An established civil servant is *un fonctionnaire titularisé. La titularisation* traditionally confers *la sécurité de l'emploi,* tenure (see above, MUTATION). There is an essential distinction in the whole of the Civil Service, *la fonction publique,* between *les titularisés,* those who have to be kept in employment, and *les auxiliaires, les contractuels*, les vacataires,* those appointed, *nommés,* on a temporary basis, *à titre temporaire.* The latter can be *licenciés,* dismissed, or, as it is sometimes more politely expressed, *remerciés.* An article in *Le Monde,* 11 February 1982, commenting on the preference of French teachers for schools in the South, *le Midi*,* rather than the North, observed that *Tous les collégiens et lycéens de l'Hexagone* ont droit à des enseignants titulaires et qualifiés.*

train, n.m. – note the expression *un train de mesures,* a batch, series of measures.

tribunal, n.m. – has the more general meaning of court of law in addition to the more limited meaning of the English word tribunal. Thus an habitual offender, *un récidiviste,* is also *un habitué des tribunaux. La Gazette des Tribunaux* gives details of recent cases heard before the courts. The French equivalent of 'You will be hearing from my solicitor' is *Il y a des tribunaux en France, monsieur! Et vous aurez de mes nouvelles.* Among the many 'tribunals' (in the English sense) are: *le tribunal paritaire des baux ruraux* for settling conflicts, *des litiges,* between farm tenants and landowners, *les preneurs et les bailleurs* (see *bail**) and *le conseil des prud'hommes* for settling differences between individual employees and their employers. As for the courts, there are three levels in

France, trying cases according to their degree of seriousness: *le tribunal de police* (when judging civil cases, called *le tribunal d'instance*); *le tribunal correctionnel* (when judging civil cases, called *le tribunal de grande instance*); and *la cour d'assises* (with a parallel *cour d'appel,* for appeals against decisions of the lower courts). Verdicts of *la cour d'assises* can be quashed only on a technicality, *cassés pour vice de forme* (see above, CASSER); if this occurs the case is reheard by another *cour d'assises.* Penal offences (*des infractions,* or, in a general sense, *des délits*) are classified as: *des contraventions* (minor offences, such as minor motoring offences), tried by the *tribunal de police; des délits,* tried by the *tribunal correctionnel;* or *des crimes,* tried by the *cour d'assises.* When a person is charged with an offence, he becomes *l'inculpé;* as a defendant before one of the two lower courts, he is called *le prévenu,* and before *la cour d'assises, l'accusé.* Note also that the term very frequently used for a prisoner is *un détenu.*

trombone, n.m. – a paper clip, as well as a musical instrument.

truand, n.m. – a crook, not a schoolboy playing truant, which is *un élève qui fait l'école buissonnière.* A more general word for a criminal is *un malfaiteur.*

tutelle, n.f. – administrative supervision, or a priori control (see above, CONTRÔLE). Thus *le ministère de tutelle* of a nationalized concern is the one to which it is immediately responsible, as *le Ministère des Transports* for railways. An important function of the *préfet* (see above) that was abolished in 1982 was *la tutelle des conseils municipaux,* the right to veto decisions, *délibérations* (see above), of local councils not only on grounds of legality, *la légalité,* but also of appropriateness, timeliness, *l'opportunité**. Henceforth, it will be only in the courts that the legality of such decisions can be tested.

vacation, n.f. – not holidays (*les vacances; les grandes vacances* are the summer holidays – see RENTRÉE in IV), but either lawyers' fees, as in *il touche de fortes vacations,* legal vacations (when the courts are not sitting) or, in the singular, an auction sale (more frequently *une vente aux enchères*).

vénal, adj. – may have the derogatory connotations of the English 'venal' or may just mean 'can be bought' (as, under the *Ancien Régime, un office vénal,* an official post that could be bought). Note also *la valeur vénale,* the market value.

ventiler, v. – in addition to meaning to ventilate, also means to break down (of a total, accounts, a budget). Thus *la ventilation des dépenses* is the breakdown of expenditure. To break down a problem into its constituent parts is *décomposer* (see above).

verbaliser, v. – to make an official report against, with a view to taking legal proceedings. Also *dresser un procès-verbal,* to take down details for an official report (often shortened to *p.v.).* See also above, MINUTE.

vigueur, n.f. – note the expression *en vigueur,* in force (of regulations, laws, treaties, etc.).

'X' – in French law, when the perpetrator of an offence (for example, a theft) is not known, *on porte plainte* (you lodge a complaint) *contre X.* In filling in a form or questionnaire, the English 'insert X (or tick/US check) the appropriate box' is rendered by *cocher la case appropriée.* See also GRANDE ECOLE in IV.

II History and Politics

abusif, adj. – when Jean-Pierre Azéma and Michel Winock (*La III*^e *République*, revised edn, 1976, p.60) describe the Paris of 1870–71 as *une capitale abusive et belliqueuse*, they mean that its determination to fight on against the Prussians after the Armistice had been signed led it to assume a leadership over the provinces to which it had no right. See also ABUSIF in I.

acquis, n.m. – note *l'acquis communautaire*, the decisions taken in the EEC before the United Kingdom joined on 1 January 1973. *Les Britanniques doivent apprendre à respecter l'acquis communautaire* (The British must learn to respect what has already been decided) really means: the British must not try to change the Common Agricultural Policy, *la Politique Agricole Commune*. But for educationists, *l'acquis* is opposed to *l'inné* (in the Nature/Nurture debate). Not to be confused with *un acquit*, a receipt, as in *pour acquit*, which should precede your signature when you cash a cheque in France, or in *par acquit de conscience*, to salve one's conscience.

adhésion, n.f. – the act of joining, accession, from *adhérer à*, to join, to accede to. Britain's joining and continuing membership of the Common Market, *l'adhésion britannique au Marché Commun*. Is also used in a wider context, as in the expression *adhérer de cœur et d'esprit à une action**, to join whole-heartedly in an action.

alternance, n.f. – began to acquire, with the signature of *le programme commun* between Socialists and Communists in September 1972, a new political meaning. Thus commentators observed that no Communist Party which has succeeded in obtaining power has ever given it up, and began to ask *Les Communistes français accepteront-ils l'alternance?* – will they leave office if they lose an election? (or, more to the point, will they ever hold elections?). The election of François Mitterrand in May 1981 was widely heralded as evidence, *la preuve*, that *la Cinquième République offrait la possibilité de l'alternance, malgré vingt-trois années de domination par la droite*, the Fifth Republic offered the possibility of an opposition coming to power legally, through elections, in spite of twenty-three years of right-wing domination.

appeasement – someone who approved of the policy of the British and French governments towards Hitler in the late 1930s is still known as *un Munichois*, and the policy itself as *la politique de la reculade*, backing down. *L'apaisemement* normally means the successful calming down of pains or fears, though one can *réclamer des apaisements*, demand reassurances, for example from the government.

atlantiste, adj. – in favour of maintaining an alliance with the United States of America and links with NATO (*OTAN – Organisation du Traité de l'Atlantique Nord*) in spite of the French withdrawal from the integrated NATO command structure in 1966. Thus Annie Kriegel, one of the most distinguished contemporary political commentators in France and an ex-member of the French Communist Party, asked in an article in *Le Figaro* on 12 October 1981, entitled *Les crédos atlantistes de François Mitterrand: Est-il possible de gouverner longtemps ensemble lorsque les uns [le Parti Socialiste] sont plutôt atlantistes et les autres tout à fait acquis à Moscou?* (Can a government last long when some of its members [the Socialist Party] are favourable to the Atlantic Alliance and the others wholly on Moscow's side?). A criticism levelled by the more nationalistically-minded ex-Gaullists, such as Jacques Chirac, against Giscard d'Estaing was that of *un atlantisme excessif.*

avertissement, n.m. – a warning or a brief preface to a book, not an advertisement. The expression *une mise en garde* is also used, especially in diplomacy, and is slightly stronger than *un avertissement*. An advertisement is *la publicité* (sometimes abbreviated to *la pub*) or *une réclame*, and the small ads in a newspaper are *les petites annonces*. Brand advertising is *la publicité de marque* and product advertising on French radio *la publicité compensée*. For advertising on French radio and television, see AUDIO-VISUEL in X.

ballot – not *un ballot*, which from its meaning of 'kitbag' became a term of abuse ('nitwit') in the trenches during the First World War, but *un scrutin*. Postal ballot, *un vote par correspondance*. Proxy vote, *un vote par procuration*. However, *un ballottage* is used in an electoral context; *il y a ballottage, le député* (see below) *sortant est en ballottage*, indicates that no candidate has obtained an absolute majority of the votes cast, *des suffrages exprimés*; a second round, *un deuxième tour de scrutin*, will accordingly be necessary. In 1965, François Mitterrand's supporters drew considerable satisfaction from the fact that *il avait mis le Général de Gaulle en ballottage*, had prevented him from being elected on the first ballot. A voting paper is *un bulletin de vote*.

bonapartiste, adj., n.m. – following the example of Napoléon Bonaparte (1769–1821) and of his nephew Louis-Napoléon Bonaparte
(1808–73) in using a real or supposed breakdown of the normal
process of government to justify the introduction of an authoritarian
régime, based on direct popular support (and the use of *le plébiscite*).
H.E. has heard of a country primary-school teacher, *un instituteur de
campagne* (see below, RÉPUBLIQUE; in IV, LIBRE; in V, SECULAR) at the
beginning of this century, who on stormy, windy nights would say: *Ce
n'est pas une nuit à mettre un bonapartiste dehors*, It's not a fit night to put a
Bonapartist out of doors. See also below, BRUMAIRE, CÉSARIEN,
GAULLISTE.

bourgeois, adj., n.m., **bourgeoisie,** n.f. – middle-class, the middle
classes. *La petite bourgeoisie*, petty bourgeoisie, in Marxist terminology.
Boillot points out that *ce mot n'a pas toujours en français le sens péjoratif*
(derogatory meaning) *qu'il a en anglais*. *La cuisine bourgeoise* indeed has
no derogatory overtones, *aucun sous-entendu péjoratif*, when describing
simple, unpretentious cooking. *Vivre en bourgeois* means – or used to
mean – to live without working with your hands, often off your *rentes**.
However, there are few examples of any French intellectual using the
word with favourable connotations. One is reminded of Flaubert's
J'appelle bourgeois quiconque pense bassement, and Jacques Brel's famous
song, *Les Bourgeois*, had the untranslatable refrain: *Les bourgeois, c'est
comme les cochons, plus ça devient vieux, plus ça devient . . . con.*

brave, adj., n.m. – as an noun either a Red Indian brave or a veteran
of the Napoleonic wars. De Gaulle used the term in his offer of *La Paix
des Braves* to the Algerian *Front de Libération Nationale* (FLN) in 1959. As
an adjective, *brave* is also used in a dismissive, somewhat derogatory
way: *il est bien brave, ce sont de braves gens* – i.e. well-meaning but not
over-intelligent or socially distinguished. See also BRAVE in VI. The
normal translation of brave is *courageux*.

Brumaire, le dix-huit – 9 November 1799, the date in the Revolutionary calendar on which, in *l'an VIII de la République*, Bonaparte
carried out the military *coup d'état* which led to the establishment of *Le
Consulat* (see below) and, subsequently, to *Le Premier Empire* (1804–
14). After his nephew, Louis-Napoléon, had carried out a similar *coup
d'état* on 2 December 1851 (the anniversary of the proclamation of the
First Empire, 1804, and of the Battle of Austerlitz, 1805), he was
violently attacked by Marx in 1852 in *Le 18 Brumaire de Louis Bonaparte*.
The extent to which events have changed and the word has become
shorthand for a military takeover can be seen in *Le Monde*, 1 January
1982: *Il est trop tôt pour préjuger l'effet sur la Pologne elle-même de ce '18*

Brumaire' [13 December 1981], *le premier survenu dans un pays communiste*. It is too early to anticipate the effect which this '18 Brumaire', the first to take place in a Communist country, will have on Poland itself. See below, CÉSARIEN, GAULLISTE, THERMIDOR.

cabinet, n.m. – sometimes synonymous with the British 'Cabinet' or the American 'Administration', in the sense of 'Government' (also *un Ministère**). A cabinet reshuffle is *un remaniement ministériel*; a shadow cabinet can be translated by *un cabinet fantôme* or, more frequently, *un contre-gouvernement* (the French don't have one, however). But *cabinet* is also frequently used in the sense of 'Private Office', the group of personal advisers on whom a Minister will rely both for advice and information and for ensuring that his wishes are indeed carried out and not obstructed by the permanent officials of the Ministry. During the present century, *les cabinets ministériels* have taken on a considerable importance and, in the Fifth Republic, consist largely of higher civil servants and members of the various *Grands Corps**, who have been seconded, *détachés*, from their normal duties. The *cabinet* is run by a *directeur**, and there may also be a *chef de cabinet*, responsible for public relations, relations with Parliament, the press, etc. It is also usual for the Minister to appoint to his *cabinet* at least one *Conseiller d'Etat* (see CONSEIL D'ETAT in I) and, if his is a spending Ministry, someone from the Finance Ministry, *le Ministère de l'Economie et des Finances*. Thus a sort of 'old boy network'* is established, reducing to some extent interministerial conflicts. If a Minister has local responsibilities (for example, as *Maire* – see below – of a large town, like Mauroy in Lille and Defferre in Marseilles), he will appoint someone solely to look after the interests of his town (see below, MANDAT). Experience in *un cabinet ministériel* is essential for any bright young civil servant with political ambitions. The *hauts fonctionnaires* tend to go back to their *corps d'origine* or Ministry when the politician in whose *cabinet* they have served loses office.

The *Préfets** also used to enjoy the services of a *cabinet*, and the *Commissaires de la République* have the same privilege now that the proposed reform of local government has come into effect.

césarien, adj. – both an operation connected with childbirth (*Macduff naquit par césarienne*, 'was from his mother's womb/Untimely ripp'd') and a régime (*la Cinquième République fut considérée, à ses débuts, comme un régime césarien*). Since 1789, France has had an impressive succession of successful, unsuccessful, would-be – and occasionally reluctant – Caesars: Napoléon I (1769–1821 [1799–1814]); Napoléon III (1808–73 [1851–70]); Edmé Patrice Maurice de Mac-Mahon (1808–93 [1873–77]); Georges Boulanger (1837–91 [0]); Philippe

Pétain (1856–1951 [1940–44]); and, at least in the eyes of his political opponents, Charles de Gaulle (1890–1970 [1958–69]). *Le césarisme* may be defined as the assumption of power by a leader deriving his authority from real or supposed military prowess, generally at a moment of real or alleged national crisis.

collaborateur, n.m. – in a narrow political sense, and with a capital C, someone who accepted Marshal Pétain's policy after the famous *poignée de main*, handshake, at his meeting with Hitler at Montoire in 1940 and who worked enthusiastically for the Germans during the 1940–44 occupation. With a small c, someone who works with you, and, occasionally – euphemistically – somebody who is rewarded for doing a great deal of boring work in a junior capacity by being referred to as *un de mes collaborateurs. Voici M. Pécuchet, un de mes collaborateurs,* Here is Monsieur Pécuchet, who has done all the work (for which I take the credit); also as a contributor to a newspaper: *Il collabore au 'Figaro',* He writes for *Le Figaro*.

colon, n.m. – not a :, which is *deux points*, nor a part of the body, *le côlon*, but a colonial settler or a child at *une colonie de vacances*. In North Africa (*le Maghreb*), and especially in Algeria, France adopted from the middle of the nineteenth century the Roman policy of establishing *des colonies de peuplement* (settlements), especially after the failure of a native uprising in 1870 coincided with the defeat suffered by France in the Franco–Prussian War and the consequent cession to the German Empire of Alsace-Lorraine. French families not wishing to live in what now became part of the German Empire were offered lands confiscated from the rebels, and those who made this choice became *les pieds noirs* (so called, reputedly, because they wore black shoes, whereas the native population went barefoot), whose descendants later organized the events of 13 May 1958 which brought Charles de Gaulle back to power and led to the establishment of the Fifth Republic. A distinction is made between *le grand colon*, who owned land and derived considerable benefit from the system, and *le petit colon*, a term often synonymous with *petit blanc*, poor white. In the view of some of his critics (e.g. Pierre Nora, Conor Cruise O'Brien), Albert Camus (1913–60) had many of the attitudes of *le petit blanc*. It is not true, however, that his grandfather came to Algeria to escape the German occupation of Alsace. The family had lived in Algeria since 1840.

confident, n.m. – not the characteristic of election candidates, however hopeless their chances, but someone to whom one confides secrets, *à qui on fait des confidences*; also a character in a classical tragedy, a confidant, whose role is to listen to the protagonists. To be confident, *être confiant*; self-confidence, *la confiance en soi*.

conforter, v. – not to comfort, *réconforter,* but to strengthen, support, encourage. Well on the way to becoming a vogue word. The vulcanologist Haroun Tazieff, in an article about the dangers of earthquakes (*Le Monde,* 4 August 1982), wrote of *le confortement préventif du bâti existant,* the preventive strengthening of existing buildings. The word is frequently used also by politicians and journalists. Thus *conforter une opinion,* strengthen a view already held; *les associations seront aidées, confortées, protégées, stimulées* (M. Henry, *Ministre du Temps libre, Le Monde,* 25 July 1981) – the organizations will be helped, strengthened and protected; *il convient de conforter les succès remportés sur le front de l'inflation* – we must not let up on our success in the fight against inflation; and, referring to the anti-Jewish bomb outrages, *les attentats à la bombe,* in Paris, *dès lors, on peut affirmer que ces terroristes ne font que conforter les meilleurs supporters de Begin et Sharon en France* (*Le Monde,* 13 August 1982) – it can therefore be said that all these terrorists achieve is to strengthen the hand of Begin's and Sharon's most ardent supporters in France.

conservateur, n.m. – more likely to be the curator of a library or museum, *le Conservateur d'un musée, d'une bibliothèque,* than a political conservative, who would be *un homme de droite.* However, it would be political suicide for a French conservative politician to call himself *un conservateur* – or even, nowadays, *un homme de droite.* Most call themselves *des libéraux* or *des modérés.* See below, ORDRE MORAL; LIBÉRAL in III, FAMILLE in VI.

consulat, n.m. – a consulate in the sense of an office which looks after the interests of foreign citizens, *des ressortissants d'un autre pays.* Also the period of French history which goes from the seizure of power by Napoléon Bonaparte on 9 November 1799, *le dix-huit Brumaire* (see above), to the proclamation of the First Empire on 18 May 1804, and Napoléon I's subsequent act of self-coronation – with the blessing of Pope Pius VII – on 2 December 1804. As Jean-Louis Quermonne observes (*Le Gouvernement de la France sous la Ve République,* 1980, p. 539), the Fifth Republic appeared initially to some observers *sous les traits d'un consulat qui, une fois la crise surmontée, ferait place à la restauration d'un régime parlementaire de type traditionnel* (as a *consulat* which, once the crisis had been overcome, would give way to the restoration of a parliamentary régime of a traditional type). A not inaccurate assessment, *une appréciation* non sans perspicacité.*

contingent, adj., n.m. – philosophically, the adjective has the same meaning as in English, and is much used in the early work of Jean-Paul Sartre as synonymous with 'absurd'. *Le contingent* is the body of conscripts in the French Army, as distinct from the professionals, *l'armée de métier;* the conscripts themselves are called *les appelés.* In 1954 Pierre Mendès-France used the threat to commit *le contingent* to the war in Indo-China as a bargaining counter in the negotiations leading to the Geneva agreements which led to the establishment of a Communist-dominated North Vietnam and a supposedly independent régime in the South. From 1954 to 1962, *le contingent* was permanently involved in the Algerian war, thus greatly increasing the latter's unpopularity. It has been suggested that the collapse of the Generals' putsch in April 1961 was in part due to the fact that *les militaires du contingent* were able to listen to the news broadcasts from Metropolitan France on their transistor radios, *leurs transistors.* For *contingent* meaning a quota, see III.

courtier, n.m. – not a courtier, *un courtisan* (however, *une courtisane* is a courtesan), but a broker, as in diamond broker. A stockbroker is, however, *un agent de change* (see CHANGE in III). *Jouer les courtiers honnêtes* is to play the honest – that is, impartial – broker, but the French also use the expression *Monsieur Bons Offices* for honest broker.

cumul, n.m. – see below, MANDAT.

débonnaire, adj. – easy-going, relaxed, not debonair, which is *élégant et bien élevé.* Thus, Valéry Giscard d'Estaing's remark in *La Démocratie française* (1976), comparing the France of 1950 with that of 1975: *Si elle était réellement libérale* dans ses structures politiques, cette société exerçait de puissantes contraintes sur l'individu. Les grandes institutions sociales que sont la famille, l'école, l'Eglise et, bien entendu, l'Etat, imposaient leur autorité sans partage, même si c'était d'une manière débonnaire.* (Although it was effectively liberal in its political structures, [French] society put powerful constraints upon the individual. Those great social institutions, the family, school, the Church and, of course, the State, exercised undivided authority, albeit in an easy-going way.)

décade, n.f. – strictly speaking, a period of ten days in the Revolutionary calendar (see above, BRUMAIRE and below, THERMIDOR), and not a decade, ten years, *une décennie.* We note, however, the growing tendency of French journalists, and even academics, to use *une décade* for a period of ten years. *Un lustre* is, in addition to lustre and a chandelier (*un chandelier,* a candle-stick), a literary word for a period of five years.

décentralisation, n.f. – has been called *la grande affaire* du Septennat de François Mitterrand*. May be translated into English as devolution. It means the transfer of powers of decision from the central organs of the State to elected local bodies. The word *décentralisation* has sometimes been used incorrectly, *de façon abusive* (see above, ABUSIF) to mean the transfer of powers of decision from Paris to centrally appointed civil servants in the provinces – *le préfet** or what are significantly called *les services extérieurs des Ministères*. This is, strictly speaking, *la déconcentration*. Also used for the development of activity in the provinces: *la décentralisation industrielle, culturelle, théâtrale,* etc. It was Lamennais (1782–1854) who, in 1848, gave one of the best definitions of centralization: *La centralisation, c'est l'apoplexie au centre, et la paralysie aux extrémités*, centralization results in apoplexy at the centre and paralysis on the periphery.

défiance, n.f. – distrust, not defiance, which is *un refus obstiné, une attitude de défi*. On 29 January 1982 an article in *Paris-Match* described how, during the Second World War, *les Anglo-Américains craignaient de soutenir des mouvements de Résistance dont l'orientation* politique éveillait leur défiance,* were afraid of supporting a number of Resistance groups of whose left-wing tendency they were suspicious. *Se défier* means to distrust. However, *défier* means to defy or challenge, and *un défi* is a challenge, as in the titles of the two best-selling books, *des best-sellers,* by Jean-Jacques Servan-Schreiber: *Le Défi américain* (1967) and *Le Défi mondial* (1980).

délibération, n.f. – in addition to the meanings of the English word, *une délibération* is used in French to designate the decisions of a local council. Recent decisions by some British local councils declaring their towns 'nuclear-free zones' have a precedent in France: in the late forties, during the Cold War, a rural *conseil municipal* (see below) *vota une délibération* (adopted a resolution) *interdisant à quiconque de faire exploser une bombe atomique sur le territoire de la commune* (forbidding anyone to explode an atomic bomb within the boundaries of the commune) *et chargea le garde-champêtre de veiller à l'exécution de la délibération* (and made the village constable responsible for ensuring that the decision was respected).

demander, v. – not to demand but to request: *le 17 juin 1940, la France demanda un armistice à l'Allemagne,* asked for an armistice. To demand is *exiger,* and a demand *une exigence,* but in an industrial relations context it is *une revendication,* and when it comes from the tax-collector (*le percepteur*), *une lettre de rappel*.

démonstration, n.f. – a show of force, *une démonstration de force*, or the proof of a theory, *la démonstration d'une théorie* (whereas we use the Latin Q.E.D., the French say C.Q.F.D., *ce qu'il fallait démontrer*). Therefore, not a political excuse for holding up the traffic, which is *une manifestation* (he's gone to a demo, *il est allé à une manif*). Note, however, that *une manifestation* has other meanings: an official ceremony, as in *les manifestations du 14 juillet;* also *une manifestation artistique*. In Bordeaux, in 1982, a traffic notice read *déviation à cause de la manifestation sportive prévue,* Diversion for the sporting event (in point of fact a football match).

dénoncer, v. – not only to denounce, report somebody, but to renounce a contract or treaty. Thus Pierre Miquel writes on p. 201 of volume II of his *Histoire de la France* (1976), explaining the effects of the defensive strategy implicit in the construction of the Maginot Line by the French, *Hitler pourrait ainsi construire tranquillement sa ligne Siegfried et mettre la Ruhr à l'abri des Alliés, cependant que la Belgique dénonçait l'accord militaire de 1920 avec la France et revenait à la neutralité. La frontière du Nord, non défendue par la ligne Maginot, était désormais ouverte.* (Hitler would thus be able to build the Siegfried Line undisturbed and protect the Ruhr against the Allies, while Belgium renounced the military treaty of 1920 with France and went back to being neutral. The Northern frontier, undefended by the Maginot Line, lay open to invasion.) The debt of the modern historian to the ideas expressed by de Gaulle in *Vers l'armée de métier* in 1935 is interestingly obvious here. De Gaulle argued that the very fact of constructing the Maginot Line was a sign that the French were giving Hitler. They were telling him that he had a free hand to the East since France would in no circumstances attack Germany. What de Gaulle wanted was a professional, highly mechanized army, capable both of defending France against the German tanks and also, should the occasion arise, of intervening to protect France's allies in Eastern Europe. There is an intriguing continuity here with the later Gaullist concept of *la force de frappe tous azimuts* (see below, DÉTERRER).

député, n.m. – an elected member of the *Assemblée Nationale*. Not to be confused with deputy, *délégué,* as in Deputy Manager, *Directeur délégué.* Thus *M. Chaban-Delmas, Député-Maire* (see below) *de Bordeaux* does not mean that he is Deputy Mayor of Bordeaux but that he is both a *député* and the *maire* of *Bordeaux* (see below, MANDAT). When a *député* is appointed to ministerial office he must give up his seat in the *Assemblée Nationale* (see below, SUPPLÉANT).

déterrer, v. – not to deter, *dissuader,* but to unearth. The (nuclear) deterrent is *la force de dissuasion* and a strike force *une force de frappe*. After France's withdrawal from the NATO integrated command structure in 1966, *le retrait de la France de la structure de commandement intégré de l'OTAN*, the French General Staff, *l'Etat-major français*, talked disquietingly about *la force de frappe tous azimuts*, the ability to despatch nuclear bombs in any direction. But see below, HEXAGONE, for a more modest view. A task force may be translated as *une force d'intervention*.

division, n.f. – most of the English meanings, except a parliamentary one, probably because French MPs, *les députés*, do not go into division lobbies, but indicate whether they are *pour* or *contre* by pressing a little button in front of them. It is not necessary to be physically present to have one's vote registered. See p. 48 of *Le Nouvel Observateur* for 31 October 1981, describing a particularly agitated session at the Palais-Bourbon: *Par intervalles, on procède à un vote électronique. Les députés de permanence* courent allumer les plots dans les travées, ça se passe très vite, c'est une sorte 'd'Intervilles' étrange* – from time to time, they vote, using an electronic device. The MPs on duty dash up and down switching on the little lights in the rows of seats, it happens very quickly, it's a kind of curious 'It's a knock-out'. 'Without a division' is thus *sans procéder au vote*, and 'The House divided', *on procéda au vote*.

étiquette, n.f. – frequently used in the sense of label, as in *l'étiquette d'une boîte de petits pois*, or *toutes les étiquettes politiques*, all political tendencies. The English 'etiquette' may sometimes be rendered by *le protocole*. Thus, *il est très protocolaire*, he's a stickler for etiquette. See also ÉTIQUETTE and LABEL in III.

éventuel, adj. – not eventual, but possible, as in *une guerre éventuelle, les conditions d'un compromis éventuel*. An article on the consequences of earthquakes (*Le Monde*, 4 August 1982) talked about *des bâtiments dont est accepté l'effondrement éventuel tels que hangars*, entrepôts*, buildings such as sheds, warehouses, whose collapse is an accepted possibility. The adverb *éventuellement* has a similar meaning, comparable to *le cas échéant*, 'should the situation arise'.

exemplaire, adj. – in addition to the normal meaning of exemplary, providing an example to be imitated, can also have the sense of 'offering an illustration'. Thus Pierre Miquel, discussing French politics in 1924 in volume II of his *Histoire de la France* (1976, p. 189) writes: *L'échec des gouvernements du Cartel est exemplaire: il manifeste avec netteté l'impuissance où se trouvait alors la gauche dans l'exercice du pouvoir*, The failure of the governments of the left-wing coalition known as *Le Cartel des gauches* exactly illustrates the impotence of the Left in the exercise of power at that time. One of the points most frequently made by political commentators after the election of François Mitterrand in 1981 was that this was the first time the Left found itself in power in a strong constitutional position. The previous occasions where a left-wing government had emerged from a general election (*des élections législatives*) – *le Cartel des Gauches* of 1924; the Popular Front of 1936; 1946, with the alliance between the old Socialist Party, *la Section Française de l'Internationale Ouvrière*, the Communist Party and the new left-wing Catholic Party, the *Mouvement Républicain Populaire;* the *Front Républicain* in 1956 – had been under political systems where no single party had a majority and where the President of the Republic had no real power. In the general elections which followed the dissolution of Parliament by Mitterrand in June 1981, however, the Socialist Party won an absolute majority, and took the Communists as allies in what might superficially be seen as an onset of almost condescending generosity. The constitution of the Fifth Republic, moreover, meant that Mitterrand derived the authority inseparable from any President elected by universal suffrage, and could probably count on remaining in office until 1988. Since Mitterrand had been one of the leading opponents of the constitution of the Fifth Republic when de Gaulle came back to power in 1958, the situation was thus not without its irony. See below, GAULLISTE, and the quotation from J.-F. Revel at ORDRE MORAL.

A copy of a book is *un exemplaire*. *Une copie* is a reproduction (as in *une photocopie*) or a piece of written work at school or university.

faillir, v. – not to fail, *subir un échec, échouer,* but almost to do something (but not quite). Legend insists that Louis XIV saw one of his courtiers, *un de ses courtisans,* arriving at the trysting-place exactly at the appointed hour and said to him: *Monsieur, j'ai failli attendre,* I almost had to wait.

futile, adj. – frivolous, unimportant, trivial. Thus Raymond Aron describes on p. 80 of *Le Spectateur engagé* (1981) how, in June 1940, he slept in a train near Bayonne containing *toutes les valeurs de la Banque de France,* all the stocks and shares belonging to the Banque de France, and notes: *Au moment de la catastrophe, apparaissait le caractère futile des valeurs mobilières,* you realized how trivial paper securities are. Note that a futile attempt is *une vaine tentative, une tentative inutile**. See also TRIVIAL in X, VALEUR in III.

gaullien, adj. – related to the political style and thinking exemplified by Charles de Gaulle (1890–1970), as when *Le Monde* (2 January 1982) commented thus on Mitterrand's New Year's Eve speech: '*Tout* *ce qui permettra de sortir de Yalta sera bon.' La formule, très gaullienne, de Mitterrand présentant ses vœux aux Français a fait mouche.* ('Anything that will enable us to escape from the consequences of Yalta will be good.' Mitterrand's use of this way of speaking, so reminiscent of de Gaulle, when conveying his New Year message, was right on target.) This remark made such a favourable impression because many Frenchmen, of the Left and the Right, are convinced that most of Europe's post-war problems stem from the Yalta agreement of February 1945, to which France was not a party.

gaulliste, adj., n.m. – implies a more conscious attitude than *gaullien* of loyalty to *le Général* and to his political philosophy. During the Occupation (1940–44), Frenchmen would occasionally express this attitude by carrying two fishing rods, *deux gaulles.* Since it is considered to be very witty in France to make puns, this showed that they were *spirituels** as well as being *des patriotes* (see below). As a political doctrine, especially after de Gaulle had made plain his opposition to the Fourth Republic (1946–58) in the *Discours de Bayeux* of June 1946, Gaullism involved hostility to political parties and a wish for a strong, independent executive; an insistence on national independence, allied with a suspicion of *les Anglo-Saxons* and of *l'hégémonie américaine*; a refusal to regard Communists as anything but *des séparatistes,* coupled with a readiness to envisage a special relationship between France and Russia; a liking for the *Jacobin* (see below) tradition of centralized government and for a certain *Colbertisme** in economic matters; together with a cult of *la grandeur française* which led cartoonists, *les caricaturistes,* to evoke Louis XIV and Napoléon I. De Gaulle's preference for *L'Europe des Etats* over *L'Europe Fédérale* – that is, a dislike of any form of supranationality – brought about the crisis of 1965 in the EEC, with its accompanying *politique de la chaise vide* (the policy of the empty chair) during which for six months France did not take part in discussions or meetings while nevertheless remaining a member of the Community. The problem was solved in January 1966 by *le compromis de Luxembourg,* enabling member states to veto proposals which went against their vital interests, *leurs intérêts vitaux.* The integration of France into the Common Market during the 1958–69 period marked a move away from its traditionally protectionist economic policy. The paradoxical nature of de Gaulle's achievement is marked in two other areas. He came back to power in 1958 as a result of a right-wing conspiracy which saw him as a national hero capable of keeping Algeria French; by 1962, he had outmanoeuvred his erstwhile supporters and given Algeria independence. He devised the constitution of the Fifth Republic to ensure a period of right-wing dominance, and this succeeded for twenty-three years; in 1981, this constitution gave François Mitterrand the most secure power-base ever enjoyed by any French left-wing politician.

gentilhomme, n.m. – a gentleman only in the now very antiquated sense of a person of gentle (i.e. aristocratic) birth. Molière's *Le Bourgeois gentilhomme*, M. Jourdain, who had spoken prose all his life without realizing it, is a middle-class merchant who would like to be a member of the aristocracy. 'He's a real gentleman', *C'est un vrai gentleman,* is old-fashioned, as is *Il est très vieille France* and *C'est un monsieur très bien. C'est quelqu'un de très bien* is perhaps better.

hexagone, n.m. – a six-sided geometrical figure, and hence, by extension, *la France métropolitaine* (Mainland France), as distinct from *la France d'Outremer.* An imaginative glance at a map of France, supplemented by reference to p. 8 of Michaud and Torrès, *Nouveau Guide France* (1974), enables the six sides to be identified as follows: (1) Brest-Lille; (2) Lille-Belfort; (3) Belfort-Menton; (4) Menton-Perpignan; (5) Perpignan-Biarritz; (6) Biarritz-Brest. In French strategic thinking of 1981, *c'est l'Hexagone seul qui est sanctuarisé* (protected like a sanctuary) *par l'atome national,* perhaps a less ambitious concept of *la dissuasion,* deterrence (see above, DÉTERRER) than the Gaullist *force de frappe tous azimuts,* the ability to strike at a possible adversary, *un agresseur éventuel* (see above, ÉVENTUEL) at any point on the globe. When Raymond Aron wrote (*Le Spectateur engagé,* 1981, p. 33) that the royalist ideologist Charles Maurras (1868–1952) *était hexagonal à un degré exagéré,* he meant excessively nationalistic.

inciter, v. – often weaker than the English to incite: *le gouvernement incite les Français à épargner davantage,* the government is encouraging the French to put more money into savings. See INVITER in IV.

intégrité, n.f. – as well as its moral meaning, the word is often used in a political context, with strong nationalistic associations: *pour les Jacobins* (see below, JACOBIN) *l'intégrité nationale est menacée par le régionalisme,* the Jacobin tradition sees national identity as threatened by regionalism.

interférence, n.f. – used only of radio waves or television transmission and of linguistic interference. Political interference is *l'ingérence dans les affaires d'un pays étranger,* but the recently noted *l'ingérence abusive* dans les affaires d'autrui* seems slightly pleonastic. The corresponding verb is *s'ingérer.*

intervention, n.f. – while having the same legal and politico-military meaning as in English – *la conquête de César commença par ce que nous appellerions une intervention armée,* the conquest of Gaul by Julius Caesar began by what we would call an armed invasion – the word also has the sense of an operation, as in *une intervention chirurgicale,* and of a contribution to a debate or discussion. Thus the well-meaning Dr Guillotin, whose invention sought at one and the same time to reduce social distinctions by extending the privilege of being beheaded from the nobility to all classes and to make legalized death more humane (see RUDE in I) was described in *L'Humanité* for 9 October 1981 as *un farceur, un hâbleur, un mythomane aussi, dont chaque intervention soulevait les rires du Parlement* (a clown, a braggart, a mythomaniac, whose every speech made Parliament roar with laughter). People who make contributions to a debate or committee meeting may be called *des intervenants.*

irresponsable, adj. – as well as having the normal English meaning of irresponsible, also means not accountable for one's actions before a higher authority: *des fonctionnaires irresponsables.* As Pierre Miquel explains in *Histoire de la France,* volume II, p. 102, when writing about the President of the Third Republic: *Il était irresponsable et les gouvernements étaient responsables devant le Parlement,* he was not responsible to Parliament, whereas governments were.

isolation, n.f. – insulation (see ISOLATION in VII). Splendid Isolation, *le splendide isolement.*

issue, n.f. – exit (*issue de secours,* emergency exit) or way out, outcome, as when de Gaulle is reported by Louis Terrenoire (*Le Monde,* 16 March 1982) to have said of *les accords d'Evian* which put an end to the Algerian war in 1962, *C'est une issue honorable,* an honourable way out. Also, the end, as in *il y aura un cocktail à l'issue de l'assemblée générale,* there will be a cocktail party after the General Meeting. The point at issue, *ce dont il s'agit.*

jacobin, adj., n.m. – the puritan enthusiasm of Maximilien de Robespierre (1758–94), the most famous member of the *Club des Jacobins* (1789–99) has given the term the associations illustrated by Alain Peyrefitte's comment on de Gaulle (*Le Mal français,* 1976, p. 58): *Je m'effrayais parfois de cette rigueur jacobine. Il aurait voulu gouverner par décrets*, arrêtés*, ordonnances*, et se montrait réticent à l'égard des projets* de loi* (I was sometimes frightened by his strict Jacobin principles. He would have liked to govern by decrees, orders in council, administrative decisions, and was not keen on parliamentary Bills). *Les doctrines jacobines* also involve uncompromising republicanism, centralization (*l'Etat jacobin est unificateur*), anti-clericalism, a cult of civic virtue and of the monopolistic power of the State. Thus *Le Monde,* commenting on 14 February 1982 on the proposed reform of the state radio and television service (see AUDIO-VISUEL in X), wrote: *Le Jacobinisme n'est plus de mise en matière de radio. Qui saurait nier encore aujourd'hui le droit des individus à faire entendre leur voix?* (Jacobin habits are no longer appropriate in matters concerning the radio. Who, today, would deny the right of individuals to make their voices heard?). Robespierre's more moderate republican adversaries were known as *les Girondins* (most of their leaders came from *le département de la Gironde,* of which the *chef-lieu* (main town) is Bordeaux), and in recent years the terms Jacobins and Girondins have come to designate the respective supporters of the two conflicting tendencies in the devolution debate in France, *le débat sur la décentralisation* (see above, DÉCENTRALISATION). For the modern Jacobins, primacy must still be given to the unity (see above, INTÉGRITÉ) of the French nation, to be defended against external threats and the internal dangers of disintegration; this unity – and individual freedom – can be achieved only by a strong, centralized State. The Girondins, in contrast, are in favour of a degree of devolution, within a unitary State. Traditionally, the Jacobins were to be found on the Left of the political spectrum and the 'decentralizers' and regionalists on the Right. This is far from being true today, as may be seen from Mitterrand's decentralizing reforms in this field, and from the fact that the most ardent champion of *le jacobinisme* is de Gaulle's former Prime Minister, Michel Debré.

jouer le jeu, v. – implies less the attitude implied by Henry Newbolt's *Vitae Lampada* – 'Play up! Play up! and Play the Game!' – than the acceptance, for other people's convenience, of an occasionally arbitrary set of rules. Thus *Encounter* for November 1981 quoted Godfrey Smith in *The Sunday Times* as writing: 'Thus, when the French papers claim that "Madame Thatcher ne joue pas le jeu", the obvious temptation is to translate it as "Maggie won't play the game"; whereas it actually means "she won't play along" – a very different matter'. Similarly, when Camus pointed out in 1955 that Meursault, in *L'Etranger, est condamné parce qu'il ne joue pas le jeu,* he was referring to his hero's refusal to observe the arbitrary social conventions which say that you weep at your mother's funeral and express remorse for your crimes. The French do use the expressions *le fair-play* and *jouer franc jeu,* but never about Britain's dealings with her EEC partners. French children often say *Ce n'est pas du jeu,* It's not fair.

laborieux, adj. – working, as well as hard-working, laborious, painstaking. When, in 1974, P.T. drove a French civil servant to watch

Leeds United play Liverpool at football – *une grande rencontre, une grande manifestation sportive,* a major sporting event – the Frenchman looked at the Bentleys and Daimlers overtaking them and remarked: *Ah. Je vois que le football reste toujours le divertissement des masses laborieuses,* is still the entertainment of the toiling masses. For the nineteenth-century French bourgeoisie, the term *classes laborieuses* was often synonymous with *classes dangereuses.*

légitimité, n.f. – legitimacy, but in addition to its association with children, is often used in French in a political context to indicate the right of individuals or political groups to exercise power in the State. The question is still debated both in respect of Pétain's *Etat français* (1940–44) (see below, VICHYSTE) and of de Gaulle's government in exile. Thus, commenting on Paul Reynaud's decision to appoint de Gaulle a junior minister early in 1940, René Rémond comments (*Les Droites en France,* 1982, p. 321): *Il lui conférait, sans le savoir, la légitimité qui ferait de l'homme du 18 juin le dépositaire de la légalité républicaine* (He was bestowing on him unwittingly the legitimacy which would make the man of 18 June the guardian of Republic legality). (See below, RÉPUBLIQUE). *La légitimité du pouvoir en place,* the right of the present government to rule, is also sometimes contested by the Opposition in mid-term when public opinion polls (*des sondages*) or regional and local elections indicate that the government no longer enjoys the support of the majority of the electorate.

libéral, adj., n.m. – because of its associations with the principles of private enterprise can mean conservative as well as liberal. See above, CONSERVATEUR; and, more especially, LIBÉRAL in III.

ligue, n.f. – while *La Ligue des Droits de l'Homme,* founded in 1898 in support of Alfred Dreyfus and in opposition to the *Action Française* organization, *La Ligue des Patriotes,* is a wholly legal organization, *une ligue* also designated, especially in the thirties, an extreme right-wing faction aimed at overthrowing republican forms of government and which, when armed, was illegal. Nowadays, *La Ligue des Droits de l'Homme* is primarily concerned with the protection of civil rights, *les libertés.*

livide, adj. – still keeps the Latin sense of ghastly pale, whereas livid in English tends simply to mean furious. Thus Henri Guillemin, happy to note an occasion when Napoleon showed himself a poltroon, describes on p. 144 of his *Napoléon Tel Quel* (1969) an incident which took place on the Emperor's way to temporary exile in Elba: *Un paysan nommé Duval l'attrape par le devant de son habit et lui crie: 'Dis: Vive le Roi!'*

Et Napoléon, livide, crie: 'Vive le Roi'. Il est saisi d'épouvante. (A peasant by the name of Duval seized him by the lapel of his coat and shouted: 'Say, Long live the King!' And Napoleon, pale with fear, shouted: 'Long live the King.' He was terror-stricken.) The newspaper *Sud-Ouest* (18 December 1981) described the survivors, *les rescapés,* of a mountaineering accident as being *livides de froid et de fatigue.*

maire, n.m. – a much more important figure in French local life than the Mayor or Lord Mayor in Britain both in terms of his responsibilities and the length of his term of office, *son mandat* (see below). Each of the 36,000-odd *communes* in France has a *maire,* elected by and from the members of the *conseil municipal* for a period of six years. He is chairman and leader of the Council, and is responsible for ensuring that its decisions are carried out. But he is also a state official in the *commune,* responsible for the registration of births, marriages and deaths (*l'état civil**), for organizing elections and for taking decisions (*des arrêtés**) affecting public order and safety. Again unlike the situation in Britain, the position of *maire* is often seen as a spring-board for a national political career (see below, PARACHUTER), and many national political figures take great care to keep their local base, and indeed manage to combine their duties as *maire* with heavy responsibilities in national politics: Mauroy in Lille, Defferre in Marseilles, Chaban-Delmas in Bordeaux, Lecanuet in Rouen, Chirac in Paris (see below, MANDAT). When carrying out official public duties, *le maire* usually wears *une écharpe tricolore* (sash, not scarf). In all but the smallest *communes,* one or more *maires-adjoints* or *adjoints au maire* are elected by the Council to assist the *maire* in his duties.

mandat, n.m. – as well as meaning a sort of postal order, a mandate (as in United Nations mandate) and terms of reference (e.g. of a committee), this word means both an elective office and the period during which the office is held. Thus, in the Fifth Republic, *le mandat présidentiel est de sept ans,* the presidential term of office is seven years; the Socialist slogan *Quatorze ans, c'est trop,* Fourteen years is too long, may well have been a contributory factor in Giscard d'Estaing's defeat in May 1981. To American and British eyes, one of the most curious features of French political life is *le cumul des mandats,* the possibility for a politician to hold onerous (not *onéreux**) public offices simultaneously at local, departmental, regional and national levels. Pierre Mauroy was Prime Minister and *Maire de Lille;* Jacques Chaban-Delmas was at the same time *Président de l'Assemblée Nationale* (Speaker of the National Assembly), *Maire de Bordeaux, Président de la Communauté urbaine de Bordeaux,* and *Président du Conseil régional* (see below, PARACHUTER). The Socialists have promised to do something about this, but may not be able to overcome the opposition, even from within their own ranks. However, the one *cumul* that the British find normal – that of Minister and MP – is not allowed in France; see below, SUPPLÉANT.

ménager, v. – not to manage, *gérer,* but to show care and consideration when dealing with an individual or organization. Thus de Gaulle writes in his *Mémoires* that during the twenties *Londres ménageait Berlin pour que Paris eût besoin d'elle,* London kept on the right side of Berlin so that Paris would need the British, and Alain Guichard forecast in *Le Monde* for 30 May 1981 that the Senate would try to *ménager un président garant du bicaméralisme* (guarantor of the two-Chamber system) *contre certains de ses amis* – a reference to the liking which the Left in France has shown since the *Convention nationale* (1792–95) for a single, supreme *Chambre législative,* and which a relative moderate such as Mitterrand could be expected to resist by preventing the *Chambre des Députés* from becoming too powerful. Note also the proverbial *ménager la chèvre et le chou,* run with the hare and hunt with the hounds.

métropole, n.f. – a large town, as in *une métropole d'équilibre,* a provincial capital consciously developed in order to counterbalance the excessive centralization of French society in and around Paris and give life to what J.-F. Gravier called *le désert français* in his book *Paris et le désert français* (1947). Also *la Métropole,* the mother country, as in *Les Français de la Métropole n'éprouvaient que peu de sympathie pour leurs compatriotes d'Algérie,* were not very sympathetic towards their compatriots in Algeria.

militaire, adj., n.m. – not only an adjective (military), but also a noun (soldier), as in Clemenceau's remark *La guerre est une chose trop importante pour être confiée à des militaires,* war is too important a thing to be entrusted to soldiers. Note that *un militaire* is not only used for a member of the Army, *l'Armée de Terre,* but also for a member of the Air Force, *l'Armée de l'Air. Un aviateur* is used only for someone who actually flies. Raymond Aron observes on p. 94 of *Le Spectateur engagé* that many people thought of de Gaulle, in the 1940s, as primarily *un militaire de formation* maurrassienne,* a soldier raised on the nationalist and highly conservative ideas of Charles Maurras (1868–1952), the principal theoretician of traditional French conservative and monarchical ideas. Equivalence of rank can cause confusion: *un adjudant** is not an adjutant, but a sergeant-major; a major is *un commandant* except in Belgium, where he would be *un major**; and some years ago, at the Paris Opéra, spectators thought they were going to discover a new twist to Bizet's *Carmen* when they read in the English synopsis that

Don José was a brigadier in the Spanish army. A brigadier is *un général de brigade,* and *un brigadier* a corporal or bombardier. Male readers should note that when addressing a French officer, they should place '*mon*' before the rank; ladies may omit the 'mon' (for more on this usage see MAJOR in I).

miner, v. – to undermine, as well as to lay mines: *miner son autorité.*

municipal, adj. – in a local government context, has a wider meaning than the English equivalent, since a rural *commune* with a couple of score inhabitants still has its *conseil municipal. La municipalité* is often used for the body of members of *le conseil municipal: La municipalité au grand complet* (at full strength) *a assisté à l'inauguration de la piscine* (attended the official opening of the swimming-pool).

national, adj. – for various reasons, perhaps used more frequently than in Britain or the United States, where, respectively, 'royal' and 'federal' are possible alternatives. Some examples: *la Bibliothèque nationale, le Conservatoire national de musique, l'Assemblée nationale, la fête nationale* (14 July)), *une route nationale* (major road or highway), *l'Education nationale* (reflecting the major role of central government in French education – see IV, Education and Science, *passim*), *l'Ecole Nationale d'Administration**, etc. However, the French Navy, *la Marine nationale,* is still familiarly known as *la Royale.* Although P.T. suggests that this might have something to do with the monarchist sympathies of some of its officers, a more plausible explanation is that it originates from the location of the Chief of Naval Staff's Headquarters, *le Quartier général du Chef d'état-major de la Marine,* in the Rue Royale in Paris.

nomenclature, n.f. (or *nomenklatura,* n.f.) – in addition to having the same use as the English 'nomenclature', this word has a meaning borrowed from the Russian to indicate the class of apparatchiks who monopolize power and privilege in the USSR (*l'URSS*). Something like the List of the Great and Good in England, except that *Le Figaro* talked on 6 November 1981 about *les magasins de luxe aux pays de l'Est où des produits de luxe sont mis à la disposition de la nomenclature, c'est-à-dire des nouveaux maîtres,* luxury shops in Eastern-bloc countries where luxury products are available for the nomenclature, that is to say, the new masters (whereas anyone can buy Chinese ginger from Fortnum and Mason or Macy's even if he does not know what a Royal Commission or a Senate Committee is).

notable, n.m. – a well-known local personality or worthy. *De Gaulle* *arrivait très tôt à se procurer l'appui des notables locaux, car grâce à sa formation* de militaire* (see above, MILITAIRE) *il se rappelait toujours leur nom,* De Gaulle rapidly won the support of the local worthies, since, because of his military training, he always remembered their names. René Rémond (*Les Droites en France,* 1982, p. 106) has defined *les notables* as *ces classes qui ont une habitude héréditaire de commander, de porter la parole, de représenter, de patronner* (those classes that customarily, from generation to generation, take command, act as spokesmen, represent their areas, support worthy causes and individuals).

obédience, n.f. – not obeying orders, which is *l'obéissance,* as in *l'obéissance exigée des premiers Jésuites impliquait le principe* 'perinde ac cadaver', the obedience required of the early Jesuits implied the principle of unquestioning acceptance of orders. As in the English phrase, 'belonging to the Roman obedience', *l'obédience* implies ideological conformity, so that *de stricte obédience giscardienne, chiraquienne* means faithfully following the party line of Giscard d'Estaing or his right-wing rival, Jacques Chirac. The (perhaps ironic) expression *des sociologues de multiples obédiences,* sociologists of many different persuasions, has now made its expected appearance.

occulter, v. – another vogue word in contemporary French political discourse. Having its origin in astronomy, it means to hide from view; hence, to reduce in importance. Thus (in the context of regional reform), *ils ont occulté la notion de région naturelle* and *tout échelon intermédiaire est occulté,* they have blurred, fudged, the notion of natural region, any intermediary level is hidden from view.

océan, n.m. – When used absolutely, *l'Océan* is the Atlantic Ocean.

opportunité, n.f. – not (in spite of the regrettable tendency of some Frenchmen to use it in this way) opportunity, which is *une occasion,* as in *profiter de l'occasion* and *une occasion à ne pas manquer.* Note also the expressions *par la même occasion,* at the same time, and *à cette occasion,* on this (that) occasion. *Une belle occasion* is a splendid bargain, though not always with *une voiture d'occasion,* a second-hand car. *Opportunité,* opportuneness, is linked to *opportun,* opportune, whether something is a good idea or not at a given time. Thus Jean-Emile Vié, interviewed by *Le Nouvel Observateur* in 1981 on the decentralizing legislation of the Mauroy government, wondered whether this might not in fact produce more delays, and commented: *Avec le préfet*, qui contrôlait* la légalité et aussi l'opportunité, c'était oui ou non tout de suite.* Cf. *Le Monde,* 4 August 1982, referring to the speed-limit controversy: *le gouvernement est divisé sur l'opportunité de modifier les habitudes, bonnes ou mauvaises, de* *circulation des Français* (the driving habits of the French). The leader of one of the republican factions during the early years of the Third Republic, Léon Gambetta (1838–82), was once accused of always waiting for the opportune moment to make reforms, and therefore of anticipating *l'immobilisme* described in F.M. Cornford's 'The Principle of Unripe Time' (*Microcosmographia Academica*, 1908: 'The Principle of Unripe Time is that people should not do at the present moment what they think right at that moment, because the moment at which they think it right has not yet arrived'). Gambetta replied: *Vous allez peut-être m'accuser d'opportunisme, mais ce barbarisme cache une vraie politique'* (see below, POLITIQUE), 'You are going perhaps to accuse me of opportunism, but this barbarous term hides a genuine policy'. Closely related to *l'immobilisme* and *l'opportunisme* is *l'attentisme*, a policy of wait-and-see.

ordre moral, n.m. – a conservative – not to say reactionary – régime, especially associated with *le Maréchal* Mac-Mahon (see above, CÉSARIEN), a monarchist sympathizer who was elected President of the Third Republic in 1873 but who declined the Duc de Broglie's suggestion that he use the Army to restore the Pretender, the Comte de Chambord. He was nevertheless compelled to resign when he lost the election of 1877 to the Republicans under Gambetta. The term had already been used approvingly by Napoléon III, and was later more critically applied both to the Vichy régime (1940–44), with its slogan of *Travail, Famille, Patrie,* and to the first years of the Fifth Republic. In 1965, Jean-François Revel commented in his fascinating and iconoclastic *En France* (p. 42) that *divers Français et amis de la France sont enclins à s'imaginer que les régimes autoritaires, paternalistes, d'ordre moral, monarchistes, catholiques, impériaux, dictatoriaux, de redressement, de renouveau, d'union, de sursaut, de rassemblement, d'urgence et de résurgence qui jalonnent notre histoire depuis 1789 constituent des accidents le long d'une pure ligne démocratique et révolutionnaire. Or, bien au contraire, ces régimes sont la France normale, et ce sont les gouvernements inspirés par le peuple qui sont exceptionnels: ceux-ci occupent, en tout et pour tout, quelques mois en 1848, un total de quatre années disséminées çà et là au cours de la troisième République, et deux au trois mois après la Libération.* (Various Frenchmen and friends of France tend to think that régimes that are authoritarian, paternalistic, based on the notion of moral order, monarchist, Catholic, imperial, dictatorial, established for the purpose of recovery, renewal, union, revival, national unity, to cope with a crisis, through a resurgence of effort, and which punctuate French history since 1789, are accidents along a pure democratic and revolutionary path. And yet the exact opposite is true: these régimes are the norm in France, and the exceptions are the governments inspired by popular sentiment: in all several months in 1848, a total of four years scattered here and there throughout the Third Republic, and two or three months after the Liberation.)

parachuter, v. – not only literally, to drop by parachute – though one would not have put it past the athletic Chaban-Delmas – but to present a local electorate with an outside candidate whose election would be useful to the party in a national context. Jacques Chaban-Delmas (born 1915), one of the Gaullist '*barons*', has been *Maire* of Bordeaux (see above, MAIRE) since 1947. He was the unsuccessful Gaullist candidate in the 1974 presidential election in which Giscard d'Estaing was the victor. When he was Prime Minister (1969–72), he summarized the advantages of *le cumul des mandats* (see above, MANDAT) in the lapidary phrase: *Monsieur le Maire écrit au Premier Ministre. Je crois que la lettre lui parvient,* I think the letter reaches him.

parti, n.m., **partie,** n.f. – note that one says *un parti politique,* but *une partie de campagne* (a trip into the country); *un beau parti* (a good catch in the marital stakes, whether man or woman), but *une partie de football* (*ce n'est que partie remise,* it's only postponed, we'll meet again). The different parties in a legal case or a war are *les parties* (see PARTIE in I for *partie civile* and note *les parties belligérantes,* the countries at war), but to take somebody's side is *prendre parti pour quelqu'un,* giving the expression *parti pris* in the sense of prejudice (for PRÉJUDICE see I). *Mon parti est pris,* my mind is made up; but 'he's gone to a party', *il est allé à une surprise-partie* (very forties). A formal party is *une réception,* or *une soirée.* A less formal one is *une fête* (see TRUCULENT in X), *une fiesta,* or *un boum.* Used absolutely, *les parties* means the sexual organs, known to more puritanically minded Christians as *les parties honteuses* and to the Greeks as *les parties nobles.*

patriote, n.m. – although Paul Déroulède's (1846–1914) *Ligue des Patriotes* (1882) was a very right-wing organization, J.-P. Azéma and M. Winock (*La IIIᵉ République,* 1970, p. 41) talk about *le patriotisme qui est en France fondamentalement républicain,* indicating that *patriote* still retains to some extent its original meaning of supporting the Revolution, and therefore being rather left-wing. This was noticeable both in 1870 and 1940–44, when an invasion from the East awoke memories of 1792–3 and the Republican resistance to tyranny and reaction. During the Occupation, Communists and Gaullists alike referred to themselves as *des patriotes,* as the *francs-tireurs,* irregulars, of 1870–71 had done before them.

plastic, n.m. – not to be confused with the synthetic substance that plays such an important part in our everyday lives, *la matière plastique*, but a highly explosive substance frequently used in bomb attacks on public buildings, *des attentats à la bombe contre des édifices publics,* for example during the extreme right-wing campaign against de Gaulle's Algerian policy in the early 1960s.

plot, n.m. – for one meaning of *un plot* see above, DIVISION; for others, see dictionary. But *un plot* is not a plot (in the sense of conspiracy) – *un complot,* or a plot (of land) – *une parcelle de terrain.* The plot of a play or novel is *l'intrigue.*

politique, n.f. – *la politique* may be translated by policy or politics, and only the context indicates which is meant. Note that politician may be rendered by *homme politique,* which is neutral, or *politicien,* which is often derogatory – such a man is concerned only with his own advantage, ambition, glory or, at best, putting his party's interests before that of the wider community. Thus, *Le Monde diplomatique* of August 1982 wrote: *M. Clark aborde les questions internationales en politicien qui pense d'abord aux effets de telle ou telle décision sur l'image du président aux yeux de l'opinion américaine.* (Mr Clark approaches international questions as a [self-interested and calculating] politician who thinks primarily of the impact which such and such a decision will have on the President's image in the eyes of American public opinion.) For a comparable use of the word 'politics' in English, see the lines in the version of *God Save the Queen* still sung by P.T.: 'Confound their politics,/Frustrate their knavish tricks.' A similar distinction is made between the adjectives *politique* and *politicien* – hence, *des manœuvres politiciennes.*

populaire, adj. – most frequently, 'of or by the people' – considered as a social class – rather than 'popular' in the sense of enjoying popularity. Thus, *le Front Populaire de 1936, le Théâtre National Populaire, la littérature populaire* (dealing with working-class subjects and intended for a working-class readership) and, in former days, *la soupe populaire,* free meals for the destitute. Note also the expression *les démocraties populaires,* People's Democracies, not necessarily always popular. 'He's very popular' is best rendered by *il a beaucoup d'amis, il est très apprécié de ses collègues, on l'aime bien.*

poujadisme, n.m. – the opposition, sometimes violent, of small shopkeepers and artisans to big business and, more recently, to *les grandes surfaces* (hypermarkets), to the State, and especially to *le fisc* (see REVENU in III) has for many years been a feature of French society. In the early 1950s this opposition, allied to a form of right-wing nationalism, found expression in a political movement led by Pierre Poujade which enjoyed spectacular, if short-lived, electoral success. Since the early 1970s the cause of the small shopkeeper and artisan has also been defended by a movement led by Gérard Nicoud and the pressure has sometimes been of an extra-political type: *plastiquages*, dynamiting (see above, PLASTIC) of tax-collectors' offices (*les perceptions*; see POLYVALENT in I) and blocking motorways at the height of the holiday season. More recently, other movements with similar aims have been established: Gérard Furnon's *Français de bon sens* and Gérard Deuil's *Syndicat National des Petites et Moyennes Industries*.

président, n.m. – as in *le Président de la République* of course, but in many other contexts too. The word is the equivalent of the English words president and chairperson (*présider une réunion*, to chair a meeting). When in a cultural, voluntary (*bénévole**) organization, there is both a Chairman (who does all the work) and a President (often just a figurehead); the latter is often called in French *le Président d'honneur* (see HONORAIRE in I). Strictly speaking, a lady Chairman/ President is addressed as *Madame le Président* (Simone Veil, *Président du Parlement européen*), and *la Présidente* is reserved for a male President's wife, but this is a rule ignored (or *ignorée**?) by more and more French-speakers.

profond, adj. – deep or profound. Something of a vogue word in the expression *la France profonde*, the France of the provinces and the suburbs, the 'grass-roots' (*la base*), who do not find expression for their aspirations and fears in the traditionally Paris-dominated political institutions and party hierarchies; as such the expression has replaced the older distinction made by Maurras and *L'Action française* between *le pays légal* and *le pays réel*: the Republicans chosen by the electorate and the Monarchists reflecting the real France.

question, n.f. – means torture as well as question. Officially abolished in 1784, thus putting an end to the opportunities for instructive amusement indignantly rejected by Isabelle in Act III, Scene 4 of Racine's *Les Plaideurs* (1668), when the judge Dandin asks her if she would like to come to *voir donner la question*, see someone being tortured, observing as he does so that *Cela fait toujours passer une heure ou deux*, it will always while away an hour or two.

radical, adj., n.m., **radicalisme,** n.m. – although the adjective can have the meaning of the English 'radical', as in *une solution radicale*, it is more frequently used in referring to *le Parti radical*, the oldest French political party (founded in 1901) and one that was to play a major part in many Third Republic governments. With its strong sense of history and an almost religious attachment to the principles of 1789 (especially in its anti-clericalism), it has been traditionally *le parti des petits contre les gros, contre 'les deux cents familles', contre les trusts**, politically left of centre, economically right of centre. Indeed, if the average Frenchman, *le Français moyen*, still has *son cœur à gauche et son portefeuille* (wallet) *à droite*, he is the archetypal radical. The party is at present split in two: *le Mouvement des radicaux de gauche* (MRG), closely allied to Mitterrand's *Parti socialiste*, and *le Parti radical*, part of Giscard d'Estaing's *Union pour la démocratie française*.

rampant, adj. – not rampant, but creeping, as in *une paralysie rampante* and the recently noted *des nationalisations rampantes*.

réaliser, v. – to achieve (one's ambition), to realize (one's assets), but not – at least for the purists – to realize (become aware), which is *se rendre compte que* or *de*, though most French people do, in conversation, use *réaliser* in the latter sense. The Second World War headline *L'Etat-Major français a pleinement réalisé la stratégie allemande*, though probably apocryphal, is a not inaccurate account of how the French Army achieved the strategic objectives of the Germans by allowing itself to be lured into Belgium and Holland in May 1940. When, on 9 October 1981, *Le Monde* wrote that *depuis plus d'un an, Solidarité commence à réaliser ce qu'il exige*, it meant that the Polish workers were beginning to achieve their objectives. See above, BRUMAIRE and INTERFÉRENCE.

reporter, v. – not to report, *rapporter*, but to carry over, postpone or transfer. *La conférence a été reportée à une date ultérieure**, has been put off to a later date. In French elections, in cases of *ballottage* (see above, BALLOT) *le report des voix entre le premier et le deuxième tour* is very important, with two major parties on the Left (Socialists and Communists) and two on the Right (Gaullists and Giscardians). If a Communist candidate *se retire en faveur du candidat socialiste*, the latter can benefit from *un report de voix important**, a substantial transfer of votes.

république, n.f., **républicain,** adj., n.m. – words which have a wider and more emotive connotation than their dictionary equivalents, as do also the words *démocratie* and *démocrate*. When Jean-François Revel recalled on p. 27 of *En France* (1965) that someone had said to him in 1949 of the then French ambassador to Mexico, *Je le crois sincèrement républicain*, the implication was obvious: the ambassador could be trusted not to try to put the clock back either to the anti-Republican *Etat Français* of the Vichy period, with the slogan, *la devise*, of *Travail, Famille, Patrie* replacing *Liberté, Egalité, Fraternité;* or to one of the two Napoleonic Empires (1804–14; 1852–70); or to the monarchy of *l'Ancien Régime* (pre-1789); or, quite simply, could be trusted not to participate in or support a *coup d'état.* Robert Escarpit wrote about one of the instigators of the 1961 insurrection in Algiers: *En 1957 . . . Salan passait pour républicain,* in 1957 . . . Salan could be taken for a Republican (*Mes Généraux,* 1965). And when, in 1958, Charles de Gaulle came back to power as a result of a military *coup d'état* in Algiers, he was careful to offer the reassurance that he was *prêt à assumer les pouvoirs de la République.* However, an earnest lady told P.T. as he stood looking at the various *affiches électorales,* electoral posters, in September 1958: *Je voterai contre lui, monsieur. Je suis une vraie républicaine,* I shall vote against de Gaulle. I'm a real Republican. Nowadays, however, the term is used almost as widely by the Right as by the Left; thus the neo-Gaullists of Jacques Chirac are *le Rassemblement pour la République* (RPR), Giscard d'Estaing's own party is *le Parti républicain* (PR), and the rather conservative daily newspaper *Sud-Ouest* calls itself *un grand quotidien républicain régional d'informations.*

It took a long time to establish Republicanism as the definitive form of government in France, and throughout the Third Republic the extreme Right Wing expressed its ambition of destroying it by repeating the slogan *Il faut étrangler la gueuse* (the slut). The view that it was the régime which divided Frenchmen least and which received the most widespread support can be seen from the fact that the very conservatively-minded Adolphe Thiers said in 1872 that *la République sera conservatrice ou elle ne sera pas,* the Republic will be conservative or it will not exist, while the progressively-minded Emile Zola, referring to his own theories on the scientific basis for fiction, said, in 1882, *la République sera naturaliste ou elle ne sera pas.* In the nineteenth century, the *Café de la République* was the place at which the radicals and anti-clericals went to drink, and the *instituteurs* who taught in the *écoles communales** established in 1881 were known as *les hussards noirs de la République* – young cavalrymen whose enthusiasm for defending *la laïcité* (see LAY in V) was not diminished by the black frock-coats they wore on ceremonial occasions. Jean-Pierre Azéma and Michel Winock write (*La IIIᵉ République,* revised edn, 1976, p. 172): *Pendant la laborieuse* (see above) *mise au monde de la République, l'Eglise a résolument pris le bouclier de l'Ancien Régime, et les prêtres sont les ennemis de la République. Par contraste, l'école laïque est devenue l'école maternelle de la République, la contre-Eglise, et les instituteurs ont alors été tout naturellement les catéchistes de la foi républicaine.* (During the laborious birth pangs of the Republic, the Church resolutely took up the shield of the *Ancien*

Régime and the priests became the enemies of the Republic. By contradistinction, the secular primary school became the nursery school of the Republic, the Counter-Church, and the primary-school teachers quite naturally the catechists of the Republican faith.) Winock and Azéma were both born in 1937, but are clearly expressing their grandfathers' view that *La République* really became itself only with the establishment of a secular State by *la séparation de l'Eglise et de l'Etat* in 1905, and the declaration that *La République française ne fait les frais d'aucun culte,* the French Republic does not provide funds for any form of religious worship. Characteristically the Vichy régime of 1940–44 dropped the word *République,* called itself *L'Etat Français,* and temporarily restored religious education in State schools. The Constitution of 1958 states that *La France est une République indivisible, laïque, démocratique et sociale,* thus reasserting the traditional refusal to allow any part of *le territoire national* to be alienated by treaty, lost by military defeat, or seceded in any other way, while also proclaiming its progressive faith in social legislation. The principle of non-secession did not work too well for the Algerian *départements.*

See LIBRE in IV, LAY and SÉCULIER in V.

robinsonnade, n.f. – a Utopian dream, presumably as achieved by R. Crusoe, the description of whose adventures by D. Defoe was the one book that Rousseau (1712–78) was prepared to let Emile read as a child. Thus when Bernard Poirot-Delpech, commenting in *Le Monde* for 9 October 1981 on the presence on President Mitterrand's private staff of the very left-wing Régis Debray, remarked: *on peut trouver que la société sans classe ni Etat est une robinsonnade et lutter pour son achèvement**, you don't need to believe in the possibility of a classless society in which the State has withered away in order to struggle to bring it about.

scandale, n.m. – scandal in the sense of a shameful occurrence (*un scandale financier, politique,* etc.) but not in the sense of gossip (*des potins, des médisances,* as in the French title of Sheridan's famous play, *L'Ecole de la médisance*).

Sea-green Incorruptible – As the difficulty of translating this famous description by Carlyle of Maximilien de Robespierre (1758–94) illustrates, French tends to use general abstractions whereas English prefers more concrete imagery. In French, Robespierre is simply known as *l'Incorruptible,* rather as the 'whiff of grapeshot' of *le 13 Vendémiaire, An IV* (5 October 1795) is referred to as *la fusillade* (discharge of fire) *de la rue Saint-Roch,* or *le jour où Napoléon mitrailla les manifestants royalistes* (turned the guns on the royalist demonstrators).

Secrétaire d'Etat, n.m. – a less prestigious office than Secretary of State, and designating a Junior Minister entrusted with specific responsibilities and answerable either directly to the Prime Minister or to another Minister. A British equivalent would be Minister of State. Thus in the Mauroy government of June 1981, there were two *Secrétaires d'Etat auprès du Premier Ministre:* Jean Le Gance, *Chargé de l'extension du secteur public,* responsible for supervising the nationalization programme; and Raymond Courrière, *Chargé des rapatriés,* responsible for looking after the French people who decided to come home in 1962 when Algeria became independent. A closer equivalent to a British Secretary of State would be *un Ministre d'Etat,* of whom there were five in the government formed by Pierre Mauroy in June 1981, except that the title and rank of *Ministre d'Etat* is not related to the importance of the portfolio held, but is given either in view of the standing of the individual (under de Gaulle, the novelist André Malraux (1901–76) was *Ministre d'Etat* – could he have been less? – *chargé des affaires culturelles,* responsible for Cultural Affairs), or in order to achieve a balance between the different political tendencies in the government. The French know that the American Secretary of State is the equivalent of *le Ministre des Affaires Etrangères* (since 1981, *Relations Extérieures*). The 1936 *Front Populaire* government was the first to include women, with three *Secrétaires d'Etat.* From the point of view of status, the two pairs, Secretary of State/Minister of State and *Ministre d'Etat/Secrétaire d'Etat,* form a linguistic 'chassé-croisé', like vicar/curate and *curé/vicaire* in V, chicory/endive and *endive/chicorée* in VIII.

solidarité, n.f. – for obvious reasons very much a vogue word, but one with a long history. In a French context it is usually associated with the word *effort* and means that the middle classes must make sacrifices: *un indispensable effort de solidarité au profit des plus défavorisés, des plus démunis* (the need for everyone to help the most underprivileged and impoverished members of society) *s'impose à tous* (is essential on everyone's part) – i.e., the middle classes must pay higher taxes in order to help the poor.

soutenir, v. – not to sustain (which may be rendered in various ways, according to the context, *selon le contexte*); can often be translated by support, as in *soutenir l'action du gouvernement, soutenir la cause des minorités.* As yet, *supporter* usually means to stand, put up with, as in *il supporte courageusement ses souffrances*; but see SUPPORTER in I.

subject – If you ask a Frenchman if he is a French subject, he will reply: *Non. Je suis citoyen français.* A more official word is *un ressortissant,* a national. See also SUJET in IV.

suppléant, n.m. – a substitute is not *un substitut* (see MAGISTRAT in I). *Suppléant* comes from the verb *suppléer à*, to make up for – again, not to be confused with *supplier*, to beg. One of the guiding principles, *les idées-forces*, of de Gaulle's Constitution of 1958 was the separation of the legislative and the executive. One of the ways in which this is achieved is that, on becoming a Minister, a *député* (see above) must vacate his seat in the *Assemblée nationale;* his place is then automatically taken by his *suppléant*, who is elected at the same time as the *député*. Difficulties have sometimes arisen as a result of government reshuffles, *des remaniements ministériels: suppléants* have on occasion been reluctant to resign to allow the former Minister to regain his seat in the *Assemblée nationale* through a by-election. (A by-election is *une élection partielle*, as opposed to general elections, *des élections législatives*.) It is also the *suppléant* who takes the seat of a deceased *député* (*le siège d'un député décédé*). One supposed advantage of this system is that it reduces the number of by-elections.

suppression, n.f. – the link with *supprimer*, to abolish, makes the word more neutral than suppression, *la répression**.

survivance, n.f. – not survival, *la survie*, but vestige, remains of a tradition.

tempérament, n.m. – in a political context, is used to indicate the different tendencies, especially within the French Socialist Party: *Le mérite de François Mitterrand est d'avoir su réunir autour de lui les différents tempéraments socialistes, qui vont du marxisme du CERES au réformisme de Michel Rocard.* (The merit of François Mitterrand lies in his success in uniting around himself the different tendencies of Socialist opinion, from the Marxism of the *Centre d'Etudes et de Recherches Socialistes* to the moderate reformism of Michel Rocard.) See also TEMPÉRAMENT in III and VI.

ténor, n.m. – not only a singer with a higher voice than *une (sic) basse* (short for *une voix de basse*), but also a well-known speaker, as in *les ténors de la gauche*.

Thermidor, n.m. – the eleventh month in the Revolutionary calendar, which corresponded to July/August and which, on *le 9 Thermidor, An III* (27 July 1794) saw the fall of Robespierre (see above, JACOBIN) and the beginning of the Thermidorian reaction. Hence, in 1952, Sartre's remark to Camus in the quarrel which followed the publication of *L'Homme révolté* in 1951: *Vous avez fait votre Thermidor* – You have ceased to be a revolutionary and moved over to the conservatives (Sartre, *Situations IV*, p. 91).

tiers, adj. – third, and as a noun, third party. Thus, *Le Tiers Etat* is the Third Estate. *Sous l'ancien régime, le premier état, c'était le clergé; le deuxième, la noblesse; le tiers état, c'était les roturiers* (commoners). *Le tiers monde* is nowadays more generously called *les pays en voie de développement* (PVD). *Les pays nouvellement développés* include such countries as South Korea and Brazil. In European Community parlance, however, *un pays tiers* is any country not a member of the EEC (*la CEE*), such as the USA, Russia, China or New Zealand. *L'assurance au tiers* is third-party insurance, as opposed to *l'assurance tous risques,* comprehensive insurance (see ASSURER in I).

unique, adj. – single, only, as well as unique: *un fils unique* is an only son and *un régime à parti unique* a one-party State.

usure, n.f. – in addition to usury, also means wearing out, wearing away, and it has been suggested that one of the reasons for Giscard's defeat in May 1981 was *l'usure du pouvoir.* Note also the phrase *le mot démocratie a servi jusqu'à l'usure,* the word democracy has become worn out through over-use, and *une guerre d'usure,* a war of attrition. There is a difference between *usé,* worn out, and *usagé,* used as opposed to *neuf,* new. In *Le Monde,* 16 October 1981, Alain Clément compared the American revolution, which he saw as still full of vigour, with the revolution which took place in France in 1789 and which was *usée par ses relances perpétuelles, fatiguée par deux cents ans d'effort pour s'intégrer au patrimoine national,* worn out by the constant need to reassert itself, exhausted by a two-hundred-years-old effort to become part of the national heritage. *Un usager,* a user of a public service, should be distinguished from *un utilisateur,* a user of anything else, such as an electric razor.

versatilité, n.f. – excessive readiness to change, not versatility, *la capacité de tout faire.* See *Le Monde,* 23 February 1982: *Les rapports du pouvoir public et de la haute administration ne sauraient se fonder ni sur la versatilité, démontrée ou escomptée, des 'grands commis' ni sur l'opportunisme* (see above, OPPORTUNITÉ) *qui leur est parfois prêté.* (The relationships between the government and the higher echelons of the Civil Service can be based neither on the proven or expected fickleness of the most senior civil servants nor on the opportunism of which they are sometimes accused.)

vichyssois, vichyste, adj., n.m. – on 24 October 1981, when the banking group Paribas was rumoured to be transferring as much of its capital as possible abroad in order to avoid losing all its assets through nationalization, *L'Humanité* commented: *Le grand Patronat* *français est prêt à tout faire pour faire échec aux nationalisations. Renouant avec ses traditions vichystes, il s'appuie sur l'étranger, sur l'internationale du capital, pour porter ses coups contre le peuple de France.* (French big business is prepared to do everything to bring about the failure of the national-ization programme. Returning to its *vichyste* traditions, it is obtaining foreign support, the support of the capitalist international, in order to strike against the French people.) The French clearly have long memories, since the Vichy régime of *le Maréchal* Pétain had been over for thirty-seven years, and had anyway enjoyed a semblance of inde-pendence from the German occupiers only between the armistice of June 1940 and the German occupation of the Unoccupied Zone, *la Zone Libre*, in 1942. The authoritarian ideas of the Vichy régime, its rejection of parliamentarianism, the stress it laid on the need for a return to traditional values and for the French to adopt a penitential attitude following the defeat of June 1940, the importance it attached to agriculture rather than industry, were supported by a large section of the Catholic hierarchy in France, and certainly ran parallel to the injunction, in the Anglican Book of Common Prayer, that we should 'think much of our duties and little of our rights'. Its vision of the corporatist State led to a ban on most trade-union activity, and this explains part of the shorthand function as a Boo-word which the term has for the readers of *L'Humanité*. The view on the Marxist Left in France has always been that Vichy was part of a capitalist conspiracy to keep the working class in its place, in spite of the fact that the French Communist Party was itself moderate in its opposi-tion until the invasion of Russia by Germany on 21 June 1941 impelled it into active resistance, and that the régime itself came into being as a result of a vote by the *députés* (see above) originally elected in 1936 in an upsurge of support for the Popular Front – 569 voted in favour of giving *les pleins pouvoirs* (full powers) to Pétain, and only 80 against. The words *Vichyste* and *Pétainiste* need to be carefully distin-guished. The first implies support for the régime itself; the second, support for *le Maréchal* as the only reasonable possibility at the time and as a means of reducing suffering and privation at the hands of the victorious Germans. As Henri Amouroux put it in the title of the second volume of his *Histoire des Français sous l'Occupation*, there were in this respect in 1940 *Quarante Millions de Pétainistes*. Support for the *Révolution Nationale* preached by Vichy was less extensive. See however above, ORDRE MORAL, CONSERVATEUR.

III   Economics, Industry and Agriculture

actif, n.m. – the assets (of a firm, etc); liabilities are *le passif.*

action, n.f. – an equity share, as its full title, *une action à revenu variable,* indicates. A shareholder is *un actionnaire.* See also below, BON, OBLIGATION, PART, TITRE, VALEUR. Note that the word *action* is often used for a government project. See ACTION in V.

alléger, v. – to lighten (a burden) as in *il faut alléger le poids fiscal de certains contribuables,* we must lighten the tax burden of certain taxpayers. To allege is *alléguer. Un allègement,* a lightening; *une allégation,* an allegation.

altérer, v., **altération,** n.f. – not to alter/alteration, which is simply *changer, un changement,* but to/a change for the worse. Thus, *une altération de la balance des paiements* is a worsening, deterioration of the balance of payments.

aménager, v. – not to manage (*gérer, diriger*) but to modify, adjust, or to move into new accommodation. *L'aménagement du territoire* (land-use planning), the co-ordinated development of the French regions, was one of the principal preoccupations of French governments in the sixties and early seventies. See MÉNAGER in II.

annuité, n.f. – not an annuity, *une rente* (see below) but a yearly payment: *il va amortir ses dettes par annuités et non pas par mensualités,* he is going to pay off his debts by yearly not monthly instalments.

appointer, v. – not to appoint, *nommer*,* but to pay a salary to. Similarly, *mes appointements* are not my appointments, *mes rendez-vous,* but my salary. Note also the expressions *un salaire d'appoint,* an extra source of earnings, and *faire l'appoint,* to give the right money or change. See below, SALAIRE. *Un chauffage d'appoint* is a supplementary source of heating. Pierre Poujade (see POUJADISME in II) is now *un partisan convaincu de l'utilisation de l'alcool du topinambour comme carburant d'appoint,* that is to say a fervent advocate of the use of alcohol derived from Jerusalem artichokes as an additional source of fuel.

armer, v., **armement,** n.m. – in addition to the military meaning note the expressions *armer un bateau de la marine marchande,* to fit out a Merchant Navy ship; *désarmer un bateau,* to lay up a ship. When H.E. read on a French passenger aircraft: *Les passagers sont priés de se familiariser avec* (passengers are requested to get to know) *le plan d'armement de cet avion,* he was relieved to learn that it only meant the layout of the seats and the location of the emergency exits (*sorties de secours*), life-jackets (*gilets de sauvetage*) and oxygen masks (*masques à oxygène*).

artisan, n.m. – has much wider implications than the English 'honest artisan'. *Un artisan* is primarily a skilled worker running his own business, *qui travaille à son compte,* and employing fewer than ten workers, e.g. a plumber (*un plombier*), a joiner (*un menuisier*), a locksmith (*un serrurier*). *L'artisanat* was much encouraged by Giscard d'Estaing, supposedly as a means of reducing unemployment. *Les artisans et les petits commerçants,* small shopkeepers, form a powerful interest group (see POUJADISME in II), lower in the social scale than *les professions libérales* (see below, LIBÉRAL), but often presenting a comparable problem to *le fisc,* the Inland Revenue/US Internal Revenue Service, in that they are self-employed. The smallness is emphasized in phrases such as *l'exploitation* (see below, EXPLOITER) *est restée au stade artisanal* (see below, STADE), that is, has not yet moved into mass-production, thus implying either hand-made quality (*production faite exclusivement à la main*) or a certain backwardness. *Une bombe artisanale* is a home-made bomb; home-made jam is *de la confiture maison.* Moon-lighting, *le travail noir,* is officially considered to be reprehensible in France, since it deprives *les artisans* of work.

associé, n.m. – a partner in a firm, whereas one says *son (sa) partenaire* for one's partner in marriage, or in doubles at tennis or in bridge. *Les partenaires sociaux* are, in industrial relations, and euphemistically, the bosses and the unions.

assortir, v. – to match (as of clothes, colours). *Assorti* as an adjective may be either matching or assorted, mixed.

avantage, n.m. – advantage, except that to take advantage of someone is *profiter de quelqu'un,* whereas *avantager quelqu'un* is to place someone in a more favourable position, as in *avantager un de ses enfants par rapport aux autres,* to favour one of one's children compared to the others – a practice severely limited by the Napoleonic Code; see FERTILITY in VI.

bail, n.m. – not bail, which is *une caution* (see below, CAUTION; also CAUTIONNER in I). *Un bail* is a lease in the sense of the period for which a rental agreement is to last, and hence the agreement itself. As one can imagine in a country where property-owning rights are sacred and where, according to *Le Nouvel Observateur* of 9 January 1982, eight million people rent their accommodation, the legislation governing the relationship between owner, *le propriétaire*, and tenant, *le locataire*, is complex and controversial. In the system of *le fermage*, farming out land, which gives the word *fermier* (see below) its prime meaning of tenant farmer, only in certain circumstances can the landowner refuse to renew the lease. If *le proprétaire-bailleur* (landlord) and *le preneur* (tenant) cannot agree on the terms of renewal, the case is referred to *le tribunal* paritaire des baux ruraux*, a local tribunal containing, as the adjective *paritaire* indicates, an equal number of *bailleurs* and *preneurs* from the region. Note also the expression *un bailleur de fonds* for someone who provides financial backing for an enterprise.

banqueroute, n.f. – the French have two words for bankruptcy: *la banqueroute* and *la faillite*, the latter implying no fault on the part of the person concerned, whereas the former implies at best punishable negligence. The fact of ceasing trading is marked by *le dépôt du bilan*, when the firm's balance-sheet is lodged with the judicial authorities. *La liquidation judiciaire* is the winding-up of a firm and *le syndic* (see below) is the Official Receiver.

baraque, n.f. – not barracks (*la caserne*) but a shed.

bon, n.m. – a bond, as in *bons du Trésor*, Treasury bonds (see below, TRÉSORERIE), *bon anonyme, au porteur*, bearer bond; also coupon, voucher, slip, in various commercial contexts (see below, COUPON).

bonus, n.m. – not a bonus, *une prime* (see below), but a sum of money which you receive without expecting and sometimes without deserving it. It is also called *un boni* or *une bonification*, but *des taux d'intérêts bonifiés* are reduced rates of interest to borrowers. A no-claims bonus is, strictly speaking, *une bonification de non-sinistre* (see below, SINISTRE), but everyone says *Attention à votre bonus*, Be careful about your no-claims bonus.

cadre, n.m. – a key word, much more widely used than the English military term cadre. It means a frame or framework, but also, when referring to people, a member of the salaried staff, of middle management. The salaried staff ('white-collar') unions form part of *la Confédération générale des cadres* (or *de l'encadrement*) and are a powerful interest group in France. They constantly proclaim that *nous ne voulons pas être les vaches à lait de la société socialiste,* we don't want to be the milch-cows of Socialist society.

caisse, n.f. – not only a cash desk/US cashier, but a unit of the decentralized Social Security system and an organization that pays pensions (*la Caisse des Cadres* – see above, CADRE). When you cash a cheque in France, only *le caissier* or *la caissière* has the right actually to hand over the money.

caution, n.f. – not a caution, *une réprimande,* but bail or a financial guarantee or deposit you provide when, for example, you hire a car or rent an apartment. Note also, of a piece of information, the expression *sujet à caution,* uncertain, unconfirmed.

chaîne, n.f. – note its use as a television channel (see AUDIO-VISUEL in X) and as a production line in a factory: *Le travail à la chaîne, effectué en général par des ouvriers spécialisés* (see below), *et très souvent par des travailleurs immigrés, est extrêmement harassant*,* Work on the production line, usually carried out by semi-skilled workers and often by immigrants, is extremely exhausting.

change, n.m. – not change in general, *le changement,* or small change or the correct change, *la monnaie,* but foreign currency, as in *Bureau de change;* see also below, DEVISE. However, *un agent de change* is not a foreign exchange dealer, *un cambiste,* but a stockbroker. Note also the expressions *faire prendre le change* or *donner le change à quelqu'un,* to put someone off the scent or often to give a misleading appearance of, for instance, health or joy.

charge, n.f. – frequently has financial associations. Thus, *des personnes à charge* are dependants; *le chauffage en hiver représente une charge financière importante* (see below, IMPORTANT), in winter, heating forms a significant part of one's budget; *l'Etat prend en charge les travaux requis,* the State accepts financial responsibility for the necessary work. In the case of blocks of flats, *les charges* are the heating, water and other common costs. One of the major complaints of French businessmen is that *les charges sociales* (Social Security and other similar contributions) which they have to pay prevent them from being competitive in international markets, *compétitifs sur les marchés internationaux.* Every new government promises to *alléger* (see above) *la charge des contribuables* (see below, CONTRIBUTIONS) – to make the taxpayers pay less. For the other meanings of *une charge* (and *charger,* v., *chargé,* adj.) see dictionary, but note in particular *un cahier de charges* (or *cahier des* *charges*); this is either the tender specifications for the award of a contract (see below, MARCHÉ) or the document specifying the conditions under which a contract must be fulfilled, as in *le cahier des charges des sociétés françaises de radio et de télévision prescrit le droit de réponse et l'obligation de permettre l'expression des différents courants politiques et religieux,* the contractual obligations of the French radio and television companies prescribe the right of reply and the requirement to give air time to the different political and religious tendencies.

closed shop – *le monopole d'embauche.* Illegal in France, though practised in *les docks de Marseille,* where the Communist *Confédération générale du travail* has a monopoly, and in *l'industrie du livre* (printing and bookbinding) in Paris.

colbertisme, n.m., **colbertiste,** n.m., adj. – the policy of offering state aid to private industry inaugurated by Jean-Baptiste Colbert (1619–83), Louis XIV's Finance Minister, still remained a sufficiently important element in French economic policy for *Le Point* to write on 22 February 1982 that *par les nationalisations, la France quitte l'ère du colbertisme et entre dans celle du socialisme,* through its nationalization programme, France is moving from the Colbertist era into the Socialist era. However, by its entry into the *Communauté Economique Européenne* in 1958, France had begun to abandon the traditional protectionism also associated with Colbert, and Valéry Giscard d'Estaing may also have had this in mind when Charles Hargrove (*'L'Autre Giscard': Valéry Giscard d'Estaing vu par un Anglais,* 1981) was given to understand (p. 170) that: *Les carcans catholiques, colbertistes, gaullistes*, qui emprisonnaient la société française devaient voler en éclats, comme me le disait dans un bel élan d'enthousiasme un des collaborateurs* du président* de la République*.* (The Catholic, Colbertist and Gaullist straitjackets which imposed such restraints upon French society had to fly into pieces, in the enthusiastic words of one of the President's aides.) However, as the virtual equation of *gaulliste* and *colbertiste* indicates, V.G.E. was also giving the word its additional meaning of *dirigisme,* in contrast to his own preference (separating him from Jacques Chirac) for free enterprise. For Alain Peyrefitte, *Le Mal français* (1976), Colbert is the main baddy, so much so that he writes (p. 108): *Peu de régimes furent aussi favorables que le colbertisme à la prévarication*,* Few régimes lent themselves to misappropriation of public funds so much as Colbertism.

commande, n.f. – an order (for goods, etc.), while a command is *un ordre.* However, *les commandes (d'un avion)* are the plane's controls.

commodité, n.f. – convenience, as in *Est-ce que le monde a été fait pour la commodité de l'homme?* or *même si pour les besoins de la polémique ou les commodités de l'action on recourt encore à la vision simpliste d'une droite unique et uniforme.* (Even if, for purposes of polemical debate and the convenience of action, people still resort to the simplistic vision of a single, uniform Right.) (René Rémond, *Les Droites en France*, 1982, p. 10). A commodity is *un produit* or *un article,* whereas in the narrow financial context, commodities are *les matières premières. Commode* as an adjective means convenient, easy; as a noun, see COMMODE in IX.

communication, n.f. – several meanings: a (telephone) call, a learned paper (at a seminar), a speech (at a meeting); but note *les moyens de communication* in the sense of means of transport or means of communication.

concours, n.m. – a competition, a competitive examination (see ECOLE NATIONALE D'ADMINISTRATION in I; DEGREE, GRANDES ECOLES in IV), but also help, assistance: *je vous remercie de votre aimable concours,* thank you for your kind help and co-operation. See also CONCOURS in IV.

concurrence, n.f. – competition, as in *la concurrence déloyale* (see below, LOYAL), unfair competition.

concussion, n.f. – not concussion *(une commotion;* concussed – *commotionné),* but fiddling the books, misappropriation of public funds. See PRÉVARICATION in I, CONCUSSION in VII.

conjoncture, n.f. – the immediate situation, especially of the economy or the Stock Exchange, *la Bourse.* The adjective *conjoncturel* enables a useful distinction to be made between *le chômage conjoncturel* – unemployment due to immediate, usually external, circumstances and perhaps therefore liable to go away – and *le chômage structurel,* resulting from defects in the organization of a branch of industry, or *le chômage sectoriel,* as in Northern Ireland or the North of France, where an unbalanced concentration in linen or heavy industry has produced a permanent unemployment problem. The Common Market has adopted 'conjunctural policy' as a translation of *la politique* conjoncturelle* instead of the more elegant 'short-term economic policy'. The word can also be used in a cultural context, as when the May 1981 number of *L'Esprit* wrote of *l'indéniable sens de la conjoncture intellectuelle et morale,* the undoubted ability to write books that reflect the immediate intellectual and moral climate which characterized the then very fashionable writer Bernard-Henri Lévy.

conséquent, adj. – note the sense of consistent (see INCONSÉQUENT in V) and that of considerable, sizeable (synonym of *important* (see below), *considérable*): *les rapports du tiercé vont être conséquents,* the prize-money for the *tiercé* is going to be very large (see BOOKMAKER in VII).

contingent, n.m. – in addition to meaning the conscript army (see CONTINGENT in II), also means, in a foreign trade context, a quota. *Contingenter,* to fix a quota.

contributions, n.f.p. – not contributions (which in the context of *la Sécurité Sociale* are *des cotisations*) but taxes. Thus *les contributions directes* are direct taxes such as income tax, *l'impôt sur le revenu* (see below, REVENU); *les contributions indirectes* are indirect taxes such as *la TVA, la taxe sur la valeur ajoutée,* VAT, Value Added Tax. Note that the term *un impôt* is normally used for a direct tax and the term *une taxe* for an indirect tax (but see also below, TAXER). *L'inspecteur* or *le contrôleur* (see CONTRÔLE in I) *des contributions* is the tax inspector (the person to whom you submit your return of income and who assesses what you have to pay). Anyone paying tax is *un contribuable* and in France, as in most other industrialized countries with a history of social legislation, a large number of activities take place *aux frais du contribuable,* at the taxpayer's expense. The idea of referring to taxes as *les contributions* dates back to the Revolution of 1789, and was an attempt to involve *les citoyens* more closely in the running of the country (see Articles XIII and XIV of the *Déclaration des Droits de l'Homme et du Citoyen*). Note also *mettre quelqu'un à contribution,* to enlist someone's help.

convoi, n.m. – several meanings in addition to that of the English 'convoy'. *Un convoi de marchandises* is a goods train, while on the road *un convoi exceptionnel* is an exceptionally large lorry/US truck or a transporter.

coupon, n.m. – the usual word for a coupon is *un bon,* except for the detachable interest warrant on a share certificate, which is *un coupon. Un coupon* is most frequently a remnant of a piece of material.

délivrer, v. – normally to free, not to deliver, which is *livrer,* as in *livraison gratuite,* free delivery.

dépôt, n.m. – deposit, as well as depot. But the deposit one pays when reserving something is *les arrhes.*

déshérité, adj. – disinherited, but more frequently nowadays, when speaking of a region or country, poor in resources; and of a person, economically deprived, that is to say poor (also *économiquement faible*).

détail, n.m. – means retail as well as detail, as in *acheter au détail*, to buy retail, as opposed to *acheter en gros*, to buy wholesale. The respective traders are *des détaillants* and *des grossistes*.

détention, n.f. – not a punishment at school (*une sanction* scolaire*), which is *une retenue,* but either imprisonment or the act of possessing: *La détention de l'or est illégale en Grande-Bretagne mais pas en France, où le lingot et le napoléon sont cotés en Bourse et peuvent être négociés encore plus facilement que les bons anonymes.* (The possession of gold is illegal in Great Britain but not in France, where gold ingots and Napoleons [gold coins] are quoted on the Stock Exchange and can be bought and sold more easily than bearer bonds.)

devise, n.f. – in the singular, a motto; also foreign currency, often in the plural.

différer, v. – normally to postpone, defer (*différer un paiement, une décision*), not to differ, which is *être différent, ne pas être d'accord.*

dilapider, v. – to waste one's substance in riotous living: *il a dilapidé l'héritage* de son père.* The verb is also used metaphorically, as in *il importe que le nouveau gouvernement ne dilapide pas le capital de sympathie dont il bénéficie,* the new government must be sure not to waste the advantage of the favourable opinion it is at present enjoying. A dilapidated building, *un bâtiment vétuste, délabré.*

directeur, n.m. – the head of a ministerial department, of a newspaper, of a *collège*,* but not a director of a firm, who is *un administrateur* (see ADMINISTRER in I). In a firm, *un directeur* is a manager, but *le Président-Directeur Général* is the Chairman and Managing Director. *La direction d'une firme* is the top management of a firm.

doter, v. – not to dote on (*adorer,* etc.) or to dot as in dot the i's, which is *mettre les points sur les i,* but to provide. Thus *doter une usine de matériel* (see below) *ultra-moderne* is to provide ultra-modern equipment for a factory. *Doter sa fille* is to provide one's daughter with a dowry.

échange, n.m. – note in particular *les échanges extérieurs,* foreign trade. The Stock Exchange is *la Bourse.*

économique, adj. – economical, as well as economic. Thus: *Il y a quelques années, le chauffage au gaz était plus économique que le chauffage au mazout, mais la politique* économique du gouvernement a changé tout cela.* (A few years ago, gas-heating was cheaper than fuel-oil, but the government's economic policy has changed all that.) An economic price is *un prix réel*, whereas *un prix économique* would probably indicate the lowest possible price, rendered in English by economical. *La politique de la vérité des prix* is the policy of charging *les usagers* (see USURE in II) *d'un service public* what it actually costs without any subsidy from the taxpayer, *sans aucune subvention du contribuable*. *L'économie* is the economy but economics (as an academic discipline) is often rendered by *les sciences économiques*. *Une économie* is a saving, and note the expression *faire l'économie de*, to do without, as when *Le Figaro* showed how strong the traditional anglophobia of the French Right still remains when it wrote on 15 April 1982 of the Falklands: *Il est vraiment dommage que, par manque d'imagination, on n'ait pas fait l'économie d'une crise aussi sérieuse et, en même temps, aussi futile**. It added that *La Grande-Bretagne ne pourra pas se retrancher indéfiniment derrière les vœux d'une poignée de bergers.* (It is a great pity that, through lack of imagination, we have not been spared such a serious and, at the same time, trivial crisis . . . Great Britain can't continue indefinitely to hide behind the wishes of a handful of shepherds.) It thus recalled not only Neville Chamberlain's justification for appeasement* ('a far-off country of which we know little') but also Voltaire's (1694–1778) comment in Chapter XXIII of *Candide* (1759) that the Seven Years' War was being fought for *quelques arpents de neige vers le Canada,* a few acres of snow over there in the direction of Canada.

effectif, adj. – effective, especially in a technical sense, e.g. *le rendement effectif,* effective yield (of land or an investment). *Efficace* is more frequently used to translate effective, e.g. *des mesures efficaces*, effective measures. *Les effectifs*, strength, personnel (of a firm, etc.); thus, *À la SNCF* (French Railways) *les effectifs féminins ont augmenté de 48%, alors que les effectifs totaux ont diminué de 25%,* the number of female employees has gone up by 48 per cent, whereas the total workforce has gone down by 25 per cent. *Il a été victime d'une compression d'effectifs,* he's been made redundant (see REDONDANT in X).

énergétique, énergique, adj. – an important distinction in French, since the first refers only to resources and industry. *Les seules ressources énergétiques naturelles dont dispose la France sont le charbon et la houille blanche,* the only natural energy resources France has at its disposal are coal and hydroelectricity (literally 'white coal'). The second adjective refers to people and actions, as in *une intervention énergique de la police a dispersé les manifestants,* a euphemistic way of saying that the police beat up the demonstrators.

engin, n.m. – not an engine (*un moteur* or *une locomitive*) but a machine, a vehicle or even a device, as in *un engin explosif.*

entreprise, n.f. – as well as having the usual English meanings, is a frequently-used generic term for a firm or a company. Thus *les entreprises nationalisées* are nationalized companies and *les Petites et Moyennes Entreprises (les PME)* are small and medium-sized firms, which constitute in France a powerful interest group.

équipement, n.m. – not equipment (*le matériel,* see below) but facilities: *l'équipement hospitalier, les équipements collectifs**.

étable, n.f. – not a stable for horses (*une écurie*) but a cowshed.

étiquette, n.f. – a label, including a political one. *Un label,* however, is only the label on an article or product that guarantees that it is of good quality. *Etiquette* also means a price tag, as in *la valse des étiquettes,* a poetic way of talking about inflation. See also ÉTIQUETTE in II and LABEL below.

exécuter, v. – wider in meaning than execute. Thus, *exécuter un budget, exécuter une sonate pour piano,* to implement a budget, perform a piano sonata.

exonérer, v. – to exempt (from paying a tax, etc.).

expenses – *frais* (n.m.p.). Entertainment – *de représentation;* living – *de séjour,* also called *une indemnité de séjour* (a daily living allowance), generally given as *une somme forfaitaire**; travelling – *de déplacement. Des faux frais* are overheads, as in the old joke about *les faux frais qui sont les seuls vrais,* an intranslatable pun (*un jeu de mots intraduisible*) once described to P.T. by a Frenchman as *une plaisanterie très spirituelle**, a very witty joke.

exploiter, v. – as in the definition of the difference between capitalism and communism: *le capitalisme, c'est l'exploitation de l'homme par l'homme; le communisme, c'est le contraire,* capitalism is the exploitation of man by man; in communism the situations are reversed. Also used in the morally neutral sense of bringing out the full potential of, using for purposes of production, or developing, as in *exploiter une mine, exploiter une forêt, exploiter un brevet,* a patent (see below, PATENTE). *Un exploitant de véhicules de transport en commun* is a coach operator. *Un exploitant agricole* is often what would be known in English as a farmer (see below, FERMIER), as when *Le Monde* for 10 April 1981 gave the average household income, *le revenu moyen par ménage,* of a family of *exploitants agricoles* in 1980 as 93,600 francs, and that of a family of *salariés agricoles,* farm labourers (see below, LABOURER) as 79,300 francs. The equivalent of the British National Farmers' Union, *la Fédération nationale des syndicats* (see below) *d'exploitants agricoles* (FNSEA), is violently anti-British, and equally violently opposed to the admission of Spain and Portugal into the EEC. As its ex-President, François Guillaume, remarked in May 1980: *L'Amérique latine sera à l'Espagne ce que l'Australie et la Nouvelle-Zélande sont à la Grande-Bretagne,* Latin America will be to Spain what Australia and New Zealand are to Great Britain. *Une exploitation familiale* is a family farm.

extravagant, adj. – more often used in the sense of flamboyantly eccentric than of extravagant, which is *dépensier*.

fabrique, n.f. – not fabric, *le tissu* (see below) but a factory, usually of relatively modest dimensions and not requiring extensive and sophisticated equipment, as *une fabrique de boutons*. The more general, modern word is *une usine*; see also below, FACTORERIE. However, *fabriquer, fabricant, fabrication* are general words for to manufacture, a manufacturer, manufacturing – except for cars, aeroplanes, boats, etc., where the terms normally used are *construire, constructeur, construction*. See also below, MANUFACTURE.

facilités, n.f.p. – not often 'facilities', which is *l'équipement* (see above), *les installations*. The meaning is clear in the expressions *il a des facilités pour le dessin*, drawing comes easy to him, and *des facilités de paiement*, favourable payment terms. Note, however, *ce train comporte des facilités pour handicapés*, this train has facilities for the handicapped.

factorerie, n.f. – not a factory (*une usine*) but a trading station, especially in the colonies. See above, FABRIQUE.

fermier, n.m. – not often used in the English sense of someone who lives by cultivating his own land, though *Le Petit Robert* quotes Zola as writing: *il épousa la fille d'un fermier voisin, qui lui apporta cinquante hectares,* he married the daughter of a neighbouring farmer, who brought him a dowry of 50 hectares. It more often has the sense of tenant farmer, with generic terms such as *un exploitant agricole* (see above, EXPLOITER) and even (in spite of its derogatory connotations) *un paysan* being used where one would say farmer. *Un cultivateur* is a grower; *un éleveur*, a breeder.

Les Fermiers Généraux were a group of financiers to whom the monarchs of the *Ancien Régime* (before 1789) sold the right to raise taxes. They paid *une somme forfaitaire**, a lump sum, and pocketed the difference, and although the system worked badly enough to bankrupt the State and bring about the Revolution, it is not a bad idea in other contexts. Owners of bars in New York use a comparable franchise system. They don't therefore need to *contrôler** what happens, since the only profits the barman drinks are his own. Some theatres still sell the fairly profitable right to show people to their seats to the *ouvreuses,* usherettes, for *une somme forfaitaire* instead of paying them wages. See also BAIL above, MÉTAYER and RENTE below.

fiable, adj., **fiabilité,** n.f. – frequently used (for things) as equivalents of the English reliable, reliability: *notre robinetterie* (taps/US faucets) *est garantie dix ans: c'est une bonne preuve de fiabilité.*

fourniture, n.f. – not furniture, *des meubles, l'ameublement,* but the act of supplying; note *les fournitures de bureau,* office supplies, and *les fournitures scolaires,* school stationery.

franchise, n.f. – frankness, openness, and also, among the commercial meanings, the relatively new one of franchising, in the sense of selling someone the right to sell your products under your trade name.

fraude, n.f. – *la fraude fiscale,* an illegal activity said to be widely practised in business circles everywhere, should be translated by tax evasion. Tax avoidance, taking advantage of all the possibilities offered by the law to pay as little tax as possible, is *l'évasion fiscale. L'évasion* is escape (from prison, etc.) and *l'évasion des capitaux* the flight of capital from a country to a place of greater safety or lower taxes.

gage, n.m. – forfeit (in a game), financial security, and, in some senses, guarantee or proof: *Le gouvernement devra donner des gages aux syndicats sur l'autre grand sujet de préoccupation, le chômage* (The government will have to give the unions some guarantees on the other major subject of preoccupation, unemployment). On 2 December 1851, Louis-Napoléon (see BONAPARTISME in II) stated: *Mon nom est le gage du pouvoir fort et stable, de la bonne administration,* My name is the guarantee of strong, stable power, of good administration. For *les gages* as servants' wages, see below, SALAIRE; *un tueur à gages* is a hired killer.

gain, n.m. – among its financial meanings, note that (usually in the plural) of earnings. *Le manque à gagner* is the income you would have received if you had done something you failed or were unable to do.

gas-oil, n.m. – diesel oil (for motor vehicles).

global, adj., **globalement,** adv. – overall, on the whole, as opposed to *ponctuel, ponctuellement* (see below). Thus: *une approche globale; en France,* *les interventions de l'Etat ont été globalement bénéfiques,* in France, State aid (to industry) has on the whole been beneficial.

gracieux, adj., **gracieusement,** adv. – free of charge as well as gracious(ly). See GRÂCE in V.

gratuit, adj. – means both free of charge and gratuitous, as does also the noun *la gratuité.* Thus, *La gratuité de l'enseignement public est un des principes essentiels de la philosophie républicaine,* but *il faut essayer d'éviter la gratuité dans le travail scolaire.* (Free State education is one of the essential principles of Republican philosophy . . . we must try not to make our teaching irrelevant.) A gratuity in the sense of a tip is *un pourboire,* and in the sense of the lump sum professional soldiers receive when they leave the Armed Forces, *une prime de départ* (see below, PRIME).

hangar, n.m. – not only an aircraft hangar but also a large shed, usually of a fairly rudimentary nature, for storing machinery, etc.

immatriculation, n.f. – one's name and number as appearing on an official list: *le numéro d'immatriculation, la carte d'immatriculation à la Sécurité Sociale,* Social Security number, card. *La plaque d'immatriculation (d'une voiture)* is the number-plate (of a car); in France, the last two numbers indicate the *département* in which the car is registered (*immatriculée*).

impératif, n.m. – essential requirement, necessity.

important, adj. – large as well as, or even instead of, important. Thus when *Le Figaro* on 6 November 1981 commented on the fact that French people eat nine kilos a year of *produits surgelés,* deep-frozen food, and added that *ce chiffre n'est pas important,* it meant that this was not a high figure, not necessarily that it didn't matter, since the same article continued with the reassurance, *on ne connaît pas davantage d'intoxication* qu'avec le produit frais*,* there is no more food-poisoning than with fresh produce. *L'avion est arrivé avec un retard important,* the plane was very late. See above, CONSÉQUENT.

imposer, v. – to impose a solution or one's authority (but not oneself, since 'I don't want to impose myself' would be *Je ne veux pas abuser de votre générosité*). Note also the useful expression *cette solution s'impose,* this solution is essential. Also to raise money by taxes, as in *un produit fortement imposé,* a heavily-taxed product. Although the fact that 42 per cent of the French gross internal product (*Produit Intérieur Brut,* PIB) was collected by the State in the form of taxes in 1981 led *Le Monde* to comment on 10 November 1981 that *si la pression fiscale devait s'alourdir chez nous jusque vers 50%, notre société deviendrait une des plus lourdement imposées au monde* (if the tax burden were to rise to 50 per cent, our society would become one of the most highly taxed in the world), this was mainly by indirect taxation, *les impôts indirects, les contributions indirectes*. The low level of income tax (*impôt sur le revenu*) meant, continued the article, that *l'ouvrier français est déjà le moins imposé du monde*, the French worker is already the least heavily taxed in the world; this implied, in the words of *Le Monde*, that *en matière fiscale, au moins, la France est encore un pays méditerranéen*. Note also *les revenus imposables*, taxable income, and *le taux d'imposition*, rate of tax. See above, CONTRIBUTIONS; below, REVENU.

incidence, n.f. – repercussions. Incidence is *la fréquence*.

indélicat, adj. – note the meaning of dishonest, underhand, as when M. Jobert, when he was the Foreign Trade Minister, *le Ministre du Commerce Extérieur*, said of France's worsening trade balance, *balance commerciale: Nos concurrents sont indélicats et déloyaux* (see below, LOYAL). *Une indélicatesse* is a dishonest action.

indemnité, n.f. – an indemnity, but also an allowance given on top of one's basic pay, *le salaire de base*, to compensate for some additional expense, as in *indemnité de logement*, housing allowance, *indemnité de vie chère*, cost-of-living allowance, *indemnité de représentation*, entertainment allowance, etc.

indépendant, adj. – note the meaning of self-employed. See above, ARTISAN and below, LIBÉRAL.

index, n.m. – the index at the back of a book, the list of books condemned by the Vatican, and the forefinger. The price index or cost-of-living index is *l'indice des prix, du coût de la vie*.

indûment, adv. – note the sense of wrongfully, as when the right-wing *Le Point* on 1 February 1982 complained of *quelques intellectuels indûment privilégiés par les médias*, a few intellectuals who receive an undue amount of attention from the media.

industrieux, adj. – not industrious in the sense of hard-working, *travailleur*, but skilful. Note the expressions *vivre d'industrie* for to live off one's wits and *un chevalier d'industrie* for a crook. As in the English 'clever' and the French *brillant* (i.e. superficial) and *original**, there is thus a slipping away towards the derogatory (*péjoratif*). Industrial is *industriel*, and *un industriel* is a factory-owner or manufacturer.

label, n.m. – the stamp guaranteeing the quality of an article. See above, ÉTIQUETTE, which is the normal French word for label.

labourer, v. – to plough, not to labour in the sense of to work, which is *travailler*. *Un laboureur* is thus a ploughman; a labourer is *un manœuvre*. Note that the word worker may be translated by *un ouvrier* or *un travailleur*, the former being a manual worker and the latter a worker in general. Communist spokesmen, *les porte-parole du Parti communiste*, use *ouvrier* to denote the classical Marxist dogma of class conflict, and *travailleur* when trying to appeal to a wider audience.

laisser-faire, n.m. – the French do not talk about 'laissez-faire' economics (as opposed to *le dirigisme*, State control) but about *l'économie libérale* (see below, LIBÉRALISME). *Le laisser-faire* often implies negligence, as in the associated expression *le laisser-aller* (free-and-easiness, to the point of off-handedness). Note also the idiom *se laisser faire*, to let other people get away with it. Since the French are not good at queueing (*faire la queue; former une file d'attente*), bus-stops in Paris (request stop, *arrêt facultatif*; compulsory stop, *arrêt obligatoire*) used to be fitted with a small machine which gave you a number indicating your place in any queue (*une file d'attente éventuelle**). P.T. was once about to board a half-empty bus at the Palais Royal when an old lady carrying two heavy shopping bags, *deux cabas très lourds*, arrived regretting her lack of a *numéro. Passez, madame, je vous en prie*, he said, and got on after her. A Frenchman, recognizing from his slight Belgian accent (see IMPROVE in X) that he was obviously English, tapped him on the shoulder and said, *Il ne faut pas vous laisser faire comme cela, monsieur*, don't let them get away with it like that.

large, adj. – wide. In an article in *Le Point* for 26 October 1981, Alain Dauvergne stated that the total production of milk in the EEC corresponded, by the end of 1979, to a lake which *mesurait 10 kilomètres de long et 2 kilomètres de large sur une profondeur de 5 mètres*, was 10 km long, 2 km wide and 5 m deep. According to this article in *Le Point*, a conservative weekly review, this stemmed from the fact that in 1968, when a guaranteed price was established for milk, everybody was too preoccupied with de Gaulle's visit to General Massu at Baden-Baden in order to check that the Army was a reliable ally against the students to think about the possible consequences of setting too high a price.

libéral, adj. – a fundamental distinction exists between *les salariés* (wage and salary earners) and members of *les professions libérales,* who receive fees, *des honoraires,* directly from their clients. Architects, like lawyers who have elected to be *avocats*, avoués** or *notaires*,* belong to the *professions libérales.* So also do doctors and dentists, who will sometimes express commiseration for their British counterparts whom they see as having accepted *un régime* salarial* by working for the National Health Service. *La médicine libérale* is medicine based on private practice. It can thus be misleading to translate *les professions libérales* as 'professional people' or 'the learned professions', especially since school and university teachers in France are civil servants, *des fonctionnaires,* and consequently *des salariés* (see below, SALAIRE).

See below, LIBÉRALISME, for the political and economic implications of the word.

libéralisme, n.m. – when André Fontaine wrote in *Le Monde,* 17 June 1981, about *le libéralisme viscéral et le mépris des pauvres de l'équipe Reagan,* the Reagan team's deep-seated liberalism and disdain for the poor, he was not using the word in a way that immediately evokes for the British reader either Gladstone or David Steel. For although the adjective *libéral* has many of the associations of wishing to extend personal freedom and therefore of being traditionally left of centre, *le libéralisme* is often used in a way that makes it impossible to distinguish it from British conservatism. This is because it indicates a readiness to rely on the free play of market forces, *la loi du marché,* rather than on State control (*le dirigisme*) and a planned economy (*une économie planifiée*). It could perhaps be argued that this meaning of the word in French points to the important fact that up to now personal freedom has done best in societies with a fair measure of economic freedom as well. During the 1970s the term was used principally by supporters of Giscard d'Estaing, but since the Socialist victory of May/June 1981, *le courant libéral passera,* the liberal tendency will win, has tended to become the rallying-call of the whole Right, including the Neo-Gaullists of Jacques Chirac (see GAULLIEN, GAULLISTE in II).

An intriguing example of how differently the word 'liberal' is used at the moment in English and French occurred in July 1983. On 24 July the London *Observer,* commenting on the appointment of Mr Eric Bolton as head of Her Majesty's Inspectorate of Education, wrote: 'Mr Bolton has marked liberal views, and his findings may be as uncomfortable for the government as Miss Browne's [his predecessor's] have been'. In *Le Figaro Magazine* for 2 July, however, Louis Pauwels presented an imaginary interview with a man whom he nicknamed *'l'évidentialiste'* because of his ability to state *les évidences*.* The *évidentialiste* spoke of how the inevitable break-up of the coalition between Socialists and Communists in France would bring about *des* *élections législatives anticipées* (an early general election), which would give *une Assemblée à majorité libérale* – that is to say, conservative, in accordance with the wishes of the extremely right-wing *Figaro Magazine*.

Later on in the same issue (no. 211), the first meeting in London of the International Democratic Union (*Union Démocratique International*), of which Margaret Thatcher was the executive secretary, was described as the setting up of *cette internationale du libéralisme* and its 18 members as holding the view that *le bon fonctionnement et la prospérité d'un pays dépendent de l'existence d'une propriété privée largement répandue, de la liberté d'entreprendre et de la libre concurrence, de l'existence d'un marché efficace du travail et des capitaux, c'est-à-dire de la co-opération internationale* (the smooth running and prosperity of a country depend on the existence of widely shared private property, on free enterprise and competition, on the existence of an efficient market for labour and capital, that is to say on international co-operation).

It is unlikely that this is what the *Observer* had in mind when describing Mr Bolton as holding 'liberal views'.

librairie, n.f. – although in Montaigne's time it meant a library, it now means simply a bookshop. *Un libraire* is therefore a bookseller, whereas a librarian is *un bibliothécaire* or, for the larger libraries, *un conservateur**.

libre, adj. – not free in the sense of *gratuit* (see above). *Entrée libre* means that you can go into a shop without being obliged to purchase. See LIBRE in IV for its meaning in an educational context.

location, n.f. – not location, *l'emplacement,* but renting, hiring, or booking for a theatre, etc., as in *la location est ouverte,* already booking. Note also the expression *jouer à guichets fermés,* to play to a full house (literally: closed counter, booking office).

lot, n.m. – does not mean a 'lot', except in the expression 'job lot' as in *acheter un lot de vieux livres à la salle des ventes,* the auction rooms. Also means a prize (as in *le gros lot,* the main prize, *de la Loterie nationale*) and a plot of land; *lotir* is to divide up a piece of land, especially for building purposes, and *un lotissement* is a housing development.

loyal, adj. – not only loyal, but also fair, as in articles 85 and 86 of *Le Traité de Rome* on *la concurrence loyale et déloyale,* fair and unfair competition.

lucratif, adj. – a more neutral adjective than in English. Thus, *une* *activité lucrative* is gainful employment, and *une association sans but lucratif* a non-profit-making organization.

manufacture, n.f. – an archaic term. Nowadays the process of manufacturing is called *la fabrication.* A factory is *une fabrique* (see above) or *une usine,* but *manufacture* is used for several large State-owned factories, some dating back to the seventeenth and eighteenth centuries, which specialize in articles of quality, e.g. *la Manufacture de porcelaines de Sèvres, la Manufacture de tapisseries des Gobelins. La Manufacture de tabacs* is also run by the State. One of the most prestigious of the *Grandes Ecoles** is called *l'Ecole centrale des Arts et Manufactures.* See also above, COLBERTISME.

marché, n.m. – as well as market, means agreement to buy or sell (*conclure un marché* is to agree on terms for purchase or sale) or a contract. *Un marché public* is a public services (or public works) contract between a public body and a private firm. Strict rules are laid down for the invitation to tender, *l'appel d'offres,* and the award of the contract, *l'adjudication,* must normally be given to the lowest bidder, *le candidat le moins-disant. Les marchés publics* are particularly subject to the *contrôle** of *la Cour des Comptes*.*

marque, n.f. – among its meanings, note that of make, brand (of a product); *un produit de marque* is an article well known for its quality and, by extension, *l'image de marque* is the image (as of a politician, a public figure).

matériel, adj., n.m. – as an adjective, can normally be translated by material (except that, in *The Importance of Being Earnest,* Lady Brack-nell's 'the line is immaterial' would be *la ligne n'a aucune importance*). As a noun, the word does not mean material but equipment, as in *du matériel de bureau,* office equipment, *du matériel de camping,* camping equipment. Material(s) may be either *du tissu, de l'étoffe* (for clothes, soft furnishings, etc.), or *la matière* (of a book, where *la table des matières* is the table of contents). *Les matières premières* are raw materials. *Les matériaux* are materials for building, etc. See below, MATIÈRE.

matière, n.f. – as above, MATÉRIEL; but also matter as opposed to the mind or the soul. It is also a subject one studies at school or university, but 'what's the matter?' is *qu'est-ce que vous avez?* or *qu'est-ce qui ne va pas?* 'It doesn't matter' is *ça n'a pas d'importance.*

mesure, n.f. – frequently a measure. *Des mesures gouvernementales* are government measures; *un Inspecteur des Poids et Mesures* is a Weights and

Measures Inspector. The expression *deux poids, deux mesures* may be loosely rendered as 'Why am I being treated less favourably than him? It's unfair!' Also measurement, moderation, and extent (as in *dans une certaine mesure,* to a certain extent; *dans la mesure où* . . , to the extent that . . .). Note also (*au fur et*) *à mesure que,* as in *mon inquiétude augmentait (au fur et) à mesure que le temps passait,* as time passed, I became more and more worried.

métayage, n.m., **métayer,** n.m. – crop-sharing, crop-sharing farmer, as opposed to *le fermage, le fermier,* tenant farming, tenant farmer (see above, FERMIER). Although *le fermage* dominates in Northern and Eastern France, *le métayage* still exists in the mixed farming areas of South and South-Western France.

mutuelle, n.f. – a profit-sharing organization (especially in the insurance field). Many French people belong to a *mutuelle,* which supplements the Social Security payments they receive, especially by paying all or part of the *ticket modérateur* (see DROGUERIE in VII).

notice, n.f. – for its different meanings see dictionary, but note *une notice biographique,* a short factual account of the author of a book or film, and *une notice individuelle,* the form giving personal and career details filled in every year by established teachers, *des professeurs* titularisés*,* and used for purposes of promotion and change of post. A notice may often be translated by *un avis.* To give in one's notice is *donner sa démission,* and to give notice of is *prévenir à l'avance* or *donner un préavis de,* as in *un préavis de grève,* advance notice of a strike. To give someone notice is *congédier, licencier, remercier quelqu'un.*

obligation, n.f. – not only in a moral, religious or financial sense, but also fixed-interest stock or debentures issued (*émis*) by a company (*une société anonyme à responsabilité limitée,* SARL – a public liability company, PLC), by a nationalized concern (*une entreprise nationalisée*) or by the government. *Il détient des obligations et des actions,* he holds stock and equity shares. See also above, ACTION. Care is needed with the adjective *obligatoire.* It means compulsory (as opposed to *facultatif,* optional) as in *le service militaire obligatoire, les matières obligatoires* (compulsory subjects at school), *les dépenses obligatoires* (compulsory expenditure). When talking about stock or debentures one uses *obligataire (dividendes obligataires, marché obligataire, placement obligataire, emprunt obligataire).*

offre, n.f. – offer, bid, but note *l'offre et la demande,* supply and demand.

onéreux, adj. – not onerous, which is *pénible,* but costing money, expensive. Thus Henri Guillemin writes on p. 130 of his vitriolic *Napoléon Tel Quel* (1969): *Les alliés et les amis, du reste, n'étaient pas mieux traités. L'amitié de Napoléon leur était presque aussi onéreuse qu'une guerre – perdue d'avance – eût été pour eux. Le royaume d'Italie apportait à son souverain 30 millions par an, inscrits au budget français.* (Besides, allies and friends weren't treated any better. Napoleon's friendship was almost as costly as would have been a war which, anyway, would have been lost in advance. The Kingdom of Italy provided its sovereign with 30 million a year for the French budget.) In 1982 the French government froze the prices of school stationery, *bloqua les prix des fournitures scolaires* (see above, FOURNITURE) *pour que la rentrée* (see VACANCES in IV) *soit moins onéreuse pour les parents. Faire quelque chose à titre onéreux,* to do something against payment, as opposed to *à titre gracieux* (see GRACIEUX above).

part, n.f. – not a part, which is *une partie* and, in a play, *un rôle,* but a share, including a share in the capital of a firm. For other associations see dictionary, but note especially the expressions *faire la part du feu,* to cut one's losses, as when you chop down part of the forest to stop the fire from spreading, and *être membre à part entière,* to be a full member. *Le Petit Robert* quotes a splendidly typical dictum by Mauriac: *Le christianisme ne fait pas sa part à la chair; il la supprime* (see SUPPRESSION in II) – Christianity does not compromise with the flesh. It abolishes it.

patente, n.f. – not a patent, which is *un brevet,* but the local tax that used to be levied on all commercial enterprises; now replaced by a controversial *taxe professionnelle. Patenté,* adj. means licensed (tradesman), but also, humorously, an officially recognized expert. We read on p. 26 of René Rémond's *Les Droites en France* (1982) of *les praticiens professionnels de la politique* (professional politicians) *et ses observateurs patentés* (officially recognized political observers).

patron, n.m. – either a pattern (as for a dress) or an employer. The French equivalent of the Confederation of British Industry is *la Confédération nationale du patronat français* (CNPF), the body recognized by the government as representing private industry. See PATRON in IX.

percevoir, v. – as well as meaning to perceive, this verb means to receive money, as in *percevoir une subvention,* to receive a subsidy, and to collect taxes. *Le percepteur* is the tax-collector and *la perception* the tax-collector's office.

permanent, n.m. – a full-time official (e.g. of a trade union). *Une permanence* is a period of duty (*médecin de permanence,* duty doctor) or the place or time when an official is available for consultation by the general public: *l'assistante sociale* (social worker) *assurera* une permanence à la mairie* (town hall) *tous les mercredis de 10 heures à midi* (see PERMANENCE in IV). *Une permanente* is a permanent wave. *Le spectacle est permanent* (cinema, strip club) – it's continuous.

placement, n.m. – in addition to placing in employment (*un bureau de placement* is a Job Centre), the word means investment, as in *ce placement a bénéficié d'une bonne tenue des cours* (has held up well), or *préservez votre épargne* (your savings) *avec de bons placements.* An observation in *Sud-Ouest* for 27 August 1982 perhaps draws attention to an underlying weakness in the French economy: *Les placements financiers qui alimentent directement le capital ou les emprunts des entreprises ne représentent que 35% de l'épargne française (62% aux Etats-Unis, 59% en République fédérale),* financial investments that directly provide capital or loans for firms represent only 35 per cent of French savings (62 per cent in the United States, 59 per cent in the Federal Republic).

police, n.f. – police, of course, but also an insurance policy. Government policy, however, is *la politique du gouvernement,* and a reflationary policy *une politique de relance.* See also POLICÉ in I.

ponctuel, adj. – punctual in the sense of *quelqu'un qui arrive toujours à l'heure,* but also isolated, not forming part of an overall plan. *Le gouvernement procédait par interventions ponctuelles,* the government was going in for piecemeal measures (and not systematic reforms).

prairie, n.f. – meadow as well as prairie. Grassland is *des pâturages,* as in Henri IV's famous adage, *Labourage et pâturage sont les deux mamelles de la France* – Ploughing and pasture are the twin paps of French prosperity.

préparation, n.f. – preparation in most senses of the English word, including a pharmaceutical preparation. But note that the preparations for a specific event are *les préparatifs,* as in *les préparatifs de voyage.*

prépondérant, adj. – note the expression *la voix prépondérante (du Président)* – the (Chairman's) casting vote, as laid down in the Standing Orders, *le règlement intérieur,* of some Committees.

prestation, n.f. – the general term for benefits in a Social Security context, as in *les prestations familiales.* They may be provided *en nature* (in kind) or *en espèces* (in cash). See ALLOCATION in VI. Also, the provision of services, as in *les prestations effectuées par les professions libérales* (see above, LIBÉRAL) *et par les hôteliers, restaurateurs, coiffeurs,* etc., services provided by members of the liberal professions, hotel-keepers, restaurant owners, hairdressers, etc. The Common Market is said to be characterized by *les quatre libertés fondamentales: la libre circulation des biens, des personnes et des capitaux, et la libre prestation des services* – the free movement of goods, people and capital, and the freedom to offer services.

prime, n.f. – several financial meanings, including a free gift when you buy something, an official government or local authority grant, as in *prime de naissance, prime à la construction, prime à l'amélioration des logements sociaux* (a grant for the improvement of low-cost housing), or a gratuity (*prime de départ*). The word also means a bonus, as in *les trains en France arrivent à l'heure parce que le mécanicien touche une prime. S'il n'est pas lui-même responsable d'un retard éventuel*, il fait signer une pièce* qui le dégage.* (Trains in France arrive on time because the driver receives a bonus. If he himself is not responsible for a possible delay, he has a document signed to that effect.) See PRIMER in I.

promotion, n.f. – as well as meaning promotion and advancement (*la promotion sociale, la promotion de la femme* – see PROMOTION in I), the word is widely used in a trade context, as in *la promotion d'un livre, un article en promotion,* a special offer or the object of a special advertising campaign; also *une vente promotionnelle.*

propriété, n.f. – ownership as well as property. Thus, in Fourastié et Bazil, *Le Jardin du voisin* (1980), p. 65, we read that *les Français sont . . . fortement attachés à la propriété de leur patrimoine et notamment à l'un de ses principaux modes de constitution: l'héritage*.* (The French are . . . very strongly attached to ownership of family property and in particular to one of the principal ways in which it is built up: by inheritance.)

provision, n.f. – note the expression *faire ses provisions,* to do one's shopping (also *faire ses courses*). *Une provision* is also a credit balance in one's bank account. French banks are not very sympathetic to customers who issue cheques that bounce, *des chèques sans provision,* unless, of course, one has arranged to have an overdraft, *un découvert.* However, the provisions of an Act, of a regulation, are *les dispositions d'une loi, d'un règlement* (see DISPOSITION in I).

radiation, n.f. – note the special meanings: striking off a member of *les professions libérales* from his professional body or dismissing a civil servant (see also RÉVOCATION in I); and *radiation d'inventaire,* writing-off (of equipment).

raison sociale, n.f. – the official trade name of a company, e.g. *Le Crédit Lyonnais, La Société Electronique Bull.* When, on 4 December 1981, Mathieu Galey wrote in *L'Express* of James de Rothschild (1792–1868), one of the models for Balzac's Baron de Nucingen, that *ostentatoire, vite légendaire, son luxe devient une véritable raison sociale,* his ostentatiously luxurious life-style, which soon became legendary, also served as his trade-mark, he thus meant that what the modern tax inspector, *inspecteur du fisc,* would call *des signes extérieurs de richesse* were indeed Rothschild's trade-mark and not that they were his reason for living.

recette, n.f. – a recipe, not a receipt, which is *un reçu* or *un récépissé.* Also the local office of the Finance Ministry official *(le receveur)* responsible for making and receiving payments for central and local government bodies. Also receipts in the sense of money received: *les dépenses et les recettes.*

receveur, n.m. – as in RECETTE above, and a bus-conductor, but not a receiver of stolen goods, who is *un receleur.* The official government Receiver, called in when a firm is going bankrupt, is *le syndic.*

recycler, v. – to put back into circulation, as in *le recyclage des pétrodollars,* and also to retrain. *Je vais me recycler dans les ordinateurs,* I'm going to retrain and become a computer expert.

rentable, adj. – either profitable or financially viable (see below, VIABLE). Not rentable, which would be *(propriété) disponible pour la location,* or simply *à louer.*

rente, n.f. – not the rent, *le loyer,* but an unearned income, as received by the lazy and villainous *rentier* class in Marx. Thus when, in Mauriac's *La Fin de la Nuit* (1935), Auguste Filhot *désire une bru rentée,* it means he would like to have a daughter-in-law of independent means. *Une rente de l'Etat* is a government annuity. Economists occasionally explain the relative slowness of France to industrialize in the nineteenth century by a preference for land ownership or for *les rentes sur l'Etat* or for *la thésaurisation par le bas de laine* (keeping gold coins in woollen stockings) over *les actions à revenu variable,* equity shares. Lending money to the State in return for a supposedly guaranteed income goes back a long way in France. In 1638, Pascal's father was involved in a riot to protest against the government's decision to *rembourser des titres de rente à un sixième de leur valeur,* pay owners of government stock only a sixth of the face value of their investment. The often heard *rente de situation* means the inalienable advantage one derives from one's particular position. Thus, in *Le Monde,* 19 August 1983: *la minorité (d'universitaires français) jouit d'une rente de situation qui peut revêtir des formes tout à fait scandaleuses.* (A minority (of French university teachers) have inalienable advantages and privileges which are sometimes quite scandalous.)

réservation, n.f. – as for a plane or a train, but not in a negotiating context (this is *une réserve).* The central reservation of a dual carriageway is *la bande médiane.*

revenu, n.m. – the income of an individual or a family. Thus an incomes policy is *une politique des revenus* and income tax *l'impôt sur les revenus* (more correctly, *l'impôt sur les revenus des personnes physiques* (IRPP) – for *personne physique,* see MORAL in I). The French have only recently introduced, and on an experimental, voluntary basis, *la mensualisation de l'impôt sur les revenus,* monthly payment of income tax by deduction from one's pay packet – the equivalent of the British Pay-As-You-Earn. In the system still followed by most *contribuables* (taxpayers), *on fait sa déclaration des revenus avant le 1er février,* you put in your income tax return before 1 February. *Aucun délai* n'est imparti ni toléré,* there is no period of grace. *Une amende de 10% est appliquée pour tout retard,* you are fined 10 per cent if you are late. *Pour permettre à l'Etat de remplir ses caisses* (to fill its coffers) *et d'empêcher les contribuables d'avoir la jouissance* d'argent qui ne leur appartient pas* (to prevent taxpayers from using money that is not really theirs), *les contribuables doivent verser à deux reprises un tiers provisionnel,* taxpayers must pay, on two separate occasions, a third of the tax paid in the previous year. Any adjustment is made when the final settlement is worked out, and there is a fine of 10 per cent for any late payment, even if only by one day. In order to restrict the money supply, *limiter la masse monétaire,* the government can *avancer* (bring forward) *la date de paiement du tiers provisionnel.* If it were in a Keynesian mood and wished to *amorcer la pompe pour une relance éventuelle*,* prime the pump in view of a possible economic recovery, it could conceivably *retarder* (delay) *le tiers provisionnel.* To our knowledge, however, this has never happened. The tax authorities are *les Contributions* or *le Fisc (Le Fisc nous prend tout,* continually complains a doctor friend of H.E.'s); the tax system is *la fiscalité.* See also above, CONTRIBUTIONS, FRAUDE.

salaire, n.m. – a more widely used term than salary, since most French people are paid by the month, manual workers included. *La* *paye,* or *paie,* tends to be a regional term, occasionally indicating a wage paid *tous les quinze jours,* every fortnight. The important distinction in France is between *les salariés* (wage-earners), and *les artisans et les membres des professions libérales,* who are self-employed. We are grateful to P.T.'s friend and host Jacques Magnet, *Conseiller référendaire à la Cour des Comptes,* for the following characteristically accurate *mise au point* (clarification):

> Les fonctionnaires civils reçoivent un traitement. Les militaires reçoivent une solde. Les notaires, avoués, huissiers et autres auxiliaires de justice reçoivent des émoluments. Les membres des professions libérales (avocats, médecins, architectes, etc.) en échange des conseils qu'ils donnent à leurs clients, reçoivent des honoraires. Les employés de bureau dont le travail est principalement intellectuel reçoivent des appointements.
>
> Les ouvriers dont le travail est principalement manuel reçoivent un salaire.
>
> Les domestiques reçoivent des gages.

In practice, most people talk about their *salaire,* except for actors, actresses and musicians, who receive *un cachet.*

sauvage, adj. – not only of wild animals and admirable primitives (the noble savage is *le bon sauvage*) but also as in unofficial, uncontrolled. Thus *une grève sauvage* is a wild-cat strike; *le camping sauvage* is camping not on a recognized camp site; and *le capitalisme sauvage,* although denoting capitalism as practised by John D. Rockefeller I, Jay Gould, Andrew Carnegie, and other American businessmen whom the French used to call *des struggleforlifers,* does not necessarily imply a total ruthlessness. It simply means unchecked by State legislation or corporate self-discipline. See above, LIBÉRAL, LIBÉRALISME.

service, n.m. – among its meanings, note those of tip, service charge (*pour le service, service compris);* the cover charge is *le couvert.* See ADDITION in VIII.

siège, n.m. – seat and siege, and also the permanent headquarters of a civilian organization (a military headquarters is *un quartier général). Le siège social* of a firm is its registered office.

sinistre, n.m. – a natural disaster (its victims are *des sinistrés*) and also an accident for which one makes an insurance claim. *A la suite d'un sinistre, l'assureur est autorisé à résilier votre contrat,* after a claim the insurer may, if he so wishes, cancel or terminate your policy. To renew an insurance policy is *reconduire un contrat d'assurance*. See also SINISTRE in X.

société, n.f. – often a firm. A non-profit-making society (cultural, social, etc.) is more likely to be *un club* or *une association*. The Socialist government of Pierre Mauroy gave active encouragement to what it called *la vie associative*, leisure and self-help activities.

solde, n.f., n.m. – *la solde* is a soldier's pay; *un solde* has several meanings, including a financial balance (*l'aggravation du solde des échanges pétroliers*, the deterioration of the oil-trade balance); and, usually in the plural, a reduced price sale (*des articles soldés*, bargains). While dictionaries give *solde* in the sense of a reduced price sale as masculine, some native speakers tend, *de façon abusive**, to use it in the feminine.

souffrance, n.f. – suffering and sufferance, but note *un colis en souffrance*, a parcel awaiting delivery or collection, and *un dossier** en souffrance*, a matter waiting to be dealt with.

souscription, n.f. – a subscription for a good cause; for the purchase of a collection of books; and, occasionally, for a review or magazine. *Un abonnement* is, however, more frequently used in the last case.

spécialisé, adj. – *un ouvrier spécialisé* (OS) is a semi-skilled worker, especially one working on the production line (*la chaîne*), not a skilled one, who is *un ouvrier qualifié* or *un ouvrier professionnel*. An unskilled worker, *un manœuvre*. The term *ouvrier spécialisé* has now been replaced in official circles by *agent de fabrication*.

stade, n.m. – means, in addition to a stadium, a stage in development, as in *le stade préliminaire*.

stage, n.m. – a period of training, especially in obtaining work experience.
    A stage in a theatre is *une scène*, a stage in the sense that all the world is one is *le théâtre*, and the players are *des comédiens**. A stage in the development of an organization or one's career is *une étape*, and when *les six pays fondateurs de la CEE* abolished all internal tariffs by 1968 *avec dix-huit mois d'avance sur le calendrier**, it would be idiomatically correct to say of them that *ils ont brûlé les étapes*, they sped through the different stages, without stopping.

standard, n.m. – normally a local telephone exchange, not something by which you judge, *un critère, une norme,* or that which is always going down *(le niveau des étudiants n'est plus ce qu'il était). Une standardiste,* a female telephone operator. The acknowledged Anglicism *standard* is nevertheless also used in technical phrases such as *modèle standard et modèle de luxe.*

succession, n.f. – as in English, but note that *les droits de succession* are death duties.

surface, n.f. – as in English (in some contexts, the French use the alternative *la superficie*), but *les grandes surfaces* are very large supermarkets, hypermarkets (also *les hypermarchés*). *Un grand magasin* is a department store such as Les Galeries Lafayette, la Samaritaine, la Belle Jardinière.

surplus, n.m.p. – usually American war surpluses. In other contexts, such as EEC agricultural production, it is better to use *un excédent* and the adjective *excédentaire.* The French naturally talk about *la montagne de beurre, le lac de vin* and other imaginary geographical entities when describing *les excédents agricoles du marché commun.* They nevertheless deplore them less frequently than do the British.

Note the expression *au surplus,* meaning in addition, furthermore.

syndic, n.m. – (not to be confused with *syndicat –* see below), is either the Official Receiver or the person who manages a block of flats on behalf of the joint owners.

syndicat, n.m. – much wider in meaning than trade union, and including *syndicat d'initiative* (tourist office), *syndicat de propriétaires* (owners' association), *syndicat intercommunal* (association of *communes* for certain facilities) and *syndicat patronal* (employers' association). French trade unions are not organized by trade but by industry, thus reducing the number of demarcation disputes, *les conflits sur la répartition des tâches,* which are a feature of British industrial life. Union membership is much lower than in the United Kingdom, *le taux de syndicalisation est très inférieur à ce qu'il est au Royaume-Uni* (see above, CLOSED SHOP), and the French trade-union movement is further weakened by the fact that most unions are affiliated to different Confederations on the basis of political allegiance. Thus *La Confédération Générale du Travail* has strong Communist sympathies (*c'est le moins qu'on puisse dire –* to put it mildly), *Force Ouvrière* is basically Socialist, and *La Confédération Française Démocratique du Travail* has moved away from the sympathy with the Church that used to characterize, and to some extent still does, *La Confédération Française des Travailleurs Chré-*

tiens. The CFDT now makes the running in movements towards worker management (*l'autogestion*), and is in some ways the most radical of the three major groupings. There is also a separate Confederation for the 'white-collar' unions (*les syndicats de cadres*) and some unaffiliated unions (*les syndicats autonomes*). Joint action is thus not easy although, at factory level, the different unions often form *une intersyndicale.* A shop steward is *un délégué syndical,* not to be confused with *un délégué d'entreprise,* an elected workers' representative on the Board, *le Conseil d'Administration.*

tarif, n.m. – not only Customs tariffs but charges, both for public services such as gas, electricity, water and public transport, and for the service industries.

taxer, v. – as well as to tax (see above, CONTRIBUTIONS), the word also means to fix a statutory price for an item or a service, as part of a price control policy. France has a long tradition of price controls.

tempérament, n.m. – in addition to the meanings in II and VI, note the expression *acheter à tempérament,* to buy under a hire-purchase agreement, although *acheter à crédit* is more frequently used nowadays. *On fait un premier versement,* deposit, down-payment, *et puis on paie le solde* (see above) *par versements mensuels, par mensualités,* by monthly instalments.

tenant, n.m. – not a tenant (*un locataire,* who pays rent, *un loyer*) but someone who holds a specific view, as in *les tenants de cette thèse.* Also *les tenants et aboutissants,* the ins and outs of a question.

terme, n.m. – not a term in the school year, *un trimestre,* but an end, as in the translation of Maynard Keynes's 'In the long term, we're all dead', *A long terme, nous sommes tous morts.* Thus Pierre Birnbaum (*Les Sommets de l'Etat* (1977), p. 135) wrote of *les membres de la commission d'industrialisation du VI⁰ Plan qui a surtout favorisé le libéralisme* (see above) *économique et mis un terme à* (put an end to) *la politique de planification gaulliste,* the Gaullist policy of economic planning.

Also a date by which a sum of money must be paid, as when in Balzac's novel Maxime de Trailles tells Gobseck: *Qui a terme, ne doit rien,* 'You owe nothing while you still have time to pay', and in *acheter à terme,* to buy on credit. Note especially *devoir son terme,* to owe one's rent. See also TERME in I.

tissu, n.m. – the correct word for anatomy tissue, for fabric, for material for clothes and soft furnishings but not for tissue-paper, as in paper handkerchiefs, *des mouchoirs en papier*. In town planning (*l'urban-isme*), *le tissu urbain* is urban fabric.

titre, n.m. – note particularly the meaning of share certificate, as when the narrator in Mauriac's *Le Nœud de Vipères* (1933) imagines the anxiety with which his wife and children will go, immediately after his death, to check whether *les titres* are still there or have been spirited or given away. A good deal of the plotting in *Le Nœud de Vipères* revolves round the fact that one could own *des titres anonymes,* which could be negotiated like banknotes, and on which also one did not have to pay *des droits de succession,* death duties. The word has also the meaning of academic qualifications. The expression *à titre* . . . is frequently used in an administrative/commercial context as the equivalent of 'on a . . . basis': for example, *à titre personnel, à titre provisoire, à titre définitif, à titre officieux* (unofficially), *à titre d'essai* (on a trial basis).

traitement, n.m. – as illustration of the remarks above under SALAIRE, note the comment of Mathieu Delarue's successful bourgeois brother in Sartre's *L'Age de raison,* when in spite of being a *professeur* de philosophie* in a *lycée,* Mathieu cannot raise enough money to pay for his mistress to have an abortion: *Tu touches tous les mois un traitement assez rondelet* (a comfortable salary). As an *avocat** and thus a member of *une profession libérale* (see above, LIBÉRAL), who has to live on his *honoraires,* Jacques takes an understandably austere view of this situation, and one would well imagine his making a pun about *les traitements de faveur accordés aux fonctionnaires.*

transaction, n.f. – in addition to a commercial transaction, note the meaning an out-of-court compromise settlement, of a financial na-ture: *aboutir à une transaction avec le fisc,* reach a compromise settlement with the tax authorities.

trésorerie, n.f. – note the meaning of cash resources, and in particu-lar *des difficultés de trésorerie,* cash-flow problems. *Un trésorier* is a treasurer and *un Trésorier-Payeur Général* a senior official of the Finance Ministry at regional and national level, responsible for authorizing official payments.

trust, n.m. – a conglomerate of firms holding a dominant position in the market. In left-wing political discourse the word was used to indicate the worst evils of the capitalist economy, but has now to a large extent been replaced by the term *les multinationales.*

U-turn – no exact political equivalent. *Le Figaro* for 13 October 1981 talked about *un renversement de vapeur;* there is also *un virage à 180 degrés,* but in politics *un changement de cap* (a change of course) is more frequently used. The French also talk in the context of political economy about *le stop-and-go.*

valeur, n.f. – value, but also a general word for stocks and shares, securities, as in *des valeurs cotées en Bourse,* quoted on the Stock Exchange.

viable, adj. – viable, but note that *les viabilités* are the essential public services such as roads, water, sewerage, gas and electricity, so that *une zone industrielle entièrement viabiliséee* is a trading estate provided with all these facilities. See also above, FIABLE, RENTABLE.

virtuel, adj. – note the sense of potential: *réaliser tout ce qu'on a comme dons virtuels,* to bring out all one's potential.

IV Education and Science

Académie, n.f. – one of the twenty-six administrative units into which metropolitan France, *la Métropole**, is divided for educational purposes (the French West Indies (*les Antilles*) and French Guiana (*la Guyane*) are grouped together to form *une Académie*). Each *Académie* is headed by *un Recteur*, who is appointed by the government. There were a certain number of *mutations** after Mitterrand's victory in May 1981, and twelve *Recteurs* were *renvoyés à leur corps d'origine* (in most cases, to posts as university professors), on account of their lack of sympathy with the educational aims of the new government. *Le Recteur* is responsible both for schools and for universities in his *Académie*. He appoints teachers to primary schools (*écoles primaires*) and, in some cases, to *les collèges* (see below); these appointments are known as *des nominations** rectorales* (see NOMMER in I). He is responsible for the organization of the *baccalauréat* in his *Académie,* and the papers are set and marked at the level of the *Académie* (see below, BACHELIER and JURY). He also has the official title of *Chancelier* of the University or Universities in his *Académie*. The closest equivalent of a British University Principal or Vice-Chancellor is the *Président** de l'Université*, usually a senior professor, elected for a limited period by the *Conseil de l'Université*.

L'Inspecteur d'académie is responsible for primary schools within a *département** and for the *école normale* (see below) which trains the teachers for those schools. At national level there is *un corps d'inspecteurs généraux*, whose duties include the formulation of national education policy and the encouragement of pedagogic innovation, as well as the periodic inspection of *les professeurs de lycée et de collège* (for all these terms see below). The marks given serve as a basis for promotion (see PROMOTION in I).

apte, adj. – not 'apt' but able. When a French student told P.T. that her aunt was 'apt to knit', she was transferring into English the expression *apte à* in the sense of 'able to'. When Michel Debré said in May 1946 that the *Ecole Nationale d'Administration** should *établir un système de recrutement qui ouvre l'accès du service public à tous ceux qui, sans distinction de rang ni de fortune, sans cooptation ni favoritisme, s'y montrent aptes* (set up a method of recruitment that will provide access to public service for all those who, without consideration of social position or private means, co-optation or favouritism, show themselves to be capable of being successful), he was reiterating the Napoleonic concept of *la carrière ouverte aux talents*. See also an advertisement in *L'Etudiant* for November 1981 for the *Ecole des arts décoratifs, où on forme* (see below, FORMATION) *des décorateurs aptes à intervenir* (take part) *dans la conception et la réalisation* d'un cadre* de vie*. To be apt to do something is *être enclin à faire quelque chose, avoir tendance à, être porté à* . . .

Arts – the Faculty of Arts is *La Faculté des Lettres,* and often *et des Sciences humaines* (see below, FACULTÉ). An arts student is *un étudiant* (or *une étudiante*) *en lettres*. An art student, *un étudiant des beaux-arts*.

autrement, adv. – means not only in a different way, as in *je le ferais autrement si j'étais vous,* but also 'much more so'. Thus the American space shuttle, *la navette spatiale,* was described in *Le Monde* as *un engin autrement plus complexe qu'Ariane* (the French rocket launcher).

bachelier, n.m., **bachelière,** n.f. – not a Bachelor of Arts, of Science or of Law (*licencié ès lettres, licencié ès sciences, licencié en droit* – see below, LICENCE) but someone who has passed *le baccalauréat* (fam. *bac, bachot*), the examination taken at about the age of eighteen and which is essential if one wishes to *s'inscrire en faculté* or *à l'université,* go to university. At the *baccalauréat* one is not awarded passes in individual subjects; one passes or fails the examination as a whole. Like all examinations in France it is marked out of 20, and to pass one needs an average of 10. To obtain *la mention assez bien, bien, très bien,* one needs 12, 14 and 16 or more respectively. *Le baccalauréat* is a written examination, but candidates with an average of between 8 and 10 have *un oral de repassage* or *un oral de contrôle** (see below, ORAL), to see if they can achieve an overall pass-mark. Candidates take about eight subjects (*matières*), and must choose one of a series of groupings (*séries*), either for the *baccalauréat d'enseignement général* or the *baccalauréat de technicien*. Thus, *Baccalauréat d'enseignement général:*

Série A – *Philosophie-Lettres*
Série B – *Economique et sociale*
Série C – *Mathématiques et sciences physiques*
Série D – *Mathématiques et sciences de la nature*
Série D[1] – *Sciences agronomiques et techniques*
Série E – *Mathématiques et techniques*
Baccalauréat de technicien:
Série F – *Secteur industriel* or *Sciences médico-sociales* or *Musique et danse*
Série G – *Secteur économique*
Série H – *Informatique* (computing)

The weighting (*le coefficient*) of the different common subjects varies with the *série*. In 1983, 63.5 per cent of the candidates passed (386,041 *candidats*, 245,119 *reçus*). See below, DEGREE, PASSER UN EXAMEN.

capacité, n.f. – not only the ability of a container to hold liquid or of a person to perform tasks, but also, occasionally, a person having ability in general. Thus Pierre Miquel writes on page 126 of volume II of his *Histoire de la France* (1976), *Car la République 'sans Dieu' croyait d'abord aux 'capacités'. C'était pour les découvrir et les former qu'elle avait construit l'école laïque*. (For the 'Godless Republic' believed first and foremost in 'People of Ability'. It was to discover and train them that it had set up its secular schools.) See RÉPUBLIQUE in II and LIBRE below.

chimiste, n.m., n.f. – a chemist working at chemistry, *la chimie*. A chemist in the sense of a pharmacist, from whom one obtains drugs, is *un pharmacien*. See DROGUERIE in VII.

Classics – 'He's reading, studying, Classics', *il étudie le latin et le grec*, or even, with educated older speakers, *il fait ses humanités* (cf. the custom of describing the Professor of Latin at a Scottish University as the Professor of Humanity). But *je connais mes classiques* may be the classical authors (Greek, Roman or the French writers of the seventeenth century) or the classics (the established writers of all periods; originally those studied in class).

clever – *ingénieux, intelligent,* without any derogatory overtones in French. *Quelqu'un d'ingénieux* solves complex problems in an ingenious way. Pascal's *les demi-habiles*, the half-educated, is probably the nearest the French come to phrases such as 'too clever by half'. See ORIGINAL in V, INGÉNUITÉ in VI.

collège, n.m. – not a college in the British or US sense of the term. The *Collège de France* is a very prestigious teaching institution in Paris. All lectures are open to the public, and the *Collège de France* does not enrol students or give diplomas. Election as a *Professeur au Collège de France* is the equivalent in status of becoming a member of All Souls at Oxford, and some intellectuals – Roland Barthes (1913–80), for example – have managed to give their *leçon inaugurale*, inaugural lecture, the cultural status if not the physical dimensions of the BBC Reith lectures.

   The term *collège* is most widely used nowadays to designate the comprehensive secondary school for all pupils aged 11 to 16. In the past, largely because of the (often residential) *collèges de Jésuites*, the word was occasionally used to distinguish a Catholic secondary school from the secular *lycée*. Both the CEG (*Collège d'enseignement général*) and the CES (*Collège d'enseignement secondaire*) have now been subsumed into the *collège*. A *lycée* (full official title: *lycée classique, technique et polyvalent*) is a State institution intended primarily to receive the more academically-minded pupils from the age of fifteen; but there are also *lycées d'enseignement professionnel* (LEP), technical colleges, which provide vocational training, *la formation professionnelle*. See below, FORMATION, LYCÉE. French children *entrent en sixième (en classe de sixième)* when they leave the *école primaire* for the *collège* at the age of eleven. They *entrent en seconde* when and if they go to a *lycée* or a *lycée d'enseignement professionnel*. *Les lycéens* normally end their school career *en terminale*, the class after *première*, at the age of 18. Those pupils who leave school at the age of sixteen (*la scolarité est obligatoire en France de 5 à 16 ans*, school is compulsory in France from five to sixteen) are encouraged to take the *Brevet d'études professionnelles*, which has now replaced the *Certificat d'aptitude professionnelle*. Only the *lycées* prepare pupils for the *Baccalauréat*, which is taken at about the age of eighteen and is essential for anyone wishing to enter higher education. However, moving up into a given form is not governed by age: pupils who have difficulty in keeping up are sometimes obliged to spend a second year in the same class, *redoubler une classe;* if they are very bright, they might in exceptional cases skip a class, *sauter une classe*. Pupils preparing the competitive examination, *le concours d'entrée*, to a *Grande Ecole* (see below), enter *première supérieure* after the *Baccalauréat (première supérieure* is provided only in the larger *lycées*). Those wishing to enter *l'Ecole Normale Supérieure* (see below) are called *des cagneux*, which in this context does not mean knock-kneed but is apparently slang for lazy and which the pupils themselves humorously spell *khâgneux;* their first year in *première supérieure* is known as *hypo-cagne* and the second as *cagne*. Those wishing to enter one of the engineering *Grandes Ecoles*, such as *l'Ecole Polytechnique* or *l'Ecole des Mines* (see below, INGÉNIEUR) are in *hypo-taupe* and *taupe* (*une taupe* is a mole, both in nature and, more recently, in the security services).

communale, école, n.f. – see below, LIBRE, and *communal* in I.

composition, n.f. – in an educational context, not a piece of work written by younger pupils, which is *une rédaction*, but an end-of-term or end-of-year examination taken (*passé* – see below, PASSER UN EXAMEN) by secondary school pupils. Likewise, *une dissertation* is not an undergraduate or postgraduate dissertation in the British or American sense; the closest equivalent of this would be *un mémoire* (see also below, STAGE). A French *dissertation* is an essay in which considerable importance is attached to the plan, terms are defined, arguments for and against are set forth; in short, *une dissertation* must have a beginning, a middle and an end. The word *essai* is used in a literary but not an academic context. See also below, INTERROGATION, THÈME.

concours, n.m. – in addition to a competitive examination (see below, DEGREE, GRANDE ECOLE), can mean a competition in sport, such as *un concours hippique* (horse-race), but also help, assistance (*je vous remercie de votre concours*).

dais, n.m. – a canopy. A dais as in a lecture theatre is *une estrade.*

degree – not *un degré*, which is a step, grade or unit of measure (of temperature, or as in *le degré alcoolique d'une liqueur, vin de 10 degrés*), but *un diplôme universitaire.* Someone with a degree – a graduate – or even with any academic qualification from the *baccalauréat* upwards (see above, BACHELIER) is therefore *un diplômé.* Cf. *Roland Barthes sur Roland Barthes* (1975), p. 134: *Qui ne sent combien il est* naturel *en France d'être Catholique, marié, et bien diplômé?* Who does not feel how *natural* it is in France to be a Catholic, married and academically well-qualified? The French equivalent of the British or American first degree (BA, BSc, etc.) is roughly *la licence*, obtainable after three or four years' study. Although the different units making up *la licence* (*les unités de valeur, u.v.*) can be awarded with *la Mention Très Bien* (16/20 or more), *la Mention Bien* (14/20–16/20), *la Mention Assez Bien* (12/20–14/20) or just *Mention Passable* (10/20–12/20), these divisions play a less important role in the subsequent career of a graduate than does the class of Honours Degree in the UK (*Licence avec Mention* is the nearest translation). What matters in France are the various *concours.*

Thus entry to the *Grandes Ecoles* (see below) is by *concours,* competitive examination. One sits for these at the age of about twenty. See, however, *l'ENA* in I. Except in medicine, where there is no *Grande Ecole*, it is much better both for one's general education and for one's future career to go to a *Grande Ecole* than to *entrer en faculté.* Anyone who is a *bachelier*, that is to say who has passed the non-competitive but difficult *baccalauréat*, may *s'inscrire en faculté* at the university nearest to his or her home, although entry to some disciplines, e.g. Medicine, is restricted by the options (*séries*) chosen for the *baccalauréat.* In contrast, in 1979, there were 2183 candidates for the 316 places at the *Ecole Polytechnique*, most of whom were probably also sitting for entry to another *Grande Ecole.* The *Grandes Ecoles* also have *un concours de sortie,* with the candidates at the top having first pick of the jobs available.

Entry to the higher echelons of the teaching profession is also by *concours.* The most prestigious of these is the *agrégation*, sat after the student has obtained *une licence* and *une maîtrise* (involving at least one year's extra study). An *agrégé* in a *lycée* or *collège* is required to teach only fourteen hours a week, and receives a higher salary than his colleagues for so doing; normally, only *agrégés* are appointed to university posts. In 1979, only 6.5 per cent of the candidates who sat the examination (*qui ont passé l'examen* or *qui se sont présentés à l'examen*) were successful. One can take the *agrégation* several times, and many of the candidates who sit the examination are already serving teachers. As in many other examinations in French higher education, there is an *examen écrit* which eliminates over half the candidates. The rest are described as *admissibles à l'oral*, and at one time *la bi-admissibilité*, passing the written examination twice, was in itself enough to secure a salary increase. As with other examinations in France, the *oral* (see below) is held in public.

Until 1968 the State had to authorize the granting of degrees and other academic qualifications. Nowadays universities have the right to grant their own *diplômes*, but only those validated by the Ministry, *habilités par le Ministère*, are called *des diplômes nationaux*. This has the effect of giving them equal status, a result officially achieved in the United Kingdom by the appointment of external examiners from other universities to assess the performance of students; the other French *diplômes* enjoy only limited status, and the Ministry makes no financial provision for them. The French Education Ministry has thus what is known as *le monopole des diplômes* and, by contrast with the large number of administratively independent degree-granting institutions in the United Kingdom and the United States, reinforces the impression often given to outside observers of French life of the power, prestige and privileges of the State.

The majority of specialist secondary-school teachers, however, do not take the *agrégation*, but content themselves with the *concours* for the *Certificat d'Aptitude Pédagogique à l'Enseignement Secondaire*. The holder of the CAPES (*un certifié*) does eighteen hours' class work a week, and like all other French teachers and lecturers is paid extra for additional teaching time (*des heures supplémentaires*).

All established teachers in French State educational establishments, from the *Instituteur*, primary-school teacher, to the *Professeur de Faculté*, university professor, are civil servants, *fonctionnaires*. While *le statut de fonctionnaire* is much appreciated because of the job security it brings once one is *titularisé**, it does have disadvantages. Vacancies are not advertised, and the *proviseur* or *directeur* has no say in the appointments made to his or her school. *Le Ministère de l'Education Nationale* (called *le Ministère de l'Instruction publique* until 1932) appoints newly-qualified *agrégés* and *certifiés* to schools where there are vacancies, but cannot always guarantee to put husband and wife in the same town. One can ask for a *mutation** (posting elsewhere), and decisions are taken by a *Commission paritaire* made up of an equal number of civil servants and teachers' union representatives. See also BACHELIER above, GRANDE ECOLE below; FONCTION PUBLIQUE, NOMMER, TITULAIRE in I.

école normale, n.f. – as in American 'Normal School', an establishment responsible for training primary-school teachers (*Instituteurs, Institutrices*) and non-specialist secondary-school teachers (*Professeurs d'Enseignement Général des Collèges* – PEGC). In the educational system established in 1882, each *département** had its own *école normale.* The three levels of education, *primaire, secondaire, supérieur,* were separated to the point where the child wishing to be an *instituteur* or *institutrice* went directly to the *école normale* of his or her *département* without going to the *lycée* or obtaining the *baccalauréat* (but see below, PROFESSEUR).

Une Ecole Normale Supérieure, as its name indicates, is a much grander institution. As a *Grande Ecole* (see below), it recruits by competitive examination (*concours*) and prepares students for the *agrégation* and the CAPES (see above, DEGREE). The *Ecole Normale Supérieure de la rue d'Ulm* was the breeding ground for much intellectual and literary talent (Raymond Aron, Jean-Paul Sartre, Jules Romains). The other *Ecoles Normales Supérieures* are those at Saint-Cloud (for men), Sèvres and Fontenay-aux-Roses (for women), and the more recently established *Ecole Normale Supérieure de l'Enseignement Technique* at Cachan.

écolier, n.m., **écolière,** n.f. – not a scholar (either in the sense of someone who holds a scholarship – *un boursier,* or of an academic distinguished in his field – *un savant*) but a pupil attending a primary school (for children 6–11 years old). The generic term for pupil is *élève,* with *collégien* and *lycéen* as more specific terms. There is a tendency to use *étudiant* not only for students in higher education but also for pupils in the upper classes of the *lycées.*

épreuve, n.f. – in addition to meaning trial or ordeal, and the proofs of a book or article, is the generic term for an examination paper.

établissement, n.m. – a general word for any type of school. Only private schools (see below, LIBRE) are referred to as *des institutions.*

faculté, n.f. – although officially abolished by the 1968 reorganization of French higher education and replaced by *des Unités d'Enseignement et de Recherches* (UER), the term is still sometimes used, especially in the expression *entrer en faculté* (or *en fac*), to go to university. Note *la Faculté* (i.e. *la Faculté de Médecine*) for the medical profession.

formation, n.f. – training. A word that is being used more and more frequently in French, stressing professional, vocational objectives rather than the more general aims of *l'éducation;* thus *la formation professionnelle* is vocational training; *la formation permanente* or *continue* is continuing education, and *la formation alternée* is a sandwich course. Valéry Giscard d'Estaing once said of François Poncet: *C'est ce qu'on fait de mieux en France. Il a la formation d'un énarque et l'expérience d'un chef d'entreprise,* He is one of the best kind of people that France produces. He was trained at *l'ENA* and has had the experience of running a business. See also below, STAGE. *L'entraînement* is used in a military or sporting context, although to do one's basic military training ('square-bashing') is *faire ses classes.*

Grande Ecole, n.f. – an institute of higher education recruiting its students by competitive examination, *un concours,* and preparing them for a specific career.

The *Grandes Ecoles* thus differ both administratively and in the role they perform from the various UER (see above, FACULTÉ) and the *Instituts Universitaires de Technologie* (see below, POLYTECHNIQUE) which provide education for most of the 18+ age group in France. Indeed, the gap between them and the university sector is much wider than the separation in England between Oxbridge on the one hand and the 'provincial' universities on the other, or in America between the 'Ivy League' and the large State universities. They are much more difficult to get into than a university (see below, SÉLECTION), suffer less disruption from political agitation (see below, UNION, STUDENTS') and offer a much more favourable staff–student ratio (*taux d'encadrement*). The State-owned *Grandes Ecoles* also free students – and parents – from any immediate financial worries not only by charging no fees but also by providing what is known as a *pré-salaire:* a regular payment to the student for being there (see ENGAGEMENT in VI). Some of the more prestigious State-owned *Grandes Ecoles* are also residential, and tend to develop a sense of corporate identity lacking in normal French university life (see ECOLE NATIONALE d'ADMINISTRATION and OLD BOY NETWORK in I). From this point of view, the existence of the *Grandes Ecoles* almost certainly lowers the quality of French university life by attracting and keeping the most able students, both men and women, out of the universities. They may well also contribute to the maintenance in power of a middle-class meritocracy, since the qualities needed to succeed in the *concours d'entrée* are most frequently found in the offspring (*les rejetons*) of upper-class and upper-middle-class parents. On the other hand, they undoubtedly contribute immensely to the wealth and efficiency of modern France by the prestige which they create and maintain for the engineering profession.

The oldest of the *Grandes Ecoles* is the *Ecole Nationale des Ponts et Chaussées,* in the *Rue des Saints-Pères,* within comfortable walking distance of the *Ecole des Sciences Politiques* on the other side of the *Boulevard Saint-Germain* and *l'ENA* in the *Rue de l'Université.* It is still the training ground for some of the best civil engineers in France, who are recruited from it into the prestigious *Corps des Ponts et Chaussées.* The most famous *Grande Ecole* is the *Ecole Polytechnique,* founded in 1796, and known as *l'X* (symbol for crossed cannons). Its military origins are nowadays principally visible in the fact that its pupils, female as well as male, have a splendid uniform for ceremonial and superior social occasions. It trains engineers, many of whom also go into public administration (see PRÉFET in I) or, if they are really ambitious, through a period of further training at the postgraduate *Ecole Nationale d'Administration**.

In addition to these two State-run *Grandes Ecoles,* there are a number of both publicly- and privately-run institutions which have an equally high reputation. These include a certain number of engineering *Grandes Ecoles,* the *Ecole des hautes études commerciales* in Paris (always referred to as HEC), as well as a large number of *Ecoles supérieures de commerce et d'administration des entreprises* in the provinces. The special number (November 1981) of *L'Etudiant* devoted to *Les Grandes Ecoles* accepted 313 institutions as deserving the title; 155 of these had been recognized by the State as authorized to *délivrer le titre d'ingénieur diplômé* (see below, INGÉNIEUR). In the academic year 1981/2 there were some 97,000 students at the various *Grandes Ecoles,* and about nine times that number of *étudiants inscrits en faculté.* The criterion used by *L'Etudiant* – but there may be others – to decide which institutions could be regarded as *Grandes Ecoles* was their success in finding jobs for their graduates (*diplômés*).

habileté, n.f. – not ability (CAPACITÉ, see above) but skilfulness. Thus Pierre Miquel, *Histoire de la France* (1976) vol. II, p. 279, speaking of the impact of television during the 1965 presidential election, noted that *la jeunesse relative de Lecanuet, l'habileté de Mitterrand étaient une révélation pour les téléspectateurs, qui avaient oublié la politique,* the relatively youthful appearance of Lecanuet, the skilfulness of Mitterrand were a revelation for viewers who had forgotten what politics was like.

ingénieur, n.m. – used only in the sense of a graduate engineer, a non-graduate engineer being *un technicien.* The vast majority of French *ingénieurs* are trained in *les Grandes Ecoles* (see above); very few French universities have Engineering UER (see above, FACULTÉ), and these do not enjoy the prestige of the *Grandes Ecoles.*

intégration, n.f. – an explosive word in French educational circles, since this is what the private schools (see below, LIBRE) fear will happen to them under a Socialist government.

intellectuel, n.m. – enjoys a far higher standing than in the Anglo-Saxon world, especially on the Left. The political power and moral prestige of the intellectuals in France is said to date from the publication in January 1898 of *Le Manifeste* (manifesto) *des intellectuels en faveur de Dreyfus*, the Jewish army captain wrongly condemned for spying.

interrogation, n.f. – yet another word for examination (also *un examen*); it may be *écrite* (written examination) or *orale* (viva voce examination). An interrogation (for example, by the police) is *un interrogatoire*.

inviter, v. – often stronger than to invite. *MM. les Professeurs sont invités à communiquer les bulletins trimestriels au Proviseur dans un délai* de quinze jours,* Members of staff must let the Headmaster have the term reports within a fortnight. But note the use in the injunction in the older carriages on the Paris Métro, *interdisant aux passagers de descendre, en cas d'arrêt prolongé entre les stations, avant d'y avoir été invités par les agents de la RATP,* forbidding passengers to leave the carriage in the event of a prolonged halt between stations, before being told to do so by a member of staff of the Underground/US subway.

In *Paris-Match* for 2 September 1983, evidence for the economy drive in France was provided by the news item: *A l'Elysée les collaborateurs* du Président ont été invités à ne voyager qu'en deuxième classe,* the staff of the presidential offices have been told to travel only second-class.

jury, n.m. – in an educational context, means an examining panel or board: *jury d'agrégation, jury de baccalauréat* (see above, BACHELIER). It is part of the official duties of *un professeur* (see below) to serve on a *jury de baccalauréat,* if appointed, but he or she does get paid extra.

lecture, n.f. – a reading, which presumably is what a lecture used to be in English, and still is for some of our colleagues. A formal lecture by a visiting speaker is *une conférence;* a less formal one *une causerie.* A class or a course of lectures is *un cours,* but an *ex cathedra* lecture is *un cours magistral.* A tutorial is probably best translated as *une séance de travaux dirigés* and laboratory work as *des travaux pratiques.* For most French people the principal meaning of *un séminaire* is now probably a seminar, rather than a seminary. To read a learned paper at a seminar or a colloquium (*un colloque*) is *faire une communication;* this may be published in *les actes du colloque, du séminaire* (proceedings, transactions). To lecture someone is *lui dire ses quatre vérités, le sermonner.*

libre, adj. – free in the political sense, but note that *entrée libre* in a shop-window simply means that you are not obliged to buy anything. To go into, say, a museum without having to pay is *entrée gratuite. Une école libre,* however, is not free in the sense of not requiring fees, but rather in the sense of independent, providing an education outside the State system and one usually based on religious principles. This is because the laws establishing primary education (known at the time as *l'instruction primaire*) in 1881–2 specified that it should be not only *universelle, obligatoire** (compulsory) and *gratuite* (free) for all children up to the age of thirteen, but also *laïque* (secular). Because of its traditional alliance with the monarchy, the founders of the Third Republic (1870–1940) wished to exclude the Catholic Church from all influence on the young. In 1905 Church and State were officially separated, and in the decade before the First World War priests and nuns *(les ecclésiastiques et les religieuses)* were forbidden to teach in State schools. State education in France has remained secular – except in Alsace and Lorraine, which were part of Germany when this legislation was enacted – though less aggressively so than in the years when *l'école communale** was known by its opponents as *l'école sans Dieu* and village life was often dominated by the rivalry between the local *curé** and the *instituteur* (see below, PROFESSEUR). When applied to universities, the term *libre* tends to mean Catholic, though Aix-en-Provence, Montpellier and Strasbourg keep alive the Protestant tradition of the south and east of France by having *une faculté libre de théologie réformée* or *une faculté libre de théologie protestante.*

All régimes have nevertheless recognized the right of parents to send their children to a religious school if they so wish, and in 1981 there were just under a million pupils under eighteen in the various *établissements d'enseignement privé* as against just over four million in the *établissements d'enseignement public.* The vast majority of the *écoles libres* offer a Catholic education. But they are fee-paying, so that just as translating the English term 'Public School' by *Ecole publique* instead of *Collège privé* would be highly misleading, to translate the expression *école libre* by 'free school' would indicate in practice the opposite of what it really is. But the similarity ends there. There are more girls than boys in *le secteur privé,* and the division in French education is an ideological and not a social one. Many relatively poor parents prefer their children to have a religious education; however, in recent years, as a result of the disruptions that have occurred in State *collèges* and *lycées,* some parents have also chosen to send their offspring to one of *les écoles libres,* where discipline is reputed to be stricter. For various reasons the fees are often fairly low.

One of these is that those *écoles libres* that sign *un contrat d'association* with the Ministry of Education do receive a State subsidy in return for ministerial control of academic standards. The question of whether or not this subsidy should be given was one of the great political disputes of the Third and Fourth Republics (1870–1940; 1946–58). In 1959, the *Loi Debré* seemed to some of the left-wing opponents of the newly established Fifth Republic to be proving its reactionary nature by giving subsidies (*des subventions*) – in particular, the cost of teachers' salaries – to the *écoles libres*. *L'école unique* (i.e. the abolition of the private sector) has always been a part of the Socialist Party programme. The remark made by François Mitterrand in October 1981 (widely interpreted as a threat in Catholic circles) about the need to create *un grand service unifié et laïque de l'Education Nationale qui demeure notre objectif à terme**, one single secular system of National Education which remains our long-term objective, has caused *la querelle scolaire* to resurface. French schoolchildren in the State system have Wednesday off (it used to be Thursday) so that their parents may arrange for them to have religious instruction. See also RÉPUBLIQUE in II, SÉCULIER in V.

licence, n.f. – the first degree in a French university. See above, DEGREE, and for other meanings, LICENCE in I.

lycée, n.m. – the first *lycées* (37 of them) were established by Napoléon I in 1808 to replace the *collèges royaux* that had been abolished at the time of the Revolution. Traditionally, they were for pupils aged from eleven to eighteen and their classes went from *sixième* to *terminale* (see above, COLLÈGE). To enter a *lycée*, pupils had to pass an entrance examination, *être reçus à l'examen d'entrée en sixième;* before the creation of the *Collèges d'enseignement général* (CEG) in the 1950s, those pupils who did not sit or who sat and failed this examination would stay at the *école primaire* until school-leaving age, *la fin de la scolarité obligatoire,* at thirteen, when they would sit the *Certificat d'Etudes Primaires.* Nowadays, however, the *lycées* take pupils only at 15–16 after their four years in a *collège.* See above, COLLÈGE.

manuel, n.m. – in addition to meaning manual as in repair manual, also means text-book. *La gratuité* des manuels scolaires est en train d'être progressivement introduite en France,* provision of text-books without charge is being progressively introduced in France. Parents must still provide *les fournitures* scolaires* (notebooks, pencils, erasers, etc.), although for parents with limited resources, grants (*des bourses*) are in many cases available from *la Caisse des Ecoles* run by *le Conseil* *municipal** and/or by the Parents' Association, *l'Association de parents d'élèves* (see below). As part of the syllabus (*le programme d'études*), *les travaux manuels* are crafts, but to become *un travailleur manuel* is often seen in France as a sign of academic failure, *l'échec scolaire.*

minus, n.m. – short for *minus habens*, a half-wit, clot, a pupil barely having the opposable thumb. However, the French would probably not use the term *le pouce opposable,* or even in this context *la main préhensile,* which is the quality often referred to as distinguishing man from the other primates.

note, n.f. – the mark awarded in an examination or for any piece of school work; traditionally given not in percentages but out of 20.

oral, n.m. – *l'oral* is a traditional part of many French examinations not only in modern languages but in other subjects as well. In the *concours,* only those reaching a certain level in the written examination are allowed to sit the *oral.*

parent d'élève, n.m. – for two meanings of *parent* see VI. *Les Associations de parents d'élèves* in France are more than just school fund-raisers: their representatives sit on school governing bodies, *Conseils d'administration,* and they are grouped into a certain number of *Fédérations nationales* (according to religious affiliation or political sympathy), which constitute powerful pressure groups in educational debates.

passer un examen, v. – to sit for an examination, not necessarily to pass it (*être reçu, réussir à,* whereas to fail is *échouer, être recalé*).

pension, n.f. – the meaning of boarding-house leads to that of boarder in a school: *un (une) pensionnaire.* A day-boarder or a pupil who takes lunch in the school canteen, *la cantine scolaire,* is known as *un (une) demi-pensionnaire.* However, the French see boarding-schools either in a strictly utilitarian context, for children living in remote country areas; or as academically useful, as when a boy from the provinces could be *mis en pension à Louis-le-Grand ou à Henri IV* in Paris in order better to prepare the *concours d'entrée* to one of the *Grandes Ecoles.* There is no social advantage or prestige attached to having been at *un pensionnat* – except perhaps for the *Collèges de Jésuites* which Henry de Montherlant refers to as *Nos Maisons* – and their more limited role in continental life generally may explain why the school story is an almost uniquely Anglo-Saxon creation. *Une pension* is also a pension, as in *pension d'invalidité,* disability pension.

permanence, n.f. – when French secondary-school children have a free period or when a teacher is away, *ils sont censés* (they are supposed to) *aller en permanence,* where their private study will be supervised by *un surveillant* (see below, PROFESSEUR). The word *permanence* is also frequently used for the times when an official is available for consultation: *l'assistante sociale* (social worker) *assurera* une permanence à la mairie tous les mercredis de 10 heures à midi.* The noun *permanent* is used for a full-time official of, for example, a trade union.

physique, n.f. – physics. *La physique de Newton,* Newtonian physics. A physicist, *un physicien. Son physique,* his physical appearance.

Polytechnique, n.f. – one of the *Grandes Ecoles* (see above), not a British polytechnic, the French equivalent of which is *un Institut Universitaire de Technologie,* generally referred to by the acronym (*le sigle*) IUT. The IUT were established in 1966. There are now sixty-six of them. They award a *Diplôme Universitaire de Technologie.* Since all publicly-funded institutions of higher education in France receive their money directly from the State and not from the local authorities, there is no real equivalent of the 'binary line' supposedly separating the British universities, funded indirectly via the University Grants Committee (UGC), from the public sector polytechnics, funded via the local authorities.

professeur, n.m. – not professor, either in the English sense of the most senior rank in the university teaching profession, or in the American one of a teacher at a university, but a generic term for a teacher in a *collège* or *lycée,* or a lecturer in higher education. There is no feminine form. *Le professeur principal,* in a school, corresponds to the class or form teacher. The English 'professor' is best translated as *Professeur de Faculté.* A lecturer in a British university (US Assistant Professor) corresponds to a *Chargé de cours, Assistant de Faculté* or *Maître-Assistant;* a Senior Lecturer (US Associate Professor), to a *Maître de Conférences.*

Another generic term for a teacher is *un enseignant.* He is a teacher, *il est dans l'enseignement.*

To the traditional rigid distinction between *l'enseignement primaire* and *l'enseignement secondaire,* which lasted well into the twentieth century, corresponds the distinction between the terms *professeur (du secondaire)* and *instituteur/institutrice (du primaire).* Until after the Second World War, children of working class or peasant origin who were not clever enough to win a scholarship to go to a *lycée* (at the age of eleven) but who wished to continue their education were encouraged to do so by becoming *instituteurs* or *institutrices.* They did this by going straight from the *école primaire* at the age of sixteen to the *Ecole Normale du Département** (US Normal School) for an additional four years' study.

It used to be almost as good an idea for an ambitious French child to choose an *instituteur* as his father as it still is for an industrious Scot to be a son of the Manse. Georges Pompidou was an outstanding example, as also were the writers Marcel Pagnol (1895–1974) and Jules Romains (1885–1972). It was also usual and useful for the local *instituteur* to marry the local *institutrice*. They could share the accommodation provided, as well as their modest salaries.

Les instituteurs, primary-school teachers, were thus not required to be *bacheliers,* holders of the *baccalauréat,* the examination taken only at the *lycée,* but to have the *brevet supérieur.* The requirement that they should be *bacheliers* before entering *l'école normale* finally became universal in 1979.

It is unusual for a French *professeur* to be responsible for the activities which absorb so much of the time of his or her British colleague: supervision of pupils at play-time, collection of milk or dinner money, distribution of stationery, etc. If done at all, these activities are the work of the members of the academic lumpenproletariat known as the *surveillants (maîtres d'internat, maîtres d'externat,* familiarly *pions),* usually students working their way through their studies. Under the direction of the *surveillant général,* now known as *le conseiller d'éducation,* they are also responsible for discipline, although in the more elegant Parisian *lycées* (Louis Le Grand, Henri IV, Montaigne) this still remains the preserve of the *censeur.* The headmaster of a *lycée* is *le proviseur.* Like *professeur,* this word has no feminine form. The head of a *collège* is *le principal/la principale.*

professionnel, adj. – for the meaning 'vocational' see above, FORMATION.

scientist – he's a scientist, *c'est un scientifique* (often opposed to *un littéraire*). Note, however, among several signs that the 'two cultures' is a less marked phenomenon in France than in the Anglo-Saxon world, the fact that *le Centre National de la Recherche Scientifique* (CNRS), a State-funded research foundation, provides facilities for literary historians and philosophers as well as for microbiologists and nuclear physicists. *Une revue à caractère scientifique* is simply a learned journal, and may therefore possibly deal with literature or linguistics.

sélection, n.f. – one of the most controversial issues in French higher education, *l'enseignement supérieur.* In the same way as it is normally necessary to have obtained the *baccalauréat* before proceeding to university (see above, DEGREE), so anyone possessing the *baccalauréat* has the right, subject in some cases to the *série* taken (see above, BACHELIER), to go to the university nearest home. This results in serious overcrowding in some French universities and an alarmingly high failure rate – more than half of French students leave university without obtaining a degree or any other kind of formal qualification.

set book – *un livre inscrit au programme.* The modern language syllabus for the *baccalauréat (le programme d'études pour les langues vivantes)* normally involves selected extracts, *morceaux choisis,* rather than individual works, and French teachers visiting their colleagues in Britain have been known to express admiration (see ADMIRER in X) at coming across A-level candidates who have actually read the whole of *Andromaque* or *Madame Bovary.* Their surprise, however, pales into insignificance beside the wonder evoked in the British or American graduate at the format of the *agrégation d'anglais* (see above, DEGREE): although ten books may be *inscrits au programme,* you enter the seven-hour literature *dissertation* examination (see above, COMPOSITION) to find that there is no choice and that you have to answer one question only on one book.

stage, n.m. – not a stage in the theatre *(une scène)* or as in *le Tour de France (une étape),* but either an intensive course of limited duration or a period of practical experience, a placement (see PLACEMENT in III), intercalated in a course of study, e.g. *un stage en entreprise.* The report submitted by *le stagiaire* after a placement is *un mémoire de stage. Un (une) stagiaire* is either a person on placement or a person serving a probationary period after obtaining his/her qualifications *(un professeur stagiaire, un (une) avocat(e)* stagiaire).*

suffisance, n.f. – not only sufficiency *(J'en ai ma suffisance,* I've enough for me) but also self-satisfaction: *Il parlait avec ce rien de suffisance qui caractérise l'intellectuel écossais nommé professeur de faculté dans une université anglaise.* (He spoke with that slight touch of self-satisfaction characteristic of a Scottish intellectual appointed to a teaching position in an English university.) Note also *l'auto-suffisance* (self-sufficiency) *en matières* premières* (raw materials), etc.

sujet, n.m. – the student, not the matter studied. *C'est un brillant sujet,* He's a very clever lad. What subject are you studying? – *Quelle matière étudiez-vous?*

syllabus, n.m. – only as in 'of errors', as condemned in 1869 by the first Vatican Council. An academic syllabus is *un programme d'études* or *un cursus.*

thème, n.m. – as in English, except that *un thème latin* means prose composition from French into Latin, and *un thème anglais* a translation from French into English, whereas translation into one's mother tongue is *une version.* Hence *un fort en thème,* a clever pupil, but also a bit of a swot, *un bûcheur.* As Flaubert puts it in the *Dictionnaire des idées reçues, Au collège, le thème prouve l'application*, comme la version prouve l'intelligence.* (At school, doing prose composition well shows you are working hard, just as the ability to translate into your own language proves you are clever.) The American 'theme' – English 'essay' – is only roughly equivalent to *une rédaction* (see above, COMPOSITION). P.T. once failed to explain to a Frenchman how funny the story was of the American teacher who criticized Johnny because his theme describing a dog was identical down to the last comma with that of Jimmy on the same subject and who received the reply 'It's the same dog, Miss'.

tronc commun, n.m. – a common syllabus, core curriculum, which everybody does. Like the ability of the *Recteur* (see above, ACADÉMIE) to decree that all the schools in his area will be closed, e.g. because of bad weather (instead of leaving the initiative to individual head teachers), the requirement that certain subjects should be studied by everybody is one of the advantages which the French derive from having a more centralized educational system.

***tutorial** – une séance de travaux dirigés.* The French university system is not paternalistic, so *un tuteur* tends to suggest either a legal guardian or a stake for a young plant. *Directeur d'études* is probably as close to tutor as you can get in a French university context, and an important cultural difference lies in the speed with which one arrives in this linguistic field at *la tutelle* administrative,* the *contrôle** exercised by the central government over local authorities and other public bodies. Your thesis supervisor is your *Directeur de thèse.*

An innovation recently proposed by the French Ministry of Education is the introduction into secondary schools of *le tutorat,* a generalized system of pastoral care.

***union, students'** –* there are many reasons why British students find French universities less interesting than the institutions from which they come themselves: many undergraduates live at home and go back there in the evenings, or, if they live away from home, go back at the weekend; there is no tradition of putting on Gilbert and Sullivan operas, organizing mountaineering expeditions, chess tournaments and pram-pushing competitions; and, consequently, no umbrella organization to provide a home for the English genius for wasting time. What replaces the students' union is what the Left Wing would like to see dominating British student life: political activity, generally of a violent and destructive nature. The *Union Nationale des Etudiants de France* (UNEF) is thus more the equivalent of the National Union of Students in Britain, except that since 1971 it has been dominated by the Extreme Left. It is opposed by the *Fédération Nationale des Etudiants de France* (FNEF), a more moderate body, and is in constant competition with a number of other acronymic bodies such as the more radical CAL (*Comité d'action des lycéens*). The participation in French political life of *la jeunesse des écoles* goes back to the nineteenth century, and 1968 was only the culminating point of a long tradition of street violence. The number of students who are actually members of a union is only 4.5 per cent. Unlike the students' union in a British university, there is no closed shop (*le monopole d'embauche* or, in this context, *d'inscription*).

université, n.f. – as in English, though 'to go up to the university' is more generally *entrer en faculté*. The term *l'Université*, used in the nineteenth century to mean the whole of the secondary as well as the tertiary sector, rarely has this meaning nowadays.

vacances, n.f.p. – holidays, not vacancies (job vacancies, *des offres d'emploi;* no vacancies, in a hotel, *complet*). The duration and dates of school and university holidays are fixed by the Ministry of Education, but the dates may vary according to the *Académie*. They normally comprise one week in November (*les vacances de la Toussaint* – All Saints'), a fortnight at Christmas (*les vacances de fin d'année*), a week in February (*les vacances de février* or *les vacances de neige*), a fortnight at Easter (*les vacances de Pâques*) and about two-and-a-half months in the summer (*les grandes vacances*). The beginning of the school holidays, especially of *les grandes vacances*, is the signal for a mass exodus of French families from the towns towards the sea or the mountains; a plan which is called *l'Opération Bison Fûté* ('the cunning bison plan', so called because the arrow indicating which way you should go is being shot by a wise little Indian with the patronymic of *Bison Fûté*, Clever Bison) is put into operation, advising motorists when to leave home and recommending less congested routes, *des itinéraires de délestage*. The radio informs listeners of the bottle-necks, *les embouteillages, les bouchons*, with, inevitably, the assumption that Paris must be the starting point for everyone's journey. H.E. once heard on *France-Inter*: *Bouchon de dix kilomètres à Saint-André de Cubzac, direction Province*, in spite of the fact that Saint-André is 550 kilometres from Paris and 20 kilometres north of Bordeaux. Those who go on holiday in July are known as *les juilletistes* and those who go in August *les aoûtiens*. All attempts at staggering holidays, *l'étalement des vacances*, have until now proved to have been of no avail.

La rentrée, return to school, is also very important for the French; the word burgeons on innumerable shop-windows (*des vitrines*), encouraging families to buy clothes, books and school requisites (*des fournitures scolaires*) for their progeny. The term is also used for the beginning of the parliamentary session, *la rentrée parlementaire*, and *la rentrée de septembre* also marks the period after the summer calm, *l'accalmie de l'été*, when French trade unions attempt to launch new offensives against the government and the bosses. Thus, *la rentrée sera chaude* is, perhaps, the symbolic though not chronological or climatic equivalent of the British 'winter of discontent'. There is also *la rentrée théâtrale*, when new plays are put on in October or November, and *la rentrée littéraire*, when new books are published in the autumn.

V Philosophy, Religion and Morals

accuser, v. – note the meaning of acknowledge receipt, as in *Je vous accuse réception de votre lettre du 15 de ce mois;* and that of betray, as in *sa voix accusait une certaine fatigue,* his voice showed he was rather tired, and *accuser son âge,* to show one's age. Note also *s'accuser de ses péchés,* to make confession of one's sins. Also, to become more marked: (*en 1965*) *la coupure politique entre la France du Nord et la France du Sud tend à se confirmer, voire à s'accuser* (Serge Sur, *La Vie politique en France sous la Ve République,* 1982, p. 271), (in 1965) the political gap between Northern and Southern France tended to be consolidated, even to become more pronounced; and to bring out, to emphasize: *Il convient de présenter d'abord les caractéristiques générales qui accusent les traits de la République gaullienne** (*ibid.,* p. 275), we must present first of all the general characteristics which bring out the main features of de Gaulle's Republic.

Act of God – not *une intervention divine,* which would be benign and providential, but *un désastre naturel, une calamité.* The wider scope of English 'calamity' can often be rendered by *une catastrophe.* See also SINISTRE in III.

action, n.f. – action, but also a deed, as in a scout's good deed for the day, *sa bonne action, sa B.A.,* as regularly performed by Giscard d'Estaing when a boy. French scouts are organized according to their religious affiliations, with the Catholics in *Les Scouts de France,* those of secular (*laïque* – see below, LAY, SÉCULIER) sympathy in *Les Eclaireurs de France,* the Protestants in *Les Eclaireurs unionistes* and the practising Jews in *Les Eclaireurs israélites.* See ACTION in III for other meanings.

adepte, adj. – does not mean to be very good at something, which is *exceller à faire quelque chose, savoir très bien faire quelque chose,* but to be somebody's follower, or a firm believer in a particular religion or political creed. Thus, *de nos jours, les sectes font de nombreux adeptes parmi les jeunes,* and the macabre comment in *Le Monde* of 15/16 August 1982 on the speed-limit controversy: *il y a les partisans de la petite vitesse et les adeptes du tombeau ouvert,* there are those in favour of going slow and those intent on driving straight into the grave. *Le Petit Robert* quotes

Renan as talking about *les rares adeptes de l'église jacobine**, although
Maxime Kœssler gives this as an incorrect use.

âge de raison, n.m. – the age, about seven or eight, at which the
Catholic Church considers that children can distinguish sufficiently
between right and wrong, *le bien et le mal*, to take their first communion. For the Anglican Church, the corresponding 'years of discretion'
are not reached until the age of fourteen or fifteen, and the irony in the
title of Sartre's novel *L'Age de Raison* (1945) would emerge more
clearly in English from a correct translation as *Years of Discretion*,
instead of the generally accepted *Age of Reason*. The *Aufklärung*, or
Enlightenment, of the eighteenth century is referred to in French as *le
Siècle des lumières*.

agnosticism – although *Le Petit Robert* defines *l'agnosticisme* as the
doctrine that *tout ce qui est au-delà du donné expérimental (tout ce qui est
métaphysique) est inconnaissable*, everything that cannot be ex-
perimentally verified (everything that is metaphysical) is unknow-
able, a Frenchman who espoused this basic tenet of logical positivism
would probably describe himself more aggressively as *un libre penseur*
or *un incroyant*. The Catholic poet and pamphleteer Charles Péguy
(1873–1914), reflecting the view that the supposed neutrality in
religious matters established by the creation of *l'enseignement laïque* in
State schools in 1881 had set up *l'école sans Dieu*, once described *les
instituteurs de la Troisième République* as *des libres penseurs professionnels*.
When the French describe their national character as *cartésien, voltair-
ien, rabelaisien*, they imply that they have the cult of clear ideas
exemplified by Descartes, the happy acceptance of the reality and
pleasures of the flesh associated with Rabelais, and the disrespect for
established religion popularized by Voltaire. *L'incrédulité voltairienne*
has played a greater part in French history than the agnosticism of
Leslie Stephen in that of Great Britain. See below, SÉCULAIRE; LIBRE
in IV; RÉPUBLIQUE in II.

apologie, n.f. – used only in the Latin sense of the systematic defence
of certain actions or opinions, as in Newman's *Apologia pro vita sua* or
J.M. Stewart's book *Pascal's Apology for Religion*.
    In one of the best apologies for the agnostic attitude (see above),
Souvenirs d'enfance et de jeunesse (1883), the biblical scholar Ernest
Renan wrote: *Mon catholicisme est celui de l'Ecriture, des conciles et des
théologiens. Ce catholicisme, je l'ai aimé, je le respecte encore; l'ayant trouvé
inadmissible, je me suis séparé de lui. Voilà ce qui est loyal* de part et d'autre. Ce
qui n'est pas loyal, c'est de dissimuler le cahier des charges*, de se faire
l'apologiste de ce qu'on ignore.* (My Catholicism is that of the Bible, the

Councils and the theologians. I loved that Catholicism and I still respect it; but when I found that it no longer commanded my belief, I left the Church. This is a proof of honesty on both sides. What is not honest is to conceal the specifications of the contract, and to defend something of which one is ignorant.) It is a statement to place by the side of P.T.'s view that it is very difficult to be an unbeliever nowadays. The modern apologists have left one so little in which not to believe.

To apologize, *faire, présenter, ses excuses*. I owe you an apology, *je vous dois des excuses*. Cf. the proverb *Qui s'excuse s'accuse*.

balancer, v. – note among other meanings that of hesitating between opposing points of view; also the colloquial *je m'en balance*, I couldn't care less. Scales for weighing are *une balance*, while balance is *l'équilibre;* to lose one's balance, *perdre l'équilibre*.

ban, n.m. – *se mettre volontairement au ban de la société*, to put oneself beyond the pale of one's own accord; but also *des bans de mariage*. To ban is *interdire*, and to banish *bannir*.

bénévole, adj. – not benevolent, which is generally *bienveillant*, but unpaid, charitable, voluntary in the sense of not expecting any financial return. *Des bénévoles ont distribué des milliers de tracts*. Thus when Jean-François Revel suggested in *Paris-Match* for 4 December 1981 that the Socialist Claude Estier had encouraged *des lyncheurs bénévoles* to attack the offices of the conservative newspaper *Le Quotidien de Paris*, he was talking about an unpaid demonstration of political enthusiasm. *Bénévolement* means out of kindness. Thus, to translate 'voluntary' into French, one has the choice between *bénévole* and *volontaire*, depending on whether one wishes to stress the absence of financial return or the completely unforced nature of the decision to undertake a given activity.

candide, adj. – has less the English sense of frank (I'll be quite candid with you, *Je vais vous le dire franchement*) than that of pure or ingenuous, as is the eponymous hero, *le héros éponyme*, of Voltaire's most famous work, *Candide* (1759).

chrétienté, n.f. – not Christianity, *le christianisme*, but Christendom, the medieval political community of all Christian people.

clerc, n.m. – not quite a clerk in Holy Orders, who is *un prêtre*, but someone who has taken the first step towards priesthood by being tonsured. Hence, for the irreverent, a possible derivation of the popular expression *un pas de clerc*, meaning an elementary error. However, all the dictionaries explain this by *clerc* as meaning *petit employé subalterne* – that is, junior clerk. In most cases clerk (in an office) may be translated by *employé(e) (de bureau)*, but note that a solicitor's clerk is *un clerc de notaire* and a Clerk to a Court of Law *un greffier*. The word *clerc* is also sometimes used to mean a scholar, a learned person (synonyms: *un savant, un érudit*). Julien Benda's *pamphlet** (short polemical essay) *La Trahison des clercs* (1927) argues that imaginative writers, scientists and philosophers who forsake rational values and spiritual matters to concern themselves with emotional experiments and contemporary issues are betraying the nobility of their calling.

collecte, n.f. – not only a prayer read during a church service, but a street or house-to-house collection for a charity, *une œuvre de bienfaisance;* the collection in church is *la quête,* while *une collection* is used for a collection of, say, stamps (*des timbres-poste)*, pictures (*des tableaux*), etc. A collector (of rare objects) is not *un collecteur* (which, in modern French, has several technical meanings, including that of a main drain), but *un collectionneur.*

confirm – although *confirmer* has most of the meanings of the English word, including the liturgical one, note the expressions confirmed Communist, *communiste convaincu,* and confirmed bachelor, *célibataire endurci.*

congrégation, n.f. – not the congregation in church, which may be translated by *les fidèles,* but, from the Middle Ages onwards, a body of Christians living according to a particular set of monastic rules (see below, SÉCULIER). In 1901, *la loi sur les congrégations* required them to register officially with the State in order to obtain legal recognition, and in the decade before the First World War their members were forbidden to teach or establish schools. In 1941, the Vichy government restored the right to teach and made the obligation to register more flexible. *La Congrégation* (1801–27) was a privately established charitable organization secretly promoting the return of the Bourbons during the Empire and, during the Restoration, rumoured to possess an immense if occult influence, which it used to extend the political power of the Church – cf. Balzac's *Le Curé de Tours* (1832).

conjurer, v. – not to conjure in the most frequent meaning of the English word (*faire apparaître . . . , faire disparaître . . .*; so that a conjurer is *un prestidigitateur* or *un illusionniste*), but to entreat (*je vous conjure de ne pas faire tant de bruit)*, to exorcise (demons, etc.) and to stave off (a danger, etc.).

consacrer, v. – in addition to the liturgical meaning (*consacrer l'hostie*, to consecrate the host), the word has secular meanings: *il consacre ses heures de loisirs à la philatélie,* he devotes his leisure time to stamp-collecting (but see below, DÉVOTION); and 'a stock expression' may be translated as *une expression consacrée.*

conscience, n.f. – several rather different meanings in French. It can mean moral conscience, the awareness of right and wrong, as in Hugo's poem *La Conscience,* Rousseau's *conscience, instinct divin,* and in the expression *un directeur* de conscience,* a priest to whom a Catholic traditionally confessed his or her sins. Alternatively, it can mean consciousness, the awareness that one exists, as in Sartre's *toute conscience est conscience de quelque chose,* we cannot be aware without being aware of something. When Hamlet remarked that 'conscience doth make cowards of us all' he was using the word in this sense, which English has now lost. *Conscience* can also mean conscientiousness, but note the two adjectives *conscient,* aware, conscious, and *consciencieux,* conscientious. To lose consciousness is *perdre connaissance.*

culte, n.m. – does not normally have the pejorative associations of the English 'cult' and may usually be translated by 'worship'. Thus *le christianisme ne se réduit pas au culte,* it's not just a question of going to church on Sundays. Note also *le culte du Moi,* the extreme form of narcissistic cultivation of the inner life recommended by the novelist Maurice Barrès (1862–1923) in his early works.

curé, n.m. – not a curate, but a Catholic parish priest, who, in a large parish, may be assisted by one or more *vicaires* (not vicars). Another linguistic 'chassé-croisé', but to translate 'I met the vicar and his wife at the supermarket' by *J'ai rencontré le curé et sa femme au supermarché* would indicate instant abolition of the age-old tradition of celibacy, *la tradition séculaire* (see below) *du célibat.* The formal mode of address to a priest is *Monsieur l'Abbé,* but nowadays *Mon père* is used more frequently by the faithful. A minister of the Protestant Church in France, *l'Eglise réformée,* is *un pasteur.* See below, RÉFORME, VICAIRE.

decency – since *la décence* is primarily associated with observing the ordinary decencies of polite speech or behaviour, it is hard to render George Orwell's remark that the political solutions suggested by Dickens amounted to little more than 'simple decency'. 'A decent chap', *un type bien,* and 'it was very decent of him', *il a été très bien avec moi, il s'est comporté comme un véritable gentleman,* but decency as an abstract concept has to be rendered as *la simple honnêteté intellectuelle, les règles les plus élémentaires de la vie civilisée,* or some comparably unsatisfactory paraphrase.

décevoir, v., **déception,** n.f. – to disappoint, disappointment, and not to deceive, deception (*tromper, la tromperie*). See Jean Cau's account in *Paris-Match*, 1787, 26 August 1983, of how, after de Gaulle had abstained from shouting *Vive l'Algérie française* on his visit to Algiers on 4 June 1958, *les activistes, les gaullistes du complot s'interrogent et ruminent une vague déception,* the activists, the Gaullists involved in the so-called plot of May 1958 that had brought de Gaulle back to power, wondered about what was happening and chewed over an undefinable disappointment; see GAULLISTE in II.

dévotion, n.f. – used only in a religious context (sometimes with derogatory overtones as indicating excessive piety). In a secular context, as in 'devotion to duty', use *le dévouement*.

dimanche, n.m. – whereas a Sunday countenance has traditionally suggested the gloom engendered by a strict observance of the Sabbath, *un air de dimanche* is the more cheerful face associated with the continental Sunday. *Endimanché* differs from 'in one's Sunday best' in that it implies being over-dressed.

doute, n.m., **douter,** v. – note that *sans doute* often means that there probably is doubt, so that 'without a doubt' is best rendered as *sans aucun doute, sans nul doute*. Care must be taken not to confuse *douter* with *se douter,* to guess, suspect, as in *je me doutais qu'il ne viendrait pas,* I suspected he wouldn't come, and *je m'en doute,* I guess so.

également, adv. – mostly used now with the weak sense of also, too.

état, n.m. – in addition to the political State (cf. Louis XIV's *l'Etat c'est moi*) and *l'état civil,* one's official identity (see I), note, among innumerable other uses, *prendre un état,* an archaic way of saying to take a job, and *mes devoirs d'état,* the duties I must fulfil in the state to which it has pleased Providence to call me. Thus in Mauriac's *Un Adolescent d'autrefois* (1969), the narrator says of his mother's attempts to give an air of Christian responsibility to her privileges as *une grande propriétaire: Le devoir d'état a bon dos,* it is too easy to make an excuse of the responsibility one has on account of one's place in society.

existentiel, adj. – a vogue word that seems to have lost all contact with Sartre's philosophical system, and is often used as a straightforward synonym of *réel*.

expérience, n.f. – note the twin meanings of 'experience' and 'experiment'.

fixe, adj. – note that *une idée fixe* is an obsession and a fixed idea *une idée arrêtée**.

génial, adj., **génie,** n.m. – not genial (*jovial, bon enfant, toujours de bonne humeur*), but brilliant, full of genius, masterly. For the extent of possible misunderstandings, see Raymond Aron's description in *Le Spectateur engagé* (1981, p. 52) of National Socialism as *l'aventure d'un homme génial et pathologique,* the adventure of a pathological man of genius. *C'est un génie,* 'He's a genius', but also note *le génie militaire,* the French equivalent of the Royal Engineers, *le génie civil,* civil engineering, etc. *Un génie* can also be a genie as in *The Arabian Nights, Les Mille et Une Nuits.*

grâce, n.f. – in addition to the religious and aesthetic associations, note that one of the traditional prerogatives of the President of France is *le droit de grâce,* the right of pardon; hence *gracier un condamné,* to pardon a condemned person. When François Mitterrand was elected President in May 1981 French public opinion saw him, for some months, as enjoying *l'état de grâce,* in a state of grace. The adjective *gracieux* is ambiguous, meaning, according to context, either graceful or free of charge. Thus, *il a prêté son concours* à titre* gracieux* means he provided his services free of charge.

grief, n.m. – not grief, *du chagrin, de la douleur,* but grievance, grounds for complaint; Robert Escarpit wrote in *Le Monde* of 5 September 1961: *Je suis toujours surpris de voir des hommes s'en prendre à des objets matériels de leurs griefs envers leurs semblables.* (I am always surprised to see some people take it out on things for the grievances they hold towards their fellow-men.) Note also the technical legal expression *les griefs d'accusation du réquisitoire,* the principal heads of the prosecution's case.

hasard, n.m. – not a hazard, *un péril, un risque,* but luck, chance: *c'est le hasard qui décidera,* chance will decide; *jeux de hasard,* games of chance. Note, however, that *hasardeux* means risky not lucky (*heureux*, chanceux*). In some respects the meanings of *le hasard* and *la chance* overlap, but note that the latter often means 'good luck' – *j'ai eu de la chance; autrement, je n'aurais pas réussi à mes examens,* I was lucky, otherwise I wouldn't have passed (see in IV, PASSER UN EXAMEN) my exams.

honnête, adj. – means not only honest but also (slightly archaic) polite, well educated, seemly. The *honnête homme* of the seventeenth century was a gentleman in the sense that he never made a display of his erudition and never tried to change the subject of the conversation already being enjoyed by the group he had just joined.

impératif, n.m. – in addition to its meaning in grammar and in Kantian philosophy, this noun is often used, especially in economic and political contexts, to mean 'the imperative demands' (of a given situation).

inconséquent, adj. – rash or ill-advised. *Vous êtes inconséquent,* you're being inconsistent. Note also *une inconséquence,* a rash or ill-advised act. See CONSÉQUENT in III.

indifféremment, adv. – not only 'without much interest' but also in the sense in which the Communion Service in the 1662 Anglican Prayer Book requests that the Monarch shall 'truly and indifferently minister justice'. Thus some members of the *Service d'Action Civique* (SAC), a kind of private police force originally set up in the 1960s to help de Gaulle, and banned by the Mauroy government in July 1982, had, as *Le Monde* for 23 July 1981 put it, become by 1981 people who *offraient indifféremment leurs services à tous les mouvements politiques et aux organisations syndicales et patronales,* didn't mind which political movement they served, and whether they were on the side of the trade unions or the bosses. Notices in the lavatories of French trains in the 1950s which read *Poussez le levier indifféremment à gauche ou à droite* were wrongly translated as 'Push the lever indifferently to the left or the right'.

jansénisme, n.m., **janséniste,** adj., n.m., n.f. – the religious movement which is said to have exercised so much influence on Pascal, Racine and other writers in the seventeenth century has left French with a useful shorthand term for moral and intellectual austerity. Thus in *Le Monde* for 29 June 1949, the *Tour de France* cycle race was described in the following terms: *Ce qui prête le plus à sourire, c'est la caporalisation, et, si l'on ose dire, le jansénisme qui s'empare lentement des participants. Défense de ceci, interdiction de cela, point de fantaisie*: de la discipline, de l'ordre et de la méthode! Les coureurs n'auront point le droit de voir parents*, femmes, amis. Ils ne devront parler aux journalistes que pour leur accorder de brèves et occasionnelles interviews. C'est tout juste s'ils ne seront pas obligés de confesser leurs péchés au directeur* de la course.* (What causes most amusement is the meticulous military discipline, and what one might almost call the Jansenism which gradually takes possession of all those taking part. You can't do that, it is forbidden to do the other, there must be no frivolity. You must have discipline, order, method! The competitors will not be allowed to see their parents, their wives, their friends. They must speak to journalists only to allow them short and infrequent interviews. They are barely spared having to confess their sins to the Tour Manager.) Similarly, in *L'Express* for 26 August

1983, in the course of an enquiry into how the French saw their history, it was observed that *les Français, gourmands plus que jamais de leur passé, refusent de se convertir au jansénisme structural; et l'histoire narrative, pourfendue par les assassins de l'anecdote, est portée à bout de bras par un public conservateur et sentimental.* (The French, greedier than ever to know about their past, refuse to be converted to structuralist Jansenism; and narrative history, torn to pieces by these murderers of anecdotes, is borne aloft by a conservative and sentimental public.)

The reference here is to the *Annales* school of historical writing, which sought to replace the story of kings and queens by detailed studies of how general historical trends affected ordinary people. It had sympathies with structuralism, the fashionable movement of the sixties and seventies, in its reluctance to give much importance to individuals, and in its rejection of the idea that history could be seen in terms of how people put their intentions into practice. This was again a feature which structuralism shared with Jansenism, for the theologians of the seventeenth century refused to see man as capable of attaining salvation by what he did, and taught a version of predestination which makes Jansenism comparable to English or American Puritanism. The Jansenists also led very austere lives, but proved so unpopular with Louis XIV that in 1710, after the condemnation of the heresy in the Papal Bull *Unigenitus* in 1708, he had their main centre at Port-Royal-des-Champs razed to the ground.

juste, adj. – as well as just, fair or correct, also means tight, as in *ces souliers sont un peu justes*, these shoes are a bit tight.

lay – a lay brother is *un frère laïque;* a layman in a religious context, as opposed to *un prêtre, un religieux,* is *un laïc;* thus in the post-Vatican II Catholic Church *l'apostolat des laïcs*, the apostolate of the laity. In the extended, non-religious sense, a layman is *un profane,* and Shaw's remark about a profession being 'a conspiracy against the laity' is perhaps best rendered as *une conspiration contre les non-spécialistes, le grand public, les profanes.* In a broader context, *laïque* has the more aggressive connotation of secular. See below, SÉCULIER, and RÉPUBLIQUE in II.

malice, n.m., **malicieux,** adj. – often in French mean no more than mischief and mischievous. Note the idiomatic expression *je n'y entends pas malice,* I mean no harm.

manichéisme, n.m. – often used in French not only to describe the view that the world is ruled by the opposing and equally strong forces of good and evil, but also to depict an attitude which sees only total evil in your political opponents. Sartre wrote much about *l'attitude manichéenne de la droite française.* See also below, RÉFORME.

martyr, n.m. – a male martyr; *le martyre*, martyrdom; *une martyre*, a female martyr. One of the best remarks about martyrdom is Mme du Deffand's comment on St Denis, said to have walked from Paris to Jerusalem carrying his decapitated head in his hands: *Après tout, il n'y a que le premier pas qui coûte.* Note also the modern expressions *une femme martyre*, a battered wife, *des enfants martyrs*, battered children.

mobile, n.m. – motive (for an action, a crime, etc.); the French also use *un motif* in this sense, as well as in that of a pattern (on wallpaper, etc.).

moral, adj. – moral, as in *une action morale*, but *le moral* is the morale (of soldiers, a football team, etc.), and morality *la morale*. The moral of the story, *la moralité de la fable. Un moraliste* is a writer with a concern for the moral implications of his story or subject-matter, or one who studies the manners of the society he is living in. *Un moralisateur* is a moralizer. Note also the expressions *une personne morale* (in a legal context: a legal entity, a corporate body), and *le rapport moral* presented to the general meeting, *l'assemblée générale*, of a social, cultural, etc., organization and summarizing the main activities during the previous year.

mystification, n.f. – taking people in, either by pretending to hold opinions you don't believe in, or by organized humbug.

office, n.m. – a church service, as in *le calendrier* des offices*. A Protestant service is often referred to as *le culte* (see above). See also OFFICE in I and VIII.

original – in the sense of new, unusual, *original*, but in the sense of going back to the origins, *originel;* thus *le péché originel*, original sin, and in *Le Figaro* of 1 August 1983, *La présence au gouvernement de ministres communistes constitue la faute originelle du septennat.* (The presence in the government of Communist ministers is the original sin of Mitterrand's seven-year term of office.)

original, n.m., adj. – also sometimes has the sense of eccentric, as when Moi observes of Lui in Diderot's *Le Neveu de Rameau* (1774), *Je n'aime pas ces originaux-là*, and the critic Faguet (1847–1916) remarks of La Fontaine, *On respecta son originalité, parce qu'il n'eut jamais la sottise de la vouloir imposer ou étendre.* (People respected his eccentricity because he was never foolish enough to impose it on others or spread it in society.) Just as the English suspicion of the intellect is said to account for the often derogatory use of 'clever', so the remark by Gautier (1811–72) that *Il n'y a qu'en France que le mot original, appliqué à un* *individu, soit presque injurieux* (see INJURE in I), might suggest that the French, at least in the nineteenth century, set a high premium on social conformity.

The meaning of *original* in the sense of unique, very unusual, is illustrated by Yvette Katen's remark in *Paris et la Région Ile de France* (1980): *la concentration de fonctions aussi multiples, politique, économique, culturelle de rang national et même international est un phénomène original dans le monde.* (The bringing together in the same place of so many different functions, political, economic and cultural, of national and even international importance can be found nowhere else in the world.) However, the original building is called *le bâtiment primitif.*

parenthèse, n.f. – bracket as well as parenthesis; thus *ouvrir/fermer une parenthèse.* Note that, when a Frenchman says *entre parenthèses,* 'by the way', 'incidentally', what he is going to say may be very important.

partial, adj. – biased; partial, as opposed to total, is *partiel,* as in *des élections partielles,* by-elections, and *des examens partiels,* regular tests now held in French universities.

patronage, n.m. – not so much the help not given at the right time by Lord Chesterfield to Samuel Johnson, but rather the youth club organized in the parish. Thus Josyane, in Christiane Rochefort's *Les Petits Enfants du Siècle* (1961), is quite happy to go to catechism because *le patronage n'y était pas obligé.* When Mr Hutton, in Aldous Huxley's *The Gioconda Smile,* had once, as an undergraduate, spent a few days at a mission in the East End of London and come back with a 'profound and ineradicable disgust' for the poor and unfortunate, he had been to a *patronage. Une mission* is an attempt to convert the heathen; thus the implication of the title of Abbé Godin's and Abbé Daniel's influential book, *La France, Pays de Mission?* (1943) was that missionary activity should not be limited to the distant, pagan lands, but that France, and in particular the French working class, was dechristianized.

Le patron is the boss, but the patrons (of a hotel) are *les clients,* and a patron of the arts is *un protecteur, un mécène.* But, for a charitable or cultural organization, the British or American equivalent of *sous le haut patronage du Président de la République* would be: Patron: HM the Queen or the President of the United States.

principe, n.m. – note the difference between *par principe,* for reasons of principle, and *en principe,* in principle. When a Frenchman says *je suis d'accord en principe* or *je donne mon accord de principe,* I agree in principle, you can expect in practice serious objections.

réforme, n.f. – not only a change for the better but also the Reformation. On 12 October 1981 an article in *Le Figaro* argued that the political Manicheism (see above) which characterizes French political life *se trouve moins souvent dans les pays anglo-saxons influencés par la Réforme,* is less frequently found in Anglo-Saxon countries influenced by the Reformation. The Counter-Reformation is *la Contre-Réforme.*

respect humain, n.m. – not a respect for other human beings, *le respect de la vie humaine, le respect des opinions d'autrui,* but a fear of what other people might say that leads you to avoid doing what your conscience tells you is right. A Catholic performing her or his *examen de conscience,* examining her or his conscience before confessing, is invited to ask: *Ai-je fait preuve de respect humain?*

ressentir, v. – although *le ressentiment* means resentment, *ressentir* does not mean to resent (*s'offusquer*) but to feel (emotions).

rétribution, n.f. – not as on the Day of (*le jour du jugement*) but payment, financial or moral, for what you have done. *L'ouvrier a droit à une juste rétribution de son travail.*

salut, n.m. – a military salute, a greeting (especially among adolescents), but also eternal salvation, as in *l'Armée du Salut,* the Salvation Army. Note also the Revolutionary *Comité du Salut Public,* Committee of Public Safety.

séculaire, adj. – not secular (see below, SÉCULIER), but either happening once every hundred years (a rare use of the word); or (more frequently) age-old, as in *un arbre séculaire* and *la méfiance séculaire de la perfide Albion que l'on trouve dans toutes les classes de la société française,* the age-old mistrust of Perfidious Albion which exists in all classes of French society. Thus Georges Menant, in *Paris-Match,* 4 December 1981, expressed a widespread French attitude when he wrote: *Il est vrai que la lutte séculaire des catholiques d'Irlande du Nord est celle d'un peuple opprimé qui, même devenu majoritaire, est resté soumis à l'envahisseur, au colon* et au maître.* (It is true that the age-old struggle of the Northern Irish Catholics is that of an oppressed people which, even now it is in the majority, still remains subject to the invader, the colonialist and the master [i.e. 'the Anglo-Saxon invader and exploiter'].)

séculier, adj. – more restricted in usage than the English secular, though both languages describe the Inquisition as handing its victims over for punishment to *le bras séculier,* the secular arm. *Un prêtre séculier* is a priest who does not belong to a monastic order (from Latin *saeculum,* the world), as opposed to *un prêtre régulier,* a priest living according to a particular *règle monastique.* When secular implies an attitude of suspicion towards religion, as in The National Secular Society, a better translation is *laïque,* and the phrase *la défense de la laïcité* means the protection from interference by the Church of the secular system of state education and the secular nature of the Republic. See above, LAY; LIBRE in IV, RÉPUBLIQUE in II.

spirituel, adj. – no difference from the English in, for instance, *Les Exercices Spirituels d'Ignace de Loyola* (1491–1556). But often the word means witty, as in La Rochefoucauld's (1613–80) readiness to depict himself as *ni plus spirituel et plus raisonnable que je suis,* neither wittier and more reasonable than I am. Not to be confused with *les spiritueux,* spirits, as in wines and spirits.

superbe, adj. – while one can talk about *une journée superbe, un superbe repas,* and *il y avait des filles superbes* means that there were some marvellous-looking girls, *superbe* also means proud to the point of hubris. Thus de Gaulle in 1944 *confie, superbe, à Louis Joxe, 'Les circonstances sont contre nous. Changeons les circonstances',* loftily informed Louis Joxe, 'Circumstances are against us. Let us change the circumstances.' *La superbe* is pride.

suspicious – *Le Petit Robert* quotes Proust observing very characteristically that *Les amoureux sont si soupçonneux qu'ils flairent tout de suite le mensonge,* Anyone in love is so suspicious that he immediately senses a lie; but 'a suspicious character' is *un personnage louche.* The adjective *méfiant* and its associated *la méfiance* and *se méfier de* are the expressions most frequently used by the French themselves to express what some people consider to be an important aspect of the French national character. See ALSACIEN in IX, ÉTAT CIVIL in I, LAISSER-FAIRE in II.

temple, n.m. – the usual term for a Protestant place of worship.

ultérieur, adj. – not ulterior, *secret, caché,* but later (*je vous donnerai ma réponse à une date ultérieure* or *ultérieurement,* I shall give you my reply in due course); the opposite of *ultérieur* is *antérieur,* earlier.

valide, adj. – while it is correct to translate 'the sacraments administered by an unworthy priest are nevertheless valid' by *les sacrements administrés par un prêtre indigne demeurent valides* – one of the central points in Graham Greene's *The Power and the Glory* – the normal equivalent of valid is *valable* (*les cartes d'identité nationales sont valables dix ans,* national identity cards remain valid for ten years). *Une solution valable,* an acceptable solution. *Une personne valide*, an able-bodied person.

vicaire, n.m. – see above, CURÉ. In pre-revolutionary times (*sous l'ancien régime*), the Church in France had an excellent system of plurality of benefices. This enabled an aristocrat to *toucher le revenu d'un bénéfice*, receive income from a living, while paying someone else, *le vicaire*, to do the work. The sum paid was known as *la portion congrue*, which survives in the expression *réduire quelqu'un à la portion congrue*, to put someone on short commons, to give him insufficient food.

You would translate the sentence from Dickens's *Great Expectations (Les Grandes Espérances)*, 'Mrs Jo was going to church vicariously, that is to say, Jo and I were going', as *Mrs Jo se rendait au temple par procuration*.

VI Sex and the Family

affaire, n.f. – not an affair in the English sense of 'he is having an affair with his secretary', which would be *Sa secrétaire est devenue sa maîtresse*, or, more vulgarly, *Il couche avec sa secrétaire*, but a legal or political case or question, e.g. *L'Affaire Dreyfus, L'Affaire de Broglie, La décentralisation* sera la grande affaire du Septennat*, decentralization will be the dominant question during Mitterrand's seven-year term of office. In a sexual sense, the French talk about *une aventure* or *une liaison*. Cf. Choderlos de Laclos, *Les Liaisons dangereuses* (1784), and the translation of Graham Greene's famous novel as *La Fin d'une Liaison*. A love affair can nevertheless be *une affaire de cœur*. Note, however, *les affaires*, business, *un homme/une femme d'affaires*, businessman, -woman, *une bonne affaire*, a bargain, *ce n'est pas une petite affaire*, it is no small matter.

agréer, agrément – see I.

alliance, n.f., **alliés,** n.m.p. – see below, PARENTS.

allocation, n.f. – (not to be confused with *une allocution*, a formal speech). When talking about resources, the English 'allocation' is *l'attribution des ressources* and 'allocation' in the sense of share is *une part**. *Les allocations familiales* are family allowances. Since 1946 – and even since 1939, with *Le Code de la Famille* – these have been seen by various governments as playing an important role in *la lutte contre la dénatalité française*, the struggle against the tendency of the French population, especially in the nineteenth and early twentieth centuries, to grow less rapidly than that of its European neighbours. The general principle on which these allowances are given is that each child in a family of three or more should entitle its parents to 33 per cent of a notional *salaire de base*, basic wage. There are also other advantages: single parents, married or not and whether or not employed, receive *une allocation de parent isolé*; members of *une famille nombreuse* (three or more children) pay only 30 per cent of the standard rate on public transport; expectant mothers receive *une allocation pré-natale*, and, once the baby is born, *une allocation post-natale*. None of these benefits is taxable. However, perhaps because the purchasing value, *le pouvoir d'achat*, of family allowances rose by only 20 per cent between 1949 and 1971, and the cost of living, *le coût de la vie*, by 185 per cent, or because people won't have babies just because you pay them, the French have had a similar decline in their birth-rate since the 1960s as other Western European countries. See below, FERTILITY; INDEMNITÉ, PRESTATION, PRIME in III.

amant, n.m., **amante,** n.f. – just as the meaning of the English word lover has evolved since Shakespeare's day, so at least until the end of the eighteenth century the French word *amante(e)* meant a *fiancé(e)*. Nowadays, it has the contemporary English meaning of lover. A female lover/common-law wife might well be *une compagne. Une copine* is the equivalent of girlfriend. But note that the masculine counterparts of these two words (*un compagnon, un copain*) are not such as to arouse the concern of traditionally-minded parents. *Ami,* and especially *petit ami, petite amie,* nevertheless might well, in certain contexts, arouse the curiosity of the French *contrôleurs/inspecteurs de la Sécurité Sociale,* those officials from the Department of Health and Social Security who have the task, in Britain, of checking whether welfare payments are being correctly made. *Ami, petit ami, petite amie* can mean the same as common-law husband or wife.

ancillaire, adj. – in addition to meaning ancillary, is also used to describe sleeping with the maidservant(s), *des amours ancillaires.* The Latin origin, ancilla, maidservant, is obvious, and the word is used without erotic associations when Gide talks in *Si le grain ne meurt* (Unless it Dies) (1926) about *les plus déconcertants spécimens ancillaires,* the most curious examples of maidservants, who came to live in his grandmother's house (p. 56).

aventure, n.f. – a brief sexual affair, less binding than *une liaison: Henri de Navarre préférait aux grâces inquiétantes des dames de la cour les aventures faciles de campagnes militaires.* (Henry of Navarre preferred to the disquieting charms of the ladies of the court the easy sexual conquests available while in the field.) (Pierre Miquel, *Histoire de la France*, 1976, vol. I, p. 177).

bachelier, n.m. – a bachelor only in an academic sense, and even then a school leaver with the *baccalauréat,* not a graduate. The late nineteenth-century fear of *un prolétariat de bacheliers* thus reflected a fear of the unwise extension of secondary, not tertiary, education. A bachelor is *un célibataire,* an unmarried woman *une célibataire.* A hardened bachelor is *un célibataire endurci* or *un vieux garçon* and an old maid *une vieille fille*. An unmarried mother is *une mère célibataire*, a modern term which has replaced the traditional but more condemnatory *fille-mère*. A bachelor flat is *un appartement de garçon*, but more frequently *une garçonnière*. See also BACHELIER in IV.

brave, adj. – not brave, which is *courageux*, but honest, reliable, decent, perhaps a bit dull and certainly not fashionable. A French lady who had married beneath her once commented disparagingly on her *beaux-parents* (parents-in-law): *Oui, ce sont de braves gens.*

C'est une brave fille – 'She's a nice lass.' See also BRAVE in II.

casualty – *un mort, un blessé*, according to meaning. No generic word, except for *une victime*. *L'accident a fait beaucoup de victimes et provoqué* bien des dégâts*, The accident resulted in many casualties and caused a great deal of damage.

Christian name – just as Americans do not have Christian names but first names, so a French person has *un prénom* and not *un nom chrétien*. Except for the South, le Midi, where boys' names of Roman origin are still frequent (Marius, César) or Brittany, where Celtic names (e.g. Loïc, Gaël, Yves) are found, most French *prénoms* come from saints in the Christian calendar, and it is customary to celebrate *sa fête*, one's saint's day, as well as *son anniversaire*, birthday.

cinq à sept, n.m. – traditionally, either the time you invite your friends or colleagues home for *un apéritif* or the time of day at which you enjoy your *aventure* (see above) or *liaison*, e.g. *un cinq à sept plus hygiénique que sentimental*, when your *tempérament* (see below) is just too much for you. The expression is also used more generally, as when the conservatively-minded *Le Point* noted: *Aucun journal libre ne peut coucher dans le même lit que l'Etat, fût-ce entre 5 et 7*, No independent newspaper can enjoy the favours of the State, even on an intermittent basis.

complaisant, adj. – not complacent, which is *content de soi-même* or *suffisant*, but indulgent. Hence, *un mari complaisant*, a husband who turns a blind eye to his wife's infidelities. Graham Greene's play, *The Complaisant Lover*, uses the word in the French sense. Similarly, a group of French journalists recently demanded that the Conservative newspaper magnate M. Hersant cease to *bénéficier de ce qu'il faut considérer comme de la complaisance des pouvoirs publics* et des banques désormais nationalisées*, enjoy what must be considered as special treatment from the official authorities and the banks that are now nationalized. *Un pavillon* de complaisance* is a flag of convenience.

concubin, n.m., **concubine,** n.f. – the legal (and morally neutral) terms for common-law husband or wife.

couvrir, v. – has the same erotic meaning of 'to cover' as in English. Thus in Marcel Aymé's *La Tête des Autres* Valentin says: *Procureur* Bertolier, faites donc taire votre chienne et, si elle est en folie, faites-la couvrir.* (District Attorney, make your bitch shut up or, if she is on heat, find a mate for her.) It is an interesting example of the greater verbal freedom allowed to French playwrights in 1952. The word has also the same meanings as in English when one talks of covering up a blunder made by a subordinate or of trying to hide a scandal from the public gaze, as well as of covering an incident or a conference as a journalist.

créature, n.f. – while a morally neutral word in Fontenelle's (1657– 1757) phrase about *cette espèce bizarre de créatures qu'on appelle le genre humain*, this strange species of creatures called the human race, the word is often used to describe a woman – either favourably, as in *Oh, c'est une adorable créature*, or pejoratively, as in the account on p. 104 of Simone de Beauvoir's *La Force de l'Age* (1963) of some advice given by Sartre to a Swiss *matrone* (see below) in 1946. *La dame craignait que son fils ne fît des enfants à quelque créature: 'Alors, apprenez-lui à se retirer, Madame', lui dit Sartre. 'En effet', dit-elle, 'je lui dirai que ce conseil vient de vous, ça le frappera davantage.'* (The lady was afraid that her son might make some creature pregnant. 'Then teach him to practise coïtus interruptus, Madame', said Sartre. 'A good idea', she replied. 'I'll tell him that this advice came from you, it will make a greater impression on him.') See below, PRÉSERVATIF.

curieux, adj. – as well as having the English meanings, is used about someone who is always minding other people's business.

déranger, v. – to disturb, as in *Je ne vous dérange pas?* – I'm not disturbing you, am I?

donation, n.f. – not a donation, *un don*, but the transfer of part of an estate to one's inheritors before one's death. See below, HÉRITAGE, TESTER.

draguer, v. – not to drag, which is *tirer péniblement après soi*, as when the sheep in 'Little Bo-Peep' *rentrent la queue entre les pattes*, but to clean up a canal or sweep a stretch of sea free of mines, or to look for an occasional sexual partner. Students of French literature required in earlier periods to admire *Le Livre de mon ami* (1885) or *Le Crime de*

Sylvestre Bonnard (1881) could thus note with relief that a television programme on Anatole France presented him, according to *Le Figaro* for 6 November 1981, as *un épicurien et dragueur frénétique*, self-indulgent and a compulsive womanizer.

éligible, adj. – not an eligible bachelor, *un beau parti*, but merely someone who can legally be elected.

embrasser, v. – to kiss as well as to embrace; should be used for kiss when in doubt, in preference to *baiser*, which when used absolutely or with a person as direct object means to have sexual intercourse.

engagement, n.m. – not what precedes marriage, which is *les fiançailles*, but the act of committing yourself or other people to a particular course of action. Thus, French public opinion has been frequently assured since May 1981 that *les engagements du Président Mitterrand seront tenus*. Jean-Paul Sartre's arguments in favour of writers committing themselves and taking sides on political issues, *la littérature engagée*, were put forward in 1947 in a book entitled *Qu'est-ce que la littérature?*, a characteristic example of his inability to distinguish between 'is' and 'ought'. Candidates for the CAPES and the *agrégation* have to sign *un engagement quinquennal*, promising, if successful, to teach for five years in the State school to which they are appointed by the Ministry. A similar *engagement* to serve the State for a number of years is required of students of certain *Grandes Ecoles** in receipt not of a scholarship (*une bourse*) or grant (*une allocation* d'études*) but of *un présalaire*. See also Grands Corps de l'Etat in I, degree in IV. Note also the somewhat archaic *engager sa montre*, to pawn one's watch.

enjoy – no simple direct equivalent. Although one can say *jouir de la vie*, to enjoy life, *jouir de* also has the sense of to enjoy possession of, and *jouir* by itself quite often means to have an orgasm. 'Did you enjoy your lunch?' is best translated as *Avez-vous bien mangé à midi?*, 'Did you enjoy the book?' by *Est-ce que le livre vous a plu?*

exciter, v. – because of its frequent sexual associations in French, this word and its derivatives should be used only with extreme caution. 'It's very exciting', *C'est très passionnant*.

famille, n.f. – a larger and more imposing entity than in English-speaking countries, including as it does all possible kindred. Its inclusion in 1940 in the Vichy motto *Travail, Famille, Patrie* which replaced *Liberté, Egalité, Fraternité* shows clearly that it is also a politically loaded word. *Moi, je suis pour la famille* means 'I'm against contraception, abortion, pornography and socialism, and in favour of law and order, state subsidies to religious schools, and stiffer prison sentences for all offenders.' See CONSERVATEUR in II.

fantaisie, n.f. – whim, fancy, imagination, while a fantasy, as of an erotic nature, is *un fantasme.*

femelle, n.f., adj. – although this word does mean female, it is applied in polite usage only to animals, and not to the female of the human species.

fertility – the word *fertilité* is used only in contexts such as *la fertilité d'un sol.* Zoological or metaphorical fertility is *la fécondité.* A number of French writers have shown preoccupation with human fertility. In 1899, Emile Zola (1840–1902) published an edifying novel entitled *Fécondité*; in 1918, Guillaume Apollinaire (1880–1918) dealt more amusingly with the same subject in *Les Mamelles de Tirésias* (whose subtitle, *drame surréaliste*, claims to be the first use of the adjective *surréaliste*); and in 1961, Christiane Rochefort (1920–   ) published in her novel *Les Petits Enfants du Siècle* a very amusing attack on the use of family allowances, *les allocations familiales*, as a means of encouraging large families. Some demographers have argued that *la dénatalité française* (in 1800, with 28 million inhabitants, France had the largest population of any European country outside Russia; by 1913 it had fallen to fourth place; between 1935 and 1938 the French population suffered a net loss) was an unintended result of Article 745 of the *Code Civil* of 1804. This abolished primogeniture and instituted the system of *le partage égal du patrimoine*, the equal division of the property to be inherited (see below, HÉRITAGE). The French are consequently said to have limited the number of children they had to keep the family inheritance intact. Other demographers dispute this explanation. According to the 1981 statistics, French women are producing on average only 1.96 children, whereas 2.1 would be needed *pour assurer le remplacement des générations*, to maintain the replacement rate. See above, ALLOCATION, and below, TESTER. On 7 January 1982 *Le Monde* noted that *les couples inféconds sont ceux qui divorcent le plus fréquemment, quelle que soit la durée du mariage*, infertile couples have the highest divorce rate, irrespective of how long they have been married.

fiasco, n.m. – among other meanings, an unanticipated inability to rise to the occasion. The novelist Stendhal wrote about it well in *Armance* (1827).

fille, n.f. – except when talking about babies or very small children

(*Est-ce une fille ou un garçon?*), still a dangerous word to use without the qualifying adjective *jeune*, since for older speakers it can mean *une fille de joie*, a prostitute. When Prince Charles married Lady Diana Spencer, the French newspapers made a point of reassuring their readers that she was *une vraie jeune fille*, unquestionably a virgin. Thus the (probably untranslatable) *Il y a des jeunes filles comme il faut, et d'autres comme il en faut*. The French make a very clear distinction between *une petite fille* (before the age of puberty) and *une jeune fille* (once she has reached this age): *Elle n'a que treize ans, mais elle fait déjà jeune fille*, She's only thirteen, but she's no longer a little girl.

fortune, n.f. – as in English, but note *un homme à bonnes fortunes*, a successful philanderer, and the meaning of emergency, makeshift in such expressions as *des réparations de fortune*, temporary repairs.

frais, adj. – cool or even cold. Fresh water is *eau douce, eau potable*. *Vivre d'amour et d'eau fraîche*, 'to live on love and fresh air'. In a French restaurant, to be sure that it is chilled, don't ask just for *de l'eau*, but always for *de l'eau fraîche*. But fresh meat is *la viande fraîche*, as in Perrault's *Le Petit Poucet* (Tom Thumb), *L'ogre flairait à droite et à gauche, parce qu'il sentait la viande fraîche*, the ogre sniffed here, there and everywhere, because he could smell fresh meat; nowadays, it would usually mean that it is not frozen, *congelée, surgelée*.

fruit sec, n.m. – dried fruit, but also a distinctly unprecocious young man, or an unsuccessful student. *C'est un fruit sec*, he's a bit of a drip.

gai, adj. – has not so far acquired the exclusive meaning of homosexual, since an advertisement for a yellow pullover in *Le Point* for 29 October 1981 depicted a bearded, obviously virile young man, also wearing blue trousers and a blue spotted tie, and carried the slogan *Laissez les costumes tristes aux hommes pas gais*, leave sombre clothes to cheerless men. However, there is a *revue mensuelle masculine* entitled *Gai pied* (see *Le Monde*, 28 March 1982), and the title may also evoke the slang *prendre son pied*, to achieve orgasm: *T'as eu ton pied?* 'Did you come?'. When French people use the word *gai* in the sense of homosexual, they often endeavour to pronounce it as in English.

A derogatory word for male homosexuals is normally *une tante* or *une tapette*, though in the prison slang of Jean Genet's novels they are also called *des cloches* (corresponding to 'punks' in US convicts' slang, as in Jack Abbot's *In the Belly of the Beast*) in contrast to their more active lovers, *des marles* (*des mâles*). To come out, in the sense of to proclaim oneself a homosexual, is *se déclarer*, though the decision of André Gide to do this with the publication of *Corydon* in 1924 is nowadays little discussed.

hagard, adj. – as English haggard when applied to falcons, but does not always have the English sense of very tired. *Il avait l'œil hagard*, he was wild-eyed.

harassant, adj. – tiring. To harass, *harceler*. Police harassment, as when a policeman tries to stop adolescents sneaking into football matches without paying, is *la persécution systématique de la jeunesse par une police fascisante*. See CHAÎNE in III.

héritage, n.m. – possessions transferred on death to another person, inheritance. *En cinq ans, il a dilapidé l'héritage qu'il a reçu de son père*, In five years, he went through the inheritance left him by his father. A legacy is *un legs*. The English 'heritage' can often be translated as *le patrimoine*, a word favoured in certain circles in France, to indicate what is handed down continuously from one generation to the next either at a national level (e.g. *le patrimoine artistique*, the nation's art treasures) or within the family. Thus, a recent advertisement read *protégez votre patrimoine des effets de l'inflation*, protect your family wealth from inflation, and a Frenchman once told H.E. that *l'impôt sur les plus-values* (capital gains tax) *serait la fin du patrimoine familial français*, would be the end of any possibility of keeping French family property together.

heureux, adj. – not only happy, but in some contexts successful too, as in *l'heureux candidat a remercié ses électeurs*, the successful candidate thanked his electors. In certain cases may also indicate sexual success, as in Balzac's remark about Lucien de Rubempré, who is having a passionate affair (not *une affaire* – see above) with the actress Coralie: *Heureux tous les jours, ses couleurs avaient pâli, son regard était trempé des moites expressions de la langueur*. (He made love every day, which made his face look pale and his eyes moist and languorous.) (*Illusions perdues*, Garnier, 1961, p. 440)

hôte, n.m. – the French have the same word for host and guest; however, *une hôtesse* is used only for hostess and *un (une) invité(e)* is often used for guest, presumably to avoid the ambiguity.

impotent, adj. – not sexually impotent, *impuissant*, but crippled.

ingénuité, n.f. – distinguish between *ingénuité*, simple-mindedness, the quality of being *ingénu* (cf. Colette's novel, *L'Ingénue libertine*, 1909) and *ingéniosité*, ingenuity in the sense of cleverness, the quality of being ingenious, *ingénieux*. See CLEVER in IV.

ingrat, adj. – not only ungrateful but fruitless, sterile, as in *une terre ingrate*, and awkward, as in *l'âge ingrat*, early adolescence.

introduire, v. – is to show someone into a room, etc., not to introduce someone, which is *présenter*.

luxure, n.f. – not luxury, which is *le luxe*, but lechery, as in the Ten Commandments (as quoted in *Quid 1981*, p. 527), *luxurieux point ne seras, de corps ni de consentement*, thou shalt not be lecherous in body or intent.

magot, n.m. – not what some anglers use, *un asticot*, but one's savings, a nest-egg, often kept according to legend *dans un bas de laine*, in a woollen stocking (see RENTE in III).

male chauvinist pig – un affreux phallocrate.

malthusianisme, n.m. – not only birth-control, as in *les pratiques malthusiennes*, but also a refusal to invest and develop. Thus Pierre Birnbaum writes on p. 118 of *Les Sommets de l'Etat* (1977) that *les hauts fonctionnaires issus le plus souvent de l'ENA* doivent lutter contre le malthusianisme très profond d'une partie importante du patronat français et lui imposer souvent des mesures économiques qui ne rencontrent guère son assentiment. C'est le début d'un nouveau colbertisme* dont le but est de permettre l'indépendance de l'Etat.* (Senior civil servants, most of whom are graduates of *l'ENA*, are obliged to fight against the deep-rooted Malthusianism of a large section of French business, and in particular to force upon it economic measures it is not really in agreement with. This is the beginning of a new form of *Colbertisme* aimed at making the State independent.)

marier, v. – to marry off, or perform the marriage ceremony. To take in marriage is *épouser* or *se marier avec*. Thus *au cours d'une seule et même année il a épousé sa femme et marié sa sœur*, in the same year he married his wife and married off his sister. Since the creation of a secular republic in France by *la Séparation de l'Eglise et de l'Etat* in 1905, *c'est le maire* qui marie les époux*, the mayor performs the legally valid marriage ceremony, *tout passage devant le curé étant purement facultatif et n'ayant aucune force de loi*, any subsequent ceremony performed by the priest being purely optional and having no legal force. However, see below, UNIR. Synonym of *époux: conjoint(s)*.

matrone, n.f. – used favourably only to describe the wife of a Roman citizen. Otherwise, an overbearing middle-aged woman, definitely not of the upper class.

parent, n.m. – can mean, especially in the plural, either parent or relative; you have to decide from the context which is meant. Strictly speaking, *des parents* are blood relations whereas for relations by marriage (*par alliance* – *une alliance* is also a wedding ring) one should use *des alliés*; thus sometimes in *des faire-part de décès*, official announcements of bereavement, one reads *les parents et alliés*. More usually, however, *parents* is the generic term. In this context, whereas in English the word orphan is normally used only for a child who has lost both parents (like Jack Worthing in *The Importance of Being Earnest, Il importe d'être Constant*), the French also use the expressions *orphelin(e) de père, orpheline(e) de mère.*

plaisir, n.m. – when used absolutely is usually sexual pleasure, as in the passage to which *l'Avocat Impérial* (the equivalent during the Second Empire of *le Procureur de la République* or *l'Avocat Général*) took such exception in his *réquisitoire* (see AVOCAT in I) against *Madame Bovary* in 1857: *Ses convoitises, ses chagrins, l'expérience du plaisir et ses illusions toujours jeunes, comme aux fleurs le fumier, la pluie, les vents et le soleil, l'avaient par gradations développée, et elle s'épanouissait dans toute la plénitude de sa nature.* (Her longings, her disappointments, the experience of sexual pleasure and her still youthful illusions had, as manure, rain, wind and sunlight do to flowers, gradually developed her, and she blossomed forth in all the fullness of her nature.) This is not to say that the word cannot be used without these specific associations, as in such expressions as *Au plaisir (de vous revoir)* or *Je viendrai avec plaisir*, but care is obviously needed.

préservatif, n.m. – a male contraceptive, so called because before the legalization of birth control in 1967 such devices could be sold only as a protection against *les maladies vénériennes*. Female devices include *le diaphragme* (Dutch cap/US diaphragm), *le stérilet* (coil/US IUD) and *la pilule. L'interruption volontaire de grossesse* (IVG) – the technical term for *l'avortement*, abortion – was legalized in 1974, but the law is very strict, especially in respect of the date by which the abortion must be carried out. Since 1983, part of the cost of abortion is reimbursed by *la Sécurité Sociale*. The half million or so illegal abortions carried out before then on women who could not afford to have the operation performed in the UK or Switzerland were the work of the ironically named *faiseuses d'anges*. For Sartre's recommended use of coïtus interruptus see above, CRÉATURE.

public, adj. – note that *une maison publique* is a brothel, not a place where you drink (*un café, un bistrot*, etc.). Before being closed down by Marthe Richard in 1946, licensed brothels, *maisons closes*, were also known as *maisons de tolérance*. Legend insists that when André Gide tried to plead the case for religious toleration to Paul Claudel, he received the reply: *La tolérance? Nous avons des maisons pour cela, me semble-t-il*. See also COLLECTIF in I.

regretté – when used as an adjective rather than as a past participle, means 'late' in the sense of deceased, e.g. *le regretté Professeur X.*

relations, n.f.p. – contacts, friends, as in *il a essayé d'exploiter ses relations dans le monde de la fonction publique*, he tried to use his friends in the Civil Service. For relations in the sense of relatives use *des parents*. See above, PARENT.

romance, n.f. – not a romance, *un roman d'amour, une idylle*, but a song. The title of Verlaine's collection of poems *Romances sans paroles* (1874) evokes Mendelssohn's *Songs without Words*.

satyre, n.m. – note the colloquial meaning of *un obsédé sexuel*, someone suffering (and making others suffer) from satyriasis. A satire is *une satire*.

sentimental, adj. – sometimes rather stronger than 'sentimental'; the title of Flaubert's novel *L'Education sentimentale* (1870) might be better translated as 'The Education of the Heart'.

serviette, n.f. – a table napkin, as well as an attaché case or a towel. *Une serviette hygiénique*, a sanitary towel/US sanitary napkin. See SANITAIRE in VII.

sexe, n.m. – both gender and the male or female sexual organ as in *un cache-sexe*, a G-string. Used absolutely, it can mean all women. *Une personne du sexe* is archaic, ecclesiastical usage for a woman. The title of Simone de Beauvoir's feminist essay *Le Deuxième Sexe* (1949) reflects her view of women as a sex made to take a back seat by men.

stoppeuse, n.f. – a female hitch-hiker or someone who will do invisible mending, fine darning/US repairing while you wait.

surprendre, v. – nowadays, more or less synonymous with *étonner* meaning to surprise. However, according to legend, when the nineteenth-century lexicographer Littré's wife discovered him *en flagrant* délit d'adultère* (in the act of adultery), and said *Je suis surprise*, he is reputed to have replied, *Non, chérie, c'est moi qui suis surpris, vous êtes étonnée*, No, my dear, *I* have been caught, *you* are surprised.

tempérament, n.m. – the eponymous heroine of Flaubert's *Madame Bovary* (1857) was *de tempérament plus sentimentale qu'artiste,* had more of a sentimental than an artistic temperament, but when Zola says, in the preface to *Thérèse Raquin* (1867), *J'ai voulu peindre des tempéraments et non pas des caractères*,* he means that he is interested in general physiological and not general psychological characteristics. When Flaubert repeats the *idée reçue* that *les brunes ont plus de tempérament que les blondes,* he means that brunettes are said to be sexier than blondes. Thus you might hear of a sprightly old gentleman that *malgré ses soixante-dix ans, il a encore du tempérament* or . . . *il est encore vert,* although he's 70, he still has an eye for the girls. See TEMPÉRAMENT in II and III.

tester, v. – not only to test but also to make a will, *un testament.* Alexis de Tocqueville observes in a footnote to *De la Démocratie en Amérique* (1835, 1840) that *Au moyen âge, le pouvoir de tester n'avait, pour ainsi dire, point de bornes. Chez les Français d'aujourd'hui, on ne saurait distribuer son patrimoine entre ses enfants sans que l'Etat intervienne.* (In the Middle Ages, there were, so to speak, no restrictions as to how you made your will. Among French people today, you can't distribute your inheritance among your children without the State intervening.) As the argument in the same author's *De l'Ancien Régime et de la Révolution* (1856) recognizes, however, this freedom to leave one's property to whomsoever one wished had begun to disappear long before 1789, as a result of the interfering tendencies of the monarchy in the seventeenth and eighteenth centuries.

trivial, adj. – not trivial, which is *futile,* but vulgar, rude. Thus *dire des trivialités* is to talk smut.

trouble, n.m., adj., **troubler,** v. – these words need special care. *Troubler quelqu'un* is not to trouble someone in the sense in which the English say to their doctor 'Sorry to trouble you', *'Je m'excuse de vous déranger'*, but to disturb emotionally. In *Armance* (1827), Stendhal writes: *Madame de Malivert, troublée par de sinistres* pressentiments, ne put trouver le sommeil,* Madame de Malivert, disturbed by gloomy forebodings, couldn't sleep. The noun *trouble* can either mean disturbances, as in *les troubles de la rue,* street disturbances, or emotional disturbance, as used by Monsieur Lepage in Marcel Aymé's *Le Confort intellectuel* (1949): *C'est par elle que le trouble s'y est introduit, installé, et sa seule présence a suffi à jeter le désordre dans des esprits parfaitement pondérés*.* (It is through her that emotional disturbance has become a permanent feature of life, and her mere presence has been enough to spread disorder among the most level-headed.) It can also occasionally have the sense of sexual excitement, as when Albert Memmi describes mixed swimming parties in *La Statue de Sel* (1953) and notes *A deux ou trois reprises, j'éprouvai quelques ardeurs honteuses qui m'obligèrent à plonger pour cacher le trouble de mon corps,* On two or three occasions, I was embarrassed by the speed of my sexual reactions, and had to dive into the water. Note also, however, *des troubles cardiaques,* heart trouble, etc. The word *trouble* may be used adjectively with several meanings, but note the expression *pêcher en eau trouble,* to fish in troubled waters.

unir, v. – to unite, but *s'unir* is to marry, or come together in sexual congress. Cf. Camus's notation in his *Carnets* (Notebooks): *Les noces à Suse: 10.000 soldats, 80 généraux et Alexandre s'unissent à des Perses,* The Nuptials at Susa: 10,000 soldiers, 80 generals and Alexander take Persian wives. Pierre Viansson-Ponté also noted on page 53 of *Les Gaullistes,* 1963, that *Madame de Gaulle a écarté sans pitié de l'entourage tout divorcé ou divorcée, raye volontiers sur les listes des réceptions intimes les couples unis civilement, bat froid ceux qui tombent sous le soupçon de libertinage* (has pitilessly removed from the General's social circle any man or woman who has been divorced, feels no hesitation in striking off the list of people to be invited to a private party any couple who have had merely a civil marriage, cuts anyone dead who is suspected of leading an irregular sexual life). See MARIER above.

verge, n.f. – care is needed in the use of this word, since, in addition to its primary meaning of stick, rod or cane, it can also mean penis, as in the erotic masterpiece by Guillaume Apollinaire, *Les Cent Mille Verges.* A verge on the roadside is *un accotement.* The warning sign 'Soft Verges' is rendered by *Accotements mouvants* or *Accotements non stabilisés,* and means that you risk sinking into the soil if you drive off the road. What the British call the 'hard shoulder' of the motorway is referred to in France as *la bande d'arrêt d'urgence,* perhaps another example (see SEA-GREEN INCORRUPTIBLE in II) of the preference which French as a language has for abstract or descriptive terms where English uses more concrete or, occasionally, evocative terms.

vice, n.m. – vice, and *le vice anglais,* which the French see as flagellation. The vice squad, *la brigade des mœurs.*

vivace, adj. – not vivacious, *vif, vivant, éveillé, plein d'entrain,* but tough, hard-wearing, long-lasting. Not often applied to people, though one does talk about *la vivacité des méridionaux,* the liveliness of people from the South. *Une plante vivace* is a hardy annual.

volontiers, adv. – willingly. *Je le ferais volontiers,* I should be delighted to do it. Distinguish from *volontaire,* a volunteer, and also someone who is strong-willed. *Volontairement* means deliberately, as in *je me suis trompé volontairement*, I made a deliberate mistake.

VII Travel and Health

absorber, v. – also means to consume or to take, especially something unusual, as in *absorber un médicament*, to take a dose of medicine.

accidenté, adj. – designates someone or something that has been involved in an accident (*une voiture accidentée*), but note also *du terrain accidenté*, rough, uneven country, *un parcours accidenté*, a hilly itinerary, course.

agonie, n.f. – death throes, as in *être à l'agonie*. Ionesco has said that Samuel Beckett's characters *représentent l'humanité entière, dans sa longue agonie*, represent the whole of humanity interminably on its deathbed. Agony, *des souffrances atroces*. 'I'm in agony', *je souffre abominablement*. In the same way *agoniser* means to be in the death throes, to be dying. An agonizing reappraisal is *une révision déchirante*.

angine, n.f. – not only angina pectoris, a serious heart complaint, more specifically *de l'angine de poitrine*. Otherwise a throat infection, generally cured, like most other minor illnesses, *maladies bénignes*, in France by the insertion of *des suppositoires,* suppositories; and it is pointless to protest that *c'est à la gorge que j'ai mal*, it's my throat that hurts.

animer, v., **animation,** n.f. – very fashionable words, rather wider in meaning than animation. *Saint-Germain-des-Prés est un quartier où il y a beaucoup d'animation* means that the cafés and restaurants stay open until three in the morning, and that you have to stuff your ears with *des boules quies* (small balls of wax coated with wisps of cotton wool; available from all good chemists, *toutes les bonnes pharmacies*) if you want to get any sleep. *Un animateur* or *une animatrice* is a person who ensures that nobody relaxes when they are supposed to be enjoying themselves, and *des qualités d'animateur/trice* can always be mentioned as a point in favour of a student applying for a job as *assistant(e) d'anglais* or *moniteur/monitrice* in *une colonie de vacances*. M. Henri, *Ministre du Temps Libre* in the 1981 Mauroy government, has stated: *L'animation est une idée qui a un très grand avenir. Les métiers de l'animation seront sans doute* parmi ceux qui vont se développer très rapidement dans la prochaine décennie* (*Le Monde*, 25 July 1981). (The organization of leisure activities has a great future, and careers in leisure organization will probably be among those that will develop most quickly in the next ten years.) *Un centre* (or *une salle) de réanimation* is an intensive care unit in a hospital, not a place used in *la première bobine*, first reel, of *un film d'épouvante*, horror movie. *Un dessin animé* is a cartoon film.

appareil, n.m. – for the many meanings of this word associated with equipment, machinery, see dictionary, but it is not used for apparel, garb (*vêtements, habits**). The word is used for a partial denture, whereas a full set of false teeth is *un dentier; la denture* is the shape and configuration of one's natural teeth (*il a une bonne denture*). Louis in Mauriac's *Le Nœud de Vipères* (1933) saw himself as *un appareil distributeur de billets*, literally a bank cashpoint/US electronic teller. Fashionable expressions in a socio-economic context are *l'appareil administratif*, the State administrative system, *l'appareil éducatif*, the education system, and *l'appareil industriel*, French industry.

athlète, n.m. – not only an athlete, but also someone fairly large and well-developed.

attraction, n.f. – *Le Petit Robert* gives *vous êtes la grosse attraction*, you are the big attraction, as an Anglicism, but *les attractions* in a night-club are the floor-show.

aubergine, n.f. – not only a vegetable but also, in the past, slang for *une contractuelle*, a traffic warden. See below, CONTRACTUELLE.

ballast, n.m. – not what you put in a boat (the distinction *navire/bateau* corresponds to the difference between ship and boat in English) to ensure stability (*le lest*) but the clinker and stones placed between railway lines (a sleeper is *une traverse*). In 1944, one of the ways in which the drivers and stokers, *les mécaniciens et les chauffeurs*, sympathetic to the Allied cause made the trains run slowly and thus disrupted the rail traffic was by throwing *une pelletée de charbon dans le foyer, deux sur le ballast*, a shovelful of coal on to the fire, two on to the track.
There is also a verb *lester*, to weigh down. Jean-Paul Sartre – who, like Roland Barthes, Charles Baudelaire, Albert Camus, Alexandre Dumas *père*, André Gide, François Mauriac, Charles Péguy, Romain Rolland, Antoine de Saint-Exupéry and Emile Zola, lost his father very early in life – writes with ironic nostalgia in *Les Mots* (1964), *Un père m'eût lesté de quelques obstinations durables; faisant de ses humeurs mes principes, de son ignorance mon savoir, de ses rancœurs mon orgueil, de ses manies ma loi, il m'eût habité.* (A father would have weighed me down with a certain mulish obstinacy, making his moods into my principles, his

ignorance into my knowledge, his resentment into my pride, his fads into my law, he would have lived in me.) Also *délester* – euphemistically, to deprive someone of his/her money by legal or illegal means.

ball-trap, n.m. – a clay-pigeon shoot, found much more frequently in France than in Britain or North America. When you are ready with your shotgun (*un fusil à choke-bore, un fusil à calibre*), you shout '*Pull!*', pronounced [pyl]. Your assistant then releases a kind of saucer, which flies in the air and which you cleverly shoot down.

bendix, n.m. – a word occasionally used for a self-starter in a car. A more normal word would be *un démarreur*. Presumably named, like the washing-machine, *la machine à laver*, after its maker. More frequently used examples of the French referring to an object by the name of its inventor are *le carter*, engine casing, *le chatterton*, insulating tape (from Chatterton's compound, 1870).

bile, n.f. – has more than a purely physical sense in French. *Pourquoi s'est-il fait tant de bile à propos de quelque chose de si ridicule?* – Why did he get so angry about something so silly? Also the adjective *bilieux* (*Pourquoi a-t-il toujours cet air bilieux?*). A bilious attack, *une crise de foie.*

bombe, n.f. – not only bomb, but also a fly or insect spray. *Une bombe glacée* is an elaborate ice-cream dessert.

bookmaker – has no legal existence in France, where betting on horse races, *les paris sur les courses de chevaux*, is a State monopoly known as the *Pari Mutuel Urbain* (PMU). Most popular with the average Frenchman is *le tiercé*, where you have to name the first three horses in a designated race (such races are run on Sundays, public holidays and sometimes during the week), either *dans l'ordre d'arrivée* (1, 2, 3) or *dans un autre ordre* (1, 3, 2; 2, 1, 3; 2, 3, 1; 3, 1, 2; 3, 2, 1). The minimum stake, *la mise minimum*, is at present five francs. However serious the national or international situation, *France-Inter* and the *postes périphériques* (the commercial radio stations situated outside France but aimed at French audiences: Radio Luxembourg, Radio Monte-Carlo, Europe 1) never fail to give *les pronostics* and, after the race, the prizes, *les rapports*, of *le tiercé*, which is effectively the French equivalent of the British football pools, but more profitable, one hopes, to the Revenue, *le fisc*. There is also *le couplé*, in which you name the first two horses, and, more recently, *le quarté*, in which you name the first four horses, but neither is as popular as *le tiercé*. A relatively recent rival of *le tiercé* is *le loto*, a form of bingo also State-run (there are no bingo halls in France). *Le tiercé* and *le loto* seem to have reduced the popularity of *la loterie nationale*.

box, n.m. – a lock-up garage, or the dock in a law-court, *le box des accusés*. However, the witness box is *la barre des témoins*. Boxing is *la boxe*. See also BOX in I.

break, n.m. – an estate-car, as opposed to *une conduite intérieure*, a saloon. A private car is *une voiture particulière*.

brûler, v. – note the idiomatic *brûler une ville*, to drive through a town without stopping, *brûler un feu rouge*, to fail to stop at a red light. Hence *brûler les étapes*, to go more quickly than expected (also *prendre une avance sur le calendrier**, as when *les six pays fondateurs de la Communauté Economique Européenne*, the six founder-members of the EEC, *ont réalisé* l'union douanière en 1968 et non pas en 1970 comme prévu*, achieved the customs union in 1968 instead of 1970 as scheduled).

cabinet, n.m. – among its meanings note the place of work of a member of the medical, legal or learned professions (*cabinet médical, dentaire* – doctor's, dentist's surgery/US office; *cabinet du notaire**; *cabinet du juge d'instruction**; *cabinet de travail d'un écrivain*; *cabinet d'un agent immobilier* – estate agent's office). In the singular or plural, it can also mean a loo, *un cabinet d'aisances*. However, when Alceste tells Orante in Act I, Scene 2 of Molière's *Le Misanthrope* that his sonnet is *bon à mettre au cabinet*, he simply means, in seventeenth-century usage, that it is only fit to be locked away in a cupboard. See also CABINET in I and II.

cachet, n.m. – as well as a mark of distinction, a seal, a rubber stamp, and an artiste's fee, also means a tablet to be taken medicinally (the term *un comprimé* is used too). *Il a pris deux cachets d'aspirine, sans arriver à s'endormir*, he took two aspirins, but couldn't manage to get to sleep. Also a postal date-stamp; *le cachet de la poste fait foi*, is sufficient proof of the date of posting.

caddie, caddy, n.m. – golf is so expensive a game in France that you probably would be able to afford one if you played it, but the word also means a trolley in a supermarket (*un supermarché, un hypermarché, une grande surface*).

car, n.m. – a bus in a country area, e.g. for taking children to school, *un car de ramassage scolaire*. Also *un car de la SNCF*, replacing an uneconomic local train, *un train d'intérêt local qui a cessé d'être rentable**; an airport bus, *un car de l'aéroport*; and *un car qui assure le service entre les différentes gares parisiennes*, a bus service to take you from one Paris railway station to another. The word *bus* or *autobus* is used for regular services within a town or city. *Un bibliobus*, a mobile library.

cargo, n.m. – a merchant vessel, whose cargo is *la cargaison.*

charabanc – *un autocar* (for outings, *des excursions,* even though the Mothers' Union and Women's Institute have no equivalent in France; had they existed, Emma Bovary and Thérèse Desqueyroux might not have been so bored). *Un char à bancs* is a horse-drawn vehicle that was used to transport people in the country. Both H.E. and P.T. have spent many pleasant hours in France trying to explain such peculiarly English activities as Sunday School outings (*excursions pour les enfants qui se sont montrés fidèles à l'école du dimanche*), Bring and Buy Sales (*ventes de charité où on apporte ce dont on n'a plus besoin afin d'acheter ce dont on n'aura jamais besoin*), Sponsored Silences or Swims (*activités où on s'engage, moyennant une somme d'argent promise à l'avance par tous ceux qui ont signé sur une feuille attestant la nature non intéressée* de l'entreprise, à garder le silence pendant telle ou telle période ou à nager telle ou telle distance*), or Jumble Sales (*ventes d'objets usagés*). See ACTION in V, MORTGAGE in IX, and UNION, STUDENTS' in IV for hints as to other cultural parallels and non-parallels. Church fêtes in France are known as *des kermesses.* The nearest one can come in ethos and atmosphere to a Church fête (combined with that of the Durham Miners' Gala) is in *la Fête de l'Humanité,* the annual fund-raising event for the Communist Party newspaper, *l'Humanité,* held near Paris in September. Indeed, one is tempted to explain the appeal of the French Communist Party by its ability to satisfy such needs.

chasser, v. – to drive away or to hunt rather than to chase, *poursuivre. Chassez le naturel, il revient au galop* – *naturam expellas furca; tamen usque recurret,* throw nature out with a pitchfork, it still comes back. *Qui va à la chasse, perd sa place* – huntsmen are easily cuckolded; the expression may be used in a more general context to encourage wariness as to what may happen in one's absence.

circulation, n.f. – as in English, but also traffic, as in *La circulation est très intense le 31 juillet. C'est le début des vacances,* Traffic is very heavy on 31 July. It's the beginning of the holidays; or movement, as in *Le Traité de Rome a créé le principe de la libre circulation des travailleurs, des marchandises et des capitaux,* The Treaty of Rome established the principle of free movement of workers, goods and capital. Note also *Circulez!* – Move along there, please! If asked to do this either by *un gendarme* (in the country), *un agent de police* (in the town) or, more particularly, by a member of the CRS, *les Compagnies Républicaines de Sécurité,* units specially trained for quelling public disturbances, then do so quickly.

code, n.m. – not only a code, as in *Code civil, Code postal, Code de la route,* but also dipped headlights, as in *l'obligation de se mettre en code dans les grandes villes* (as opposed to *pleins phares*, full headlights, *feux de position*, sidelights, parking lights).

coffre, n.m. – not coffers, as in Mark Antony's 'Whose ransom did the general coffers fill', but often the boot of a car/US trunk. A safe is more normally *un coffre-fort*.

compas, n.m. – a pair of compasses, as well as a mariner's compass showing *la rose des vents*, the points of the compass. It is *la boussole* which more frequently helps you to find your way.

composter, v. – to punch a railway ticket, something which you must do before starting your journey, so that the *contrôleur** can see that you don't intend to use your ticket twice.

concussion, n.f. – fiddling the books. He's suffering from concussion, *il a été victime d'une commotion cérébrale*, or *il a été commotionné*.

conductor – in a bus, *le receveur**; in music, *le chef d'orchestre* (the leader of the orchestra is *le premier violon*).

continent, n.m. – the French mainland, especially to *un Corse*, an inhabitant of Corsica, *la Corse*, also known as *L'Ile de Beauté*. Thus in *Sud-Ouest* for 26 August 1982 H.E. read that one of the Corsican autonomist movements *avait décidé de suspendre pour l'instant ses actions sur le continent, mais de reprendre les attentats contre les intérêts continentaux sur l'île* (had decided to suspend for the present its acts of violence on the French mainland, but to resume its attacks against French interests on the island).

contractuelle, n.f. – a female civil servant who is not *titularisée** and is thus on a limited-term contract, and especially a traffic warden. Because of the purple colour of their uniform, *les contractuelles parisiennes* used to be known as *les aubergines*. This has been changed to a light blue, so that they are now also called *des pervenches*, periwinkles. They distribute *contraventions**, parking tickets, called in familiar style *contre-danses*. If you have well-placed friends at the *préfecture* or the *commissariat* (police station), you might manage to get the ticket torn up (*faire sauter une contravention*). They occasionally arrange with their heftier male colleagues, *leurs collègues plus costauds*, to affix *un sabot de Denver* (as in Colorado), a padlock the size of a giant horseshoe, on to the front wheel of an illegally parked car, *une voiture stationnée en contravention*. Alternatively, unless you are a member of *le Corps Diplomatique*, your car can be removed to *la fourrière*, the pound.

correspondance, n.f. – an exchange of letters; Baudelaire's belief in the poetic harmony of the universe; a connection when travelling, as in *il y a une correspondance à Lyon*, you'll get a connection at Lyons. A title envisaged for this book was *Correspondances, or Where to change.*

cric, n.m. – not a crick in the neck, which is *un torticolis*, but a jack for jacking up the car when you have *crevé* or had *une crevaison*, had a puncture or flat.

cure, n.f., **curer,** v. – not to cure or to get better – *guérir* renders both meanings – but to clean out, as with *un cure-dents*, a toothpick. *Une cure* is not a cure, *une guérison*, but a course of treatment; *faire une cure à Vichy*, take the waters, but also *cure d'antibiotiques, cure de vitamines*. Note also the expression *n'avoir cure de*, to pay little attention to: *le terrorisme, lui, n'a cure des frontières (Parlement européen*, 13/17 September 1982). See RUDE in I.

dancing, n.m. – a dance-hall. The French don't talk about a 'palais de danse'; and if you are invited to spend an afternoon *à l'hippodrome*, it will be to see horse-racing not a pantomime (see PANTOMIME in X).

déjection, n.f. – not dejection (*abattement, tristesse*), but either the medical term for the act of evacuating the bowels or the excrement itself, or the technical term for what is thrown up by volcanoes.

droguerie, n.f. – not a drugstore (US) or a chemist's shop but a hardware store (also *une quincaillerie*). A chemist's shop is *une pharmacie*. You need *une ordonnance*, a prescription, to buy drugs, *des médicaments*. If you are not a national, *un ressortissant*, of a Common Market country, it is essential to take out medical insurance before you visit France; if you are British, it is a sensible precaution to have obtained your E.111 from your local DHSS office before leaving the United Kingdom. Whether you go to see the doctor in his surgery/US office, *son cabinet* (see above) for a consultation, or whether he comes to see you in your hotel/villa/tent (*une visite*) you pay him directly *ses honoraires*, his fee, plus, in the latter case, *ses frais de déplacement*, his travelling expenses. If he is *homologué par la Sécurité Sociale*, on the Social Security list, approximately 80 per cent of this is *remboursable*, repayable to you. So, too, is the money you pay for *les médicaments* which fall into the same category, and *vous collerez les vignettes sur la feuille de maladie que le médecin vous aura donnée et où le pharmacien aura apposé son cachet*, you will stick on the little tabs showing how much you have paid on the sickness form which the doctor will have given you and which the chemist has stamped. You then take this form to the nearest *Caisse primaire de la Sécurité Sociale* (you will be told where it is if you ask at the *Mairie* (town hall) or the *Syndicat d'initiative* – see below), and a *mandat* international* will be sent to you *dans un délai* d'un mois*, within a month. The difference between what you have paid and the sum reimbursed is known as *le ticket modérateur* (see below, TICKET, and MUTUELLE in III). The chronic deficit of the French Social Security system has caused headaches to successive governments. Drugs, in the narcotic sense, are *des stupéfiants*, but someone who is under the influence of narcotics, *sous l'empire des stupéfiants*, may be known as *un drogué*.

erratique, adj. – quite literally wandering, as in *une douleur erratique*, a pain which keeps moving about.

éruption, n.f. – note the sense of a skin rash, as well as volcanic activity.

express, n.m. – not an express train, *un rapide*, but simply a fairly fast train. *Un omnibus* is a train which stops at every station.

fièvre, n.f. – a common and quite undramatic way of talking about a high temperature: *il a un peu de fièvre, j'ai quarante de fièvre* (104°F).

flanelle, n.f. – only as *un pantalon de flanelle*. A face flannel/US washcloth is *un gant de toilette*. To flannel, to avoid the issue by talking a lot, is *baratiner*. 'Don't flannel' – *Alors? C'est oui ou non?*

galerie, n.f. – among other meanings, note that of roof-rack on a car.

germe, n.m. – not a germ that causes disease, which is *un microbe*, but a seed, as in wheat-germ, *des germes de blé*.

hôpital, n.m. – as in English, though *une clinique* is often used to make it clear that you are in a private and not a public one. *Il est mort à l'hôpital* can still mean 'he died in an institution'. Never translate the English 'hospice' by *un hospice*, which still has marked Poor Law associations. *C'est l'infirmerie qui se moque de l'hôpital*, the pot calling the kettle black.

indicatif, n.m. – as well as the grammatical mood, also means a signature tune, as in *l'indicatif de France-Inter*, or part of a telephone number. Thus, to ring from one *département* to another, *vous composez le 16*, you ring 16; you wait for *la tonalité*, a musical phrase, and then ring the two-figured number of the *département* where your correspondent lives (*l'indicatif*), followed by her/his number. *L'indicatif* is not the same as the postal number of the *département*.

infection, n.f. – in addition to the first meaning as in English, note also that of vile smell. It is more usual to hear *c'est contagieux* for 'it's infectious', and *les maladies contagieuses* for infectious diseases.

inférieur, adj. – sometimes quite neutral in sense, as in *couchette inférieure*, lower bunk; likewise for *supérieur*.

intoxiquer, v., **intoxication,** n.f. – to poison, as when Thérèse Desqueyroux's relations said that *elle avait tort de tant fumer: elle s'intoxiquait*, she was wrong to smoke so much, she was poisoning herself (François Mauriac, *Thérèse Desqueyroux*, 1927); likewise the noun, as in *une intoxication alimentaire*, an attack of food poisoning. To intoxicate is *enivrer*.

isolation, n.f. – insulation (*thermique* – to keep heat in; *sonore* – to keep sound out). The English isolation is *l'isolement*. Note also *une insolation*, an attack of sunstroke. For Splendid Isolation, see ISOLATION in II.

libre, adj. – as in *libre-service*, in a shop, self-service. See also SELF in VIII. *Entrée libre*, you don't have to buy anything. Free, *gratuit*, as in *stationnement gratuit* (free parking), the opposite of *stationnement payant*.

licence, **driving** – *un permis de conduire. See also* LICENCE in I and IV.

lifting, n.m. – a face-lift. Another of the numerous words 'borrowed' from English though not existing as such in English; see SMOKING in IX.

liquide, adj. – note the expression *Vous voulez payer par chèque ou en liquide?* Do you want to pay by cheque or in cash?

loo/US john –'May I use the?' – *est-ce que je peux me servir des toilettes, y a-t-il des cabinets, où sont les waters, les WC* (pronounced 'Vay Say') *s'il vous plaît?* The old *vespasiennes*, originally introduced by the *Préfet* Rambuteau in 1834, have now disappeared and are being replaced in the provinces as well as in Paris by new, coin-operated, centrally-heated, automatically disinfected and clearly visible edifices. Should you be unable to find one of these, go into the largest and most expensive *café* you can see; ask for the telephone; this will almost certainly be situated next to the loo. If it is the old type that works with a *jeton de téléphone*, ask confidently for one; disappear behind the doors helpfully labelled *Téléphone/Toilettes*; re-emerge and return your *jeton* with the (for you) ambiguous sentence *Je n'ai pas eu ma communication* (I couldn't get through), *madame*. She will hand back 1F40 of the 1F60 you gave her for the *jeton*, since she knows what you're doing. Alternatively, order a cup of coffee.

Le jeton is a round, metallic disc, often of a size that will fit only one particular type of 'phone. The normal translation of 'token' offers the interesting coincidence of linking the word with a fallacious interpretation. 'A token presence' might be held to indicate the fact that you are at a meeting only to obtain what the French call *un jeton de présence*, a token which enables you to claim a fee for having attended. This was the practice in the first French revolution, where Maximilien de Robespierre *n'avait pour source de revenu que ses jetons de présence à l'Assemblée Nationale*, had no income other than his daily allowance for attendance at the *Assemblée Nationale*, and it still applies to the *Académiciens* who receive a *jeton* for turning up at a meeting of the *Académie Française*. However, the explanation in the present instance is rather more prosaic, in spite of there being no agreement as to what it is. Some say that *café* proprietors were anxious to ensure that anyone using the 'phone they had installed paid handsomely for it. They therefore refused to allow a telephone on their premises if it could be made to work with an ordinary coin of the realm, that is to say *un denier de la République*. Others observe that the slow introduction of the public telephone into France coincided with a period of high and continuous inflation. It was therefore never possible, on purely practical grounds, to have telephones which worked if one inserted a given number of francs or centimes, since this number would never in the past remain constant for long enough to make the installation of a coin box a working proposition.

A token presence is best translated by *une présence symbolique*.

maniaque, adj. – not so much a maniac (*fou à lier*) as fussy. *Lunatique*, moody, temperamental, has remained closer in meaning to the Latin etymon (lunaticus – of mood changing according to the phases of the moon) than the English 'lunatic' (*complètement cinglé*, etc.).

midi, n.m. – midday; also the South of France, like the Italian *il Mezzogiorno*. The French talk about *le Sud de la France* mainly in a geographical context; the more normal word is *le Midi*. For Northern Frenchmen, the inhabitants of the *Midi*, *les méridionaux*, are essentially characterized by their tendency to exaggeration and their dislike of hard work. *Le démon de midi* is the expression used to designate the increased sexual urges and the propensity to indulge in extra-marital relationships, reputedly experienced by men in their early middle age. In English, 'the male menopause' is conveniently used in this sense.

monnaie, n.f. – change, as in *la petite monnaie*, small change. *Est-ce que vous n'avez pas la monnaie?* Don't you have the right amount (in change)? *La Monnaie* is the Mint. Money is *l'argent*, though *la monnaie* is also currency, as in *le cours d'une monnaie*, the rate of exchange (also *le taux de change*). See DEVISE in III.

moto, n.f. – a motorbike.

nerveux, adj. – not always nervous (*inquiet*), more frequently wiry, sinewy. *Un style nerveux* – a vigorous style. *Une voiture nerveuse, un moteur nerveux* – nippy, lively, responsive, with rapid acceleration, indispensable for the popular French sport of trying to be first away at the traffic-lights.

oblitérer, v. – in addition to the sense of 'to obliterate', this verb also means to cancel, as when a postage stamp is franked in order to prevent it from being used a second time. Visitors to the *Gouffres de Padirac* should therefore be reassured rather than disturbed by the notice in the lift/US elevator to the effect that *Le courrier est oblitéré du cachet postal des Gouffres de Padirac*. It merely means that their friends will be able to see that they have visited these rather splendid underground caves, not that they will be deprived of the pleasure of reading what has been written on the postcards; literally, all mail bears the postmark of the *Gouffres de Padirac*.

omnibus, n.m. – nowadays, a train not a road passenger vehicle, which is *un bus* in town and *un car* in the country. See EXPRESS above.

ouvrable, adj. – working, as in *tous les jours ouvrables sauf le dimanche et jours fériés*, every working day except Sunday and public holidays.

palace, n.m. – not a palace (*un palais*) but a large luxury hotel.

parc de voitures, n.m. – not a car-park, *un parking* (*parking souterrain*, underground car-park; *parking-silo*, multistorey car-park), but the number of vehicles on the road. Cf. *Le Monde*, 13 February 1982: *Si on prend le nombre de tués par rapport au parc automobile, on compte pour 100.000 véhicules, 70 tués en France, 729 en Turquie (c'est le taux le plus élevé), 56 en Allemagne, 48 au Japon, 42 aux Etats-Unis, 40 en Grande-*

Bretagne. Si on compare le nombre de tués au trafic, la constatation est identique: 4,6 tués aux 100 de véhicules-kilomètres en France, 2 aux Etats-Unis, 2,3 en Grande-Bretagne, 3,3 en Italie, 4 en Allemagne, 6 en Belgique, 7,4 en Espagne ... (If you take the number of people killed in relationship to the number of cars on the road, you have 70 fatal accidents for every hundred thousand cars in France, 729 in Turkey (the highest figure), 56 in Germany, 48 in Japan, 42 in the United States, 40 in Great Britain. If you compare the number of people killed to the density of the traffic, you come up with the same result: 4.6 people killed for every 100 cars to the kilometre of road in France, 2 in the United States, 2.3 in Great Britain, 3.3 in Italy, 4 in Germany, 6 in Belgium, 7.4 in Spain.) Note *le parc automobile d'une grande entreprise*, the fleet of cars of a big firm. Cf. also *le parc hôtelier français*, the number of hotels in France. *Un parc-mètre* is a parking meter.

Pas-de-Calais, n.m. – Straits of Dover, as well as being a *département** in the North of France. When Napoléon I said *Du sublime au ridicule il n'y a qu'un pas*, some brave soul is said to have replied: *Oui, Sire, et c'est parfois le Pas-de-Calais*. The English Channel is *la Manche* (literally: sleeve), and during the Occupation a Paris waiter is reputed to have said, while helping a German officer on with his greatcoat: *Que c'est difficile de passer la manche (Manche)*.

patente, n.f. – see III, PATENTE. Patent medicine is *une spécialité pharmaceutique*.

pétrole, n.m. – petroleum, oil, as in North Sea oil, *le pétrole de la Mer du Nord, que les Anglais devraient bien partager avec leurs partenaires européens*, North Sea oil, which the English ought to share with their European partners, and the slogan used in France's energy-saving campaign, *Nous n'avons pas de pétrole, mais nous avons des idées*, we have no oil, but we have ideas. French agriculture is often referred to by the French as *le pétrole vert*. Petrol/US gas is *l'essence. Le carburant* is often used as a synonym for *l'essence*. The French talk not about the number of kilometres they do to the litre, but the number of litres they need to travel one hundred kilometres. See the advertisement *Je fais du 4, 5 aux cent. Qui suis-je?* And the reply, written upside down: *Renault 5 GLT. Le fuel* (or *le mazout*) is domestic heating oil. *Le brut* is crude oil, as well as champagne which has not yet undergone its second fermentation. For cooking, lubricating or painting one uses *l'huile*, though normally of different kinds. *Le gas-oil* (or, sometimes, *le gasole*) is diesel-oil for a motor-vehicle.

pile, n.f. – a battery for a torch (*une lampe de poche*), *un transistor* or *un walkman* (sound walky). But a car-battery is *une batterie*. Piles, *des hémorroïdes*.

point, n.m. – note particularly *un point de côté*, a stitch, while running. The points in a car-engine are *les vis platinées*.

province, n.f. – the provinces, as opposed to Paris, and to be distinguished from *la Provence*, the South of France around Avignon. Félix Boillot makes a nice point when he contrasts 'county people' (*tout ce qu'il y a de bien dans la région*) with 'country people' (*des gens de province*). It is hard to say whether it is *le provincial* or *le banlieusard* (commuter) who is considered to be more beyond the pale by Parisians, all apparently oblivious of the fact that they are *des provinciaux déracinés*, uprooted provincials.

radio, n.f. – note the meaning of X-ray as well as radio; for the French radio, see AUDIO-VISUEL in X. *Un radio* is a wireless operator on board ship.

rage, n.f. – not only fury but also violent toothache (*une rage de dents*) and rabies.

resident – more normally called *un habitant*. 'Parking for residents only' – *Stationnement réservé aux riverains. Une résidence* is an up-market modern block of flats, *un immeuble de grand standing, haut de gamme*.

Riviera – the French talk about *la Côte d'Azur*, using the Italian word to describe only the Italian coast.

rupture, n.f. – a break, as in *rupture de négociations*. A rupture, *une hernie*.

sanitaire, n.m. – the washing and toilet facilities in a house or flat. As an adjective, is also used for health and medical care, as in *un avion sanitaire*, ambulance plane.

secteur, n.m. – a sector, but also the mains, as in *un rasoir électrique qui marche sur pile* (battery) *ou sur secteur*.

serviette, n.f. – a towel as well as a table-napkin, and a briefcase (in the latter case, also *un porte-documents*). *Serviette hygiénique*, sanitary towel/US napkin. Idiomatic expression: *Ne mélangeons pas les torchons* (dishcloths) *et les serviettes* – There are two separate issues here.

sleeper – Boillot warns against translating 'he's a bad sleeper', *il est sujet à des insomnies*, by *c'est un mauvais coucheur*, a disagreeable character. On a train, a sleeper is *un wagon-lit*; as part of the railway track, *une traverse*. See above, BALLAST.

spider, n.m. – not a spider (*une araignée*), but the dicky-seat in a twenties-style roadster.

starter, n.m. – the choke. The starter (of a car) is *le démarreur*. 'It started first go', *J'ai démarré au quart de tour* – literally, as soon as I turned the key 45 degrees.

stop, n.m. – a road sign, *un panneau de signalisation*, indicating that you do not have the traditional *priorité à droite*; *faire du stop*, to hitch-hike (done not by raising a thumb in the direction you want to go, but by standing facing the traffic and holding a piece of cardboard displaying your destination). See STOPPEUSE in VI.

store, n.m. – not a large shop, *un grand magasin*, but a window blind, occasionally of metal. *Pur protéger leurs vitrines en cas d'émeute, les marchands baissent leurs stores*, to protect their windows in the event of a riot, shopkeepers lower their blinds.

substitut, n.m. – a deputy public prosecutor (see MAGISTRAT in I). 'I can find you a substitute' – *Je peux vous trouver quelqu'un pour me remplacer*. Also *un suppléant**. 'It's only a substitute' – *Ce n'est qu'un succédané, un produit de remplacement, un ersatz*.

syndicat d'initiative, n.m. – local tourist information office, an invaluable source of help both if you write in advance, and on the spot, *sur place*. Often situated at or near *la Mairie*, and frequently closed – like many other offices in France – between 12 and 2.

tansad, n.m. – pillion seat on *une moto*, a motorbike.

tension, n.f. – note the meaning of high blood-pressure, as in *j'ai de la tension*. However, *le médecin m'a pris la tension* means the doctor took my blood-pressure.

ticket, n.m. – a ticket only in the Métro or on a bus; otherwise a ticket is *un billet*, or, in the theatre, *une place*. The Paris Métro (but not the RER, *le Réseau Express Régional*) works on the simple principle of an inclusive price, *une somme forfaitaire**, for any single journey, however long. It is best to buy *un carnet de tickets*, originally a booklet of tickets (you get ten). For *ticket modérateur*, see above, DROGUERIE.

touché, past participle – in addition to the English meanings is sometimes used for someone afflicted by an illness, *il est gravement touché par la maladie.*

tourniquet, n.m. – both a device for stopping bleeding and a turnstile or revolving door (*un tambour*).

tramp, n.m. – a tramp steamer. A tramp is *un clochard.*

trappe, n.f. – not a carriage or a trap but a trap-door. Also the Trappist order of monks.

turc, n.m. – as well as meaning Turk, is occasionally also used in the masculine to designate *un cabinet à la turque*, an Asian, squatting type loo/US john as still occasionally found on the more primitive camp sites, *les campings les moins bien aménagés.* In 1969, *le turc* at *Le camping municipal d'Amiens* had a timing device, *une minuterie*, which made it flush very copiously at 95-second intervals. *Une minuterie* is also the automatic switch which you press to put the lights on before dashing upstairs in your hotel and which extinguishes them just as you are looking for your key. *C'est pour économiser l'électricité, monsieur.* The French justify *le turc* on hygienic grounds, and they are still being installed in motorway rest areas (*aires de repos*).

valide, adj. – the word *valable* is more frequently used in the sense of valid, as in the notice in Métro stations: *Au-delà de cette limite les billets ne sont plus valables*, Tickets invalid beyond this point. *Valable* is also used to mean acceptable, defensible: *votre hypothèse/point de vue est tout à fait valable; c'est un travail valable.*

van, n.m. – a horse-box, whereas a van is *une camionnette.*

végétation, n.f. – in the singular as in English, but in the plural, adenoids.

VIII Food and Drink

accommoder, v. – to prepare (a dish) and not to accommodate, *loger*.

addition, n.f. – not only the art of adding up, but also the bill in a restaurant, also jocularly referred to as *la douloureuse* (because of the pain it causes) or *le coup de fusil* (because it often comes as such a surprise) or even *la multiplication*. Most French people check, *vérifient*, the bill carefully, and, in *Les Carnets du Major Thompson* (1954), Pierre Daninos makes Major Thompson say of his friend Monsieur Taupin that *s'il ne trouve pas d'erreur, il semble déçu. S'il en déniche une, il est furieux*, if he doesn't find a mistake, he looks disappointed. If he unearths one, he is furious. One asks whether service is included: *Est-ce que le service est compris?* 'In addition' is *en plus*.

alcoolique, adj. – is applied to people *atteints d'alcoolisme* as well as to alcoholic drinks, more properly called *des boissons alcoolisées*. Ordinary *vin de table* is classified according to the number of *degrés d'alcool* (10°, 11°, 12° etc.). *L'alcool à brûler* is methylated spirits. Sometimes, however, *l'alcool* is used in the sense of the US hard liquor.

alimentaire, adj. – used more widely than in English; as in *les produits alimentaires*, foodstuffs, *l'hygiène alimentaire*, eating what is good for you (cf. *suivre un régime*, to keep to a diet), *une pension alimentaire*, alimony, *une intoxication alimentaire* (see INTOXICATION in VII), food-poisoning, *une besogne alimentaire*, work that one does to earn one's bread and butter, rather than doing something creative like writing poetry, and – in time of war – *un blocus alimentaire*, preventing food from reaching the enemy. Successive French governments have encouraged *l'industrie agro-alimentaire*, the food-processing industry, as a means of reducing surpluses of fresh fruit and vegetables.

anglaise, adj. – *une assiette anglaise* is a plate of cold meats. See also below, CRÈME.

asparagus, n.m. – non-edible asparagus fern, as used in bunches of flowers. Asparagus is *une asperge*.

ballon, n.m. – a wine glass. *Un ballon d'oxygène*, an oxygen cylinder, but also used metaphorically in the sense of a whiff of oxygen, a boost or a booster (as to the economy). *Un ballon* is also a balloon and an inflatable ball as used in football, whereas *une balle* is a bullet and a small non-inflatable ball as used in tennis, etc.

blonde, n.f. – a glass of light beer, pale ale, as opposed to *la bière brune*, brown ale. *Le tabac blond*, American tobacco. *Des blondes* are American cigarettes. In a totally different context, *des cheveux blonds*, fair hair, and *des cheveux très blonds*, blond hair.

boîte, n.f. – can be a box (or a night-club; short for *une boîte de nuit*), but also a tin, as *une boîte de sardines*. On his first visit to France, in 1949, P.T. was confronted at dinner with *sardines au beurre*, cold sardines, as an *hors-d'œuvre*. He complimented his hostess on their excellence and was told *Oui, monsieur, ce sont des sardines de Munich*, Yes, they are Munich sardines. His host had to explain that this meant *achetées en septembre 1938, au moment de la crise de Munich*, bought in September 1938, at the time of the Munich crisis, adding that his wife had bought enough at that time to last them all through *les événements de 40, l'Occupation et la Libération* and pointing out that *la sardine, cher monsieur, a cette particularité de se bonifier en boîte*, the sardine has the peculiarity of improving in the tin.

boucherie, n.f. – a butcher's shop, but note that the French make a distinction between *une boucherie* and *une charcuterie*, a pork-butcher's, where in addition to pork, *du porc*, you can buy ham, pâté, etc. Many *charcuteries* also sell *des plats cuisinés, à emporter*; comparison with the Anglo-Saxon 'take-away'/US 'take out' immediately shows how great cultural differences are.

cabaret, n.m. – also, in earlier days, the equivalent of a pub/US saloon. Just as Ma, in Laura Ingalls Wilder's *Little House on the Prairie*, considered that one saloon in a town is one saloon too many, so Mme Vingtras, in Jules Vallès, *L'Enfant* (1879), had a horror of the Demon Drink which showed itself by a dislike of *le cabaret*.

café, n.m. – not normally a place to eat in, which is *un restaurant* or *une brasserie*.

cake, n.m. – not an individual cake, which is *un gâteau* or *une* *pâtisserie*, but a sort of fruit cake. It can be cooked at home, in a rectangular shaped tin, and in that case is delicious. It corresponds to what the French think of as an English light fruit cake, and although any similarity may be accidental, the result can be most pleasing. *Du cake* is, however, also sold in *cafés*, in slices often wrapped in cellophane, and is kept immediately available, *sur le zinc*, on the counter, at the bar. Unlike sardines (see above, BOÎTE), it does not improve with keeping.

Canterbury lamb – the French are only too aware that this comes from New Zealand (see end of entry for EXPLOITER in III), even though we may claim, *prétendre**, that it is home-grown, *un produit indigène, de provenance britannique*. While lamb in England is traditionally raised by the rich to be eaten by the poor, in France it is more often the other way round, even though Jacques Vingtras (see above, CABARET) was sometimes forced by his mother virtually to live off the stuff. Note that *un gigot* is a leg of lamb, a great delicacy to be eaten almost raw, *saignant*, in its own gravy, *la sauce* (see below), and without mint sauce, *sauce à la menthe*, regarded by the French as final proof of the fact that, as Tony Mayer put it in *La Vie anglaise* (1954), *on mange très mal outre-Manche*, you eat very badly on the other side of the Channel.

cantine, n.f. – a more generic term than canteen, since the refectory or school dining-hall is *la cantine de l'école*.

casserole, n.f. – a saucepan, not a casserole or even a casserole dish. In France, as a general rule, the only meat dishes that are cooked in the oven (*au four*) are roasts (*des rôtis*); French housewives, *les maîtresses de maison* or *les ménagères* (not *les femmes de ménage*, daily helps), cook all other meat dishes on the hob, *sur le fourneau*. A possible paraphrase for a casserole would be *un plat de viande et de légumes mijoté au four et que l'on sert dans le plat de cuisson*, a meat and vegetable dish cooked slowly in the oven and served in the dish in which it was cooked. A possible equivalent of a casserole dish would be *une cocotte en grès* (earthenware), whereas *une marmite* is, or was, usually of cast-iron and suspended above the open range. *Une cocotte-minute* (also *un auto-cuiseur*) is a pressure-cooker.

cave, n.f. – not a cave (*une caverne*) but a cellar, as in the refrain of the traditional song: *Dans une cave où il y a du bon vin*, in a cellar where there's good wine.

cherry, n.m. – cherry brandy, not sherry (*vin de Xérès*) or the

American drink known as *un sherry-cobbler*, much consumed in the early novels of Jean-Paul Sartre. It consisted of sherry, lemon, sugar and fruit-juice but is not specifically held responsible for the *nausée* (nausea) which revealed the world's essential absurdity (see CONTINGENT in II) to Roquentin in *La Nausée* (1938) and Mathieu in *Les Chemins de la Liberté* (1945–9).

chicorée, n.f. – as a vegetable, *chicorée frisée* is an endive or curly endive. See below, ENDIVE.

chips, n.m.p. – (pronounced 'sheeps') are potato crisps; chips in the sense of 'French fries' are *des pommes frites* or *des frites*, and in gambling *des jetons*. Chips as in microchips for a computer, *un ordinateur*, are *des puces*. Blue Chips on the Stock Exchange (*la Bourse*) are *des valeurs sûres*.

claret – *le Bordeaux rouge. Un vin clairet* is a light, rather pale red wine. *La clairette* is a sparkling white wine from the Midi. Tante Marie (see below, CRÈME) recommends drinking *le Bordeaux rouge chambré, c'est-à-dire à la température de la pièce*, but tells us to *se souvenir que le Bourgogne et les vins blancs se boivent frais* (cool). This is confirmed by R. Dumay in his *Guide du Vin* (1981); he states on p. 326 that *l'usage se répand, à raison selon moi, de boire frais certains rouges, surtout s'ils sont légers et jeunes: Arbois, Beaujolais, Bourgueil, Riceys, vins de Touraine . . .*, the custom is growing, rightly in my view, of drinking certain red wines cool, especially if they are light and young.

confection, n.f. – quite literally the making of something, as in *des gâteaux de sa confection*, cakes which she made herself. Also ready-made clothing: *On peut très bien distinguer un petit bourgeois d'un grand bourgeois. Le premier porte des vêtements de confection, du prêt-à-porter, le deuxième a ses vêtements faits à la main, sur mesures, chez son tailleur.* (It is very easy to tell a member of the lower middle class from a member of the upper middle class. The former wears ready-made clothes, off the peg; the latter has hand-made clothes, made to measure by his tailor.) Confectionery (and a confectioner's shop) is *une confiserie*, and a confectioner is *un confiseur; la trève des confiseurs* (literally: confectioners' truce) is the period preceding Christmas and the New Year, *les fêtes de fin d'année*, when the unions refrain from industrial action and the government defers announcing unpleasant decisions. *Un confectionneur* makes clothes. *Pierre Mendès-France était fils d'un confectionneur aisé*, a prosperous tailor's son.

contrôlé, adj. – *un vin d'appellation d'origine contrôlée* is one made under certain carefully defined conditions from grapes grown on a vineyard, *un vignoble*, which has been named by the *Office National du Vin* as producing that particular *appellation (Côtes du Rhône*, etc.). See also CONTRÔLER in I.

côtelette, n.f. – a chop, as in lamb chop.

coupe, n.f. – not normally a cup, *une tasse*, except in a sporting context, e.g. *la Coupe du Monde*, and in the proverb, *il y a loin de la coupe aux lèvres*, there's many a slip 'twixt the cup and the lip. Note *une coupe de champagne*, a glass of champagne.

crème, n.f. – cream, but don't be disappointed if *crème fraîche* is not fresh cream. It is a delicious form of sour cream, to be eaten by itself if you are to appreciate the full flavour. Tante Marie, the French equivalent of Mrs Beeton, does not give the recipe, and it is difficult to find it outside France. Unlike Miss Jean Brodie and the London *Times*, the French do not often talk about 'la crème de la crème'. The term *le gratin* indicates those at the top, but belongs to a much less refined register. *La crème anglaise* is custard.

crudités, n.f.p. – uncooked vegetables served as *hors-d'œuvre*. A crudity is *une grossièreté* or *une trivialité* (see TRIVIAL in VI).

déguster, v. – to taste (wine, etc.). *Dégustation gratuite*, free wine-tasting. To disgust is *dégoûter*. Did anyone really see the notice 'Disgusting oysters' outside a Boulogne café?

endive, n.f. – chicory.

farce, n.f., **farcir,** v. – in a culinary context, stuffing, to stuff, as in *des aubergines farcies, des tomates farcies*, stuffed aubergines, stuffed tomatoes.

gloria, n.m. – as 'in excelsis Deo', but also a drink similar to Irish coffee, but with brandy mixed with the coffee and sugar and without cream. In Flaubert's *Madame Bovary* (1857), Charles Bovary's disreputable father likes *des glorias longuement battus*; and quite fancies Emma as well at one point.

grappe, n.f. – a bunch, especially of grapes. See below, RAISIN.

grille, n.f. – the French use *un gril* for grilling (*griller*) food. *Une grille* is a grid, schedule, metal fence or gate.

lard, n.m. – not lard, *le saindoux*, but (more or less) bacon.

limon, n.m. – alluvial clay. A lemon is *un citron*; a lime, *une lime* or *une limette*. The soft drinks are respectively *la citronnade* and *la limonade*. *Un citron pressé*, fresh lemon juice, is healthier, more agreeable, and more expensive.

lunch, n.m. – the meal following a wedding ceremony; may be at any time of the day, like our wedding breakfast. Lunch is *le déjeuner*.

marmelade, n.f. – not marmalade, *la confiture d'orange*, but a mixture of fruits cooked in sugar (also *une compote de fruits*). Note *quelle marmelade!* – what a mess!

office, n.f. – a pantry. See also OFFICE in I and V.

offrir, v. – to give as well as to offer. *Il nous a offert un très bon déjeuner*, he invited us out to a splendid lunch.

paraffine, n.f. – paraffin wax, used in making candles, grease-proof paper (*du papier sulfurisé* or *du papier imperméable*) and even to give consistency to some kinds of preserves (*conserves*). Paraffin to use in a stove is *du pétrole lampant*.

parmentier, adj. – with potatoes in it, since it was Antoine Parmentier (1737–1813) who popularized the potato in France. *Hachis parmentier* is shepherd's pie; *une omelette parmentier* is an omelette with sliced boiled potatoes in it.

plongeur, n.m. – not only a diver, from *plonger*, to dive, but somebody who does the washing-up in a restaurant, *qui travaille à la plonge*, as George Orwell did in *Down and Out in Paris and London*. The French translation, *La Vache enragée* (from the idiomatic expression *manger de la vache enragée*, to be on one's uppers) was a favourite book of Albert Camus's, and for a long time was better known in France than *Animal Farm (Les Animaux Partout)*. Diving is *la plongée* (e.g. *sous-marine*).

pot-de-vin, n.m. – not a jar of wine but sometimes a tip, usually a bribe. *Une bribe* is therefore not a bribe; it is a fragment, a snatch of, especially in *des bribes de lettres, de conversation*.

primeur, n.f. – not a primer in the decorating context, *une première couche*, or at school, *un manuel de base*, but early-season vegetables for which the French are prepared to pay astronomic prices. Farmers, *les agriculteurs, les exploitants agricoles*, in South and South-West France fear that, when Spain and Portugal join the Common Market, *lorsque l'Espagne et le Portugal adhéreront au Marché commun*, French *primeurs* will not be able to command such high prices. Also used metaphorically for first view, first hearing: *je vous donne la primeur de mon dernier poème*. See also PRIME in III and PRIMER in I.

prune, n.f. – a plum. A prune is *un pruneau*, but *des pruneaux d'Agen* are a liqueur-soaked delicacy having little in common with prunes and custard, *des pruneaux et de la crème anglaise*.

raisin, n.m. – a grape, but *du raisin* means grapes. Raisins, *raisins secs*; currants, *raisins de Corinthe*; sultanas, *raisins de Smyrne*.

recette, n.f. – not only money received (*les recettes de l'Etat*, State revenue; *les films porno font encore recette*, are still box-office successes), but also recipe. See also RECETTE in III.

salade, n.f. – in a restaurant, unless further defined (*de tomates, niçoise, de fruits*), means *une salade verte*. At the greengrocer's, *chez le marchand de légumes*, you would be expected to specify what type of salad you want to buy – *laitue, frisée, batavia*, etc. Also *quelle salade!* – what a mess! Boillot suggests *quand j'étais un blanc bec* for 'in my salad days', but a better rendering of Cleopatra's remark might be *du temps de ma jeunesse folle*, for *blanc bec* implies both inexperience and pretentiousness.

sauce, n.f. – also means natural gravy for meat dishes (also *du jus de viande*) and a liquid preparation of spices for fish dishes. Most French housewives, *maîtresses de maison*, would be horrified at the idea of using gravy-browning. Readers might recall the remark attributed to Francesco Caraccioli (1752–99) and frequently, though incorrectly, to Voltaire, that there are in England sixty different religious sects, but only one sauce.

saucisse, n.f. – a small sausage eaten hot, often designated by its place of origin: *de Strasbourg* (beef); *de Francfort* (mixture of veal and pork), etc.

saucisson, n.m. – a large sausage, generally eaten cold in slices, as part of an *hors-d'œuvre* or at a picnic, *où les gens vont saucissonner*.

scotch, n.m. – not only whisky but a brand name for a widely used adhesive tape/US cellophane tape or Scotch tape; thus, *Je va. scotcher ce paquet*, put sellotape round this parcel.

self, n.m. – a self-service restaurant; now being joined by *le fast-food* as the name of the establishment as well as what you eat there.

sobre, adj. – abstemious, simple; also as in *un style sobre et dépouillé*, a simple and restrained style. *La sobriété*, restraint, as when Philinte tells Alceste in *Le Misanthrope* (Act I, Scene 1): *La parfaite raison fuit toute extrémité/Et veut que l'on soit sage avec sobriété.* (True reason eschews all exaggeration, and demands that we be wise in a restrained way.) He's quite sober, *il n'a rien bu*. However, the appeal for *la sobriété au volant*, 'don't drink and drive', may be reinforced by *l'alcotest*, the breathalyzer.

tempérance, n.f. – virtually synonymous with *sobriété*, but with no suggestion of 'total abstinence'. Boillot maintains that *le néphalisme* means *l'abstention complète de boissons alcooliques*, total abstinence from alcoholic beverages, but the word is not in the seven-volume *Robert*. You might look quite a long time in France before finding a temperance hotel. Total abstainers are *des croix-bleu*.

zeste, n.m. – means zest only in the sense of a slice of orange or lemon peel; otherwise, zest may be rendered by *entrain, enthousiasme*.

IX Clothes and Houses

accommodation, n.f. – the physiological act of adaptation, e.g. of the eye to a change of light. *Un accommodement* is the fact of coming to terms with someone, as in Tartuffe's reassurance to Elmire in Act IV, Scene 5 of Molière's play *Le Tartuffe* (1667): *Le ciel défend*, de vrai, certains contentements/Mais on trouve avec lui des accommodements.* (Certain satisfactions are, it is true, forbidden by God; but it is not impossible to come to some arrangement with Him.) For ACCOMMODER see VIII. Accommodation is *un logement.* 'I'm looking for accommodation', *je cherche un appartement, je cherche à me loger.*

aérer, v. – to air in the sense of ventilate (*aérer une chambre, un lit*), but see VENTILER in I. To air the sheets is *finir de faire sécher les draps*, but we have not met anyone in France who has an airing cupboard. *Un centre aéré* is a holiday playgroup for town children.

allée, n.f. – a tree-lined avenue, not an alley, which is *une ruelle, une venelle.*

alsacien, adj. – pertaining to Alsace. *Une brasserie alsacienne* is a place where you eat *la choucroute* and other delicacies from Eastern France. An Alsatian dog, as kept in a minute *appartement* to express your *peur du voisin* and your *méfiance d'autrui*, is *un berger allemand.* See SUSPICIOUS in V.

antiquités, n.f.p. – when used in the plural, often means antiques. H.E. once saw an exclusive up-market furniture store called *Les Antiquités de demain.*

bain, n.m. – a public or Turkish bath. In a house, a bathroom is *une salle de bains* but the actual fixture is *une baignoire.* A swimming-bath is *une piscine.* To take a bath is normally *prendre un bain,* and to bathe *se baigner. Etre dans le bain* is to be implicated (e.g. in a scandal), while *mettre quelqu'un dans le bain* is to put someone in the picture, and *un bain linguistique* is a *stage** of total-immersion language training.

baskets, n.m.p. – rubber-soled shoes, as worn when playing basketball, *lorsqu'on joue au basket.* A basket is *un panier.*

bassin, n.m. – not a wash-basin, *un lavabo,* nor a kitchen sink, *un évier,* but an ornamental pond in a garden or, in sick-room parlance, a bedpan. Note also its geographical meaning as in *le Bassin parisien, le Bassin d'Arcachon,* and its anatomical meaning of pelvis.

blouse, n.f. – sometimes a blouse but frequently a smock. *Les blouses blanches* are the members of the medical profession (because of their white coats). A blouse is often *un chemisier.* Note also *un blouson,* a waist-length jacket, often made of leather, as in *les blousons noirs,* young French delinquents of the 1950s.

bonde, n.f. – a plug for a bath or wash-basin.

brassière, n.f. – not a brassiere, *un soutien-gorge,* but either a baby's long-sleeved vest or, as on the ferry from Royan to La Pointe de Grave, *une brassière de sauvetage,* a life-jacket. More frequently, however, this is known as *un gilet de sauvetage.* Not to be confused with *une brasserie,* which is either a brewery or a rather chic eating house where you can obtain expensive meals at any time of the day.

builder – *constructeur* or more frequently *entrepreneur de bâtiments,* rather than *bâtisseur* which tends to have wider, more symbolic associations, as in *un bâtisseur d'empire.* Since most French town-dwellers still live in flats, *appartements,* rather than *maisons individuelles* (see below, PAVILLON), the small, speculative builder is a less conspicuous character in French life than is the large *société* de construction* or *société immobilière* which has the capital to put up *une résidence* (an up-market block of flats), *un grand immeuble* or even *un building (toujours grand).* A property developer is *un promoteur.* For building society, see below, MORTGAGE.

canadienne, n.f. – a fur-lined jacket, as worn by J.-P. Sartre in many photographs.

carpette, n.f. – a rug. A carpet is *un tapis.* A fitted carpet is *une moquette* (see below).

charge, n.f. – an expense, a charge made for a service. Thus, for your *appartement,* you pay *le loyer* (see below, RENTE), *le gaz, l'électricité et les charges,* services. See also CHARGE in I and III.

château, n.m. – not a castle, which is *un château fort,* where *le donjon* is the keep, and the dungeon *le cachot,* but a large country house, practically a stately home, as in *les châteaux de la Loire*; also, an estate, *une propriété*, in the wine-growing country around Bordeaux. *Un château d'eau* is a water tower. *La vie de château* – as at Blandings Castle in the novels of P.G. Woodhouse: an idyllic existence.

commode, n.f. – not a commode, which is *une chaise percée*, but a chest of drawers. See also COMMODITÉ in III.

costume, n.m. – a man's suit, still known as *un complet-veston* (or just *un complet*), as well as what you wear on stage. *Un bal costumé* is a fancy-dress ball. *Un dîner de têtes*, as readers of Jean Anouilh's one adult play, *Pauvre Bitos* (1956) will remember, is a dinner party where you wear modern dress but make up your face and hair to resemble those of an historical character.

culotte, n.f. – a pair of knee-breeches, as in *les sans-culottes*, who showed their membership of *les classes laborieuses** by wearing long, modern-style trousers and not the breeches and hose of formal eighteenth-century dress; a pair of women's pants (*un slip* – see below – is used more frequently nowadays for a garment worn by men and women); a pair of trousers, as in *c'est sa femme qui porte la culotte*. The 'culottes' fashionable in England in 1982 were, according to *Le Point* on 12 October 1981, known as *knickers – Appelez-le knickers, bermuda, corsaire, jupe-culotte, saracel, comme vous voulez. Si la mode ne fait pas rire, ce n'est plus la mode.* (Call them . . ., as you wish. If what is fashionable doesn't make you laugh, it's no longer fashionable.) See below, PANTALON.

froc, n.m. – a monk's cowl, as in the expression *jeter le froc aux orties*, to give up the ecclesiastical state, and as worn by Balzac when staying up all night (*passer une nuit blanche*) writing. A woman's frock is *une robe*.

fuel, n.m. – fuel oil, not fuel, *le combustible*.

fuser, v. – not to fuse the lights, which is *faire sauter les plombs* or *les fusibles*, but to run like wax or to burst out (*les lumières fusent partout*).

galoche, n.f. – a clog. Galoshes (Brit. Eng.), overshoes (US) are *des caoutchoucs*. 'You can tell her mother wore clogs', *On voit bien que sa mère portait le foulard* (headscarf). This expression, immortalized in Mauriac's novels, has its origin in the social convention, observed in certain parts of France at the turn of the century, that only middle-class women wore hats; a peasant woman would seem to be adopting airs above her station if she wore a hat. It would probably not be readily understood by many young French people today, in an age when clothes are not such clear social indicators. We have found no stock phrase (*une expression consacrée*) corresponding to the English North Country proverbial expression 'Clogs to clogs in three generations'. However, on p. 42 of Michel Tournier's *Gilles et Jeanne* (1983), Gilles de Rais's grandfather explains to him, on 15 November 1432, that he is now one of the richest lords in the kingdom but that he must nevertheless bear in mind the fact that *'les petits-fils dilapident ce que les grands-pères ont accumulé'* (grandchildren waste the fortune their grandparents have built up). The idea is clearly the same, though the absence of a comparable expression might well indicate that the French have, since the fifteenth century, been able to *mieux protéger leur héritage*, look after their inheritance better than the English.

grange, n.f. – a barn, whereas its modern British meaning might be translated as *un manoir*.

habit, n.m. – not a habit, *une habitude*, but a monk's or nun's habit as well as formal evening dress for men, as in *L'avantage de l'habit, c'est qu'on peut porter toutes ses décorations, ce qui n'est pas le cas quand on est en smoking* (The advantage of tails is that you wear all your decorations, which you can't do if you're wearing a dinner jacket) (see below, SMOKING). *Les habits* are clothes, costume, etc. Note that although in English fine feathers make fine birds, in French *l'habit ne fait pas le moine*, habits don't make monks.

hôtel, n.m. – as in English, but can also mean a private house of some importance in a town. *Ils ont un hôtel dans le seizième, un appartement rue de l'Université, sans compter la résidence secondaire en Dordogne. Ils ne peuvent donc pas crier misère,* They have a large private house in the 16th *arrondissement* (one of the more exclusive districts in Paris), a flat/US apartment in the *rue de l'Université*, to say nothing of a second home in the Dordogne. So they can't plead poverty.

inhabité, adj. – uninhabited, whereas inhabited is *habité*.

interrupteur, n.m. – note the sense of electric switch, also called *le commutateur* or just simply *le bouton*.

jaquette, n.f. – a morning coat for a man (*les messieurs en jaquette et pantalon rayé*, pin-striped trousers) and a short coat for a woman. A man's jacket is *un veston* or *une veste* (see below, VESTE).

moleskine, n.f. – imitation leather.

moquette, n.f. – not only moquette on a sofa, armchair or three-piece suite (*un canapé avec deux fauteuils assortis**) but also wall-to-wall carpeting.

mortgage – the generally accepted translation – *une hypothèque* – is sometimes misleading. The French noun and corresponding verb *hypothéquer* stress the disadvantages of the financial arrangement involved, as in *les Anglais ont hypothéqué le pétrole** de la Mer du Nord pour s'acheter dix années de vie facile*, the English have mortgaged North Sea oil to buy ten years' easy life. What you need to buy a house and beat inflation is *un prêt immobilier*, which you will *amortir par mensualités*, pay off in monthly instalments, while at the same time being able to *déduire les intérêts de votre revenu imposable*, deduct the interest from your taxable income (see IMPOSER in III). You will not get a loan to purchase your home so easily from *une société** immobilière* in France as you would from a building society in the United Kingdom, since the former is mainly a company that buys and sells property or invests money in it. The Nonconformist spirit of self-help which led to the establishment of the first building society in Birmingham in 1775 was not a feature of French nineteenth-century working-class life; and French banks do not traditionally make the type of long-term loans that are a feature of house purchase in the Anglo-Saxon world. It is only in the last twenty-five or so years that specially favourable arrangements have existed for house purchase in France in the form of *comptes d'épargne-logement* involving an initial period of regular investment before a loan is made, *un prêt est consenti*. These are now run by banks as well as by *des sociétés de crédit mutuel* (see MUTUELLE in III) and State- and municipal-run organizations, such as *le Crédit foncier* and *les Caisses d'Epargne*. A useful metaphorical expression, especially in a political context, is *lever une hypothèque*, to get rid of an obstacle to achieving something.

nouveautés, n.f.p. – fancy goods or newly published books. *Un magasin de nouveautés*, a draper's shop.

pantalon, n.m. – normally used in the singular, except in (archaic) a woman's pants, and *les pantalons de golf*, plus-fours.

patron, n.m. – not only the boss, but a (dress-) pattern. A patron (of the arts) is *un mécène*, and a hotel patron *un client* (as in *parking réservé aux clients de l'hôtel*). See PATRON in III.

pavillon, n.m. – not only a flag (*un paquebot battant pavillon britannique*), a military tent, and the wing of a building, as in *le pavillon des* *agités* in a psychiatric hospital and the title of the French translation of Solzhenitsyn's famous novel (*Le Pavillon des cancéreux*), but also a small, detached suburban house, the dream, or so it seems, of most French city-dwellers. *L'univers pavillonnaire* is a possible equivalent of 'suburbia'. See also COMPLAISANT in VI.

polo, n.m. – a polo-necked sweater.

privacy – you can have *chasse gardée, défense d'entrer,* and *propriété privée* (private shooting, no entry, and private property) but there seems to be no generic term; in the same way, there seems to be no standard equivalent of 'Trespassers will be prosecuted'. 'I like my privacy' – *Je n'aime pas qu'on vienne me déranger, je n'aime pas qu'on vienne chez moi sans y avoir été invité, je tiens à mon intimité.* The French equivalent of 'an Englishman's home is his castle' is *le charbonnier est maître dans sa maison* or *chez lui. Des privautés* is over-familiarity, often of an amorous sort.

pyjama, n.m. – normally used in the singular. If Roland Barthes's (1913–81) 1954 essay *L'écrivain en vacances* in *Mythologies* (1957) is any guide, the French still wore in the fifties what were known in the twenties and thirties as beach pyjamas; it is said that a photograph of François Mauriac in *Le Figaro littéraire* inspired the sentence, *Je sentirais sans doute délicieusement fraternelle une humanité où je sais par les journaux que tel grand écrivain porte des pyjamas bleus.* (I should doubtless have a delicious fellow-feeling for a human race in which I know through the newspapers that a certain great writer wears blue beach pyjamas.)

rente, n.f. – see this word in III for unearned income, etc. The rent is *le loyer,* as paid by a tenant, *un locataire.* See also CHARGE above.

robe, n.f. – an ordinary dress for women as well as a formal garment, a gown, for lawyers, as in *la noblesse de robe* (the pre-Revolutionary legal nobility) and *les robins* (an archaic pejorative term for lawyers), or an academic gown, also called *une toge.*

room – the generic term is *la pièce.* Other, more specific words are: *le bureau,* office or study; *la chambre à coucher,* also *d'amis* (spare room), *de bonne* (maid's room, usually at the top of the house or apartment block), *d'enfants* and, of course, *des Députés; la salle de bains, de classe, à manger, d'attente (à la gare).* In modern flats you will find *le living.* In addition to *le salon,* drawing-room, lounge, note *le salon d'attente (chez le médecin, le dentiste), de beauté, de thé* and *de l'Automobile* (Motor Show).

slip, n.m. – not a woman's slip, *une combinaison, un jupon*, but a pair of men's or women's underpants, or swimming trunks.

smoking, n.m. – a dinner jacket. As Proust observes (in *Le Côté de Guermantes*), *on donne à toute chose plus ou moins britannique le nom qu'il ne porte pas en Angleterre*, we call everything vaguely British by a name that it does not have in England. Contrariwise, of course, we call *un dancing* 'a palais de danse', eat in a café and imagine that the French often talk about 'la crème* de la crème'. Note *un brushing*, a blow-dry, *un living*, a living-room, *le footing*, walking, *un planning*, a master timetable, *un pressing*, a dry cleaner's, *un tennis*, a tennis court, *un golf*, a golf course, *le jumping*, show-jumping, *le cross*, cross-country, *un billard*, a billiard-table, *un lad,* a stable-lad. *Un pub* in France is fashionable and very expensive, and *le fast-food* is spreading rapidly.

stopper, v. – to stop, but also to do invisible mending. See STOP-PEUSE in VI.

studio, n.m. – not an artist's, which is *un atelier*, but either a cinema, a radio or television studio, or a one-bedroom flat. *J'ai trouvé un studio dans le quinzième. C'est beaucoup mieux que la chambre de bonne que j'avais dans le seizième.* (I've found a one-bedroom apartment in the 15th *arrondissement* (not a fashionable district in Paris). It's much better than the maid's room I had in the 16th) (see above, HÔTEL). Traditionally, and especially in Paris, the maid's rooms are small, on the top floor and accessible only by the staircase.

study – *un bureau (de travail)*, for a don (*professeur de faculté*) or a writer. *Une étude* is a solicitor's office as well as his practice. See also CABINET in I.

tapisserie, n.f. – wallpaper as well as tapestry. *Le Petit Robert* gives *la tapisserie de Bayeux* as *un usage abusif**, pointing out that it is in fact *une broderie* (embroidery). *Faire tapisserie* (at a dance), to be a wallflower.

veste, n.f. – not a vest but a jacket. A man's vest is *un gilet de corps*, or *un gilet de peau*, as in an article in *Le Monde* on 29 December 1976 by Thomas Cazemages entitled *Portrait du parfait technocrate* and containing the interesting question: *Combien de polytechniciens* (see POLYTECHNIQUE in IV) *ont vu leur carrière brisée à cause d'un gilet de corps apparent sous une chemise en nylon ou de souliers jaunes étincelants au bas d'un pantalon bleu?* (How many *polytechniciens* have seen their career ruined by having their vest showing through a nylon shirt, or shining light-brown shoes beneath blue trousers?) Note *retourner sa veste*, to change sides in a controversy. As an article of female clothing, a vest is *une chemise*.

X Literature, the Arts and the Media

academic, academy – *académique* is often a pejorative term in French, just as 'academic' frequently is in English; however, an academic is *un universitaire*, an academic subject is *une discipline universitaire*, and an academic child, perhaps with the suggestion of being a bit of a swot, may appropriately be rendered as *un fort en thème**. (Note that the French call a gifted child *un enfant surdoué*, since all French children are by definition *doués*.) In French, *académique* is most frequently used when discussing painting or another of *les beaux-arts*, the fine arts, and implies a cold, over-formal style. An academic approach, attitude or discussion would be best rendered as *une façon trop théorique d'aborder le sujet, une attitude abstraite, une discussion sans portée pratique*.

L'Académie Française was founded by Richelieu in 1634, with a membership of forty writers alleged to be *immortels*, and is best known as the guardian of the purity of the French language. It is frequently criticized for its slowness in producing a new edition of its famous Dictionary, and for its failure to elect the more original authors such as Balzac, Baudelaire, Camus, Diderot, Flaubert, Malraux, Molière, Sartre and Zola. There is no English or American equivalent. French scientists have *l'Académie des Sciences* and French artists *l'Académie des Beaux-Arts*, but neither enjoys the prestige of *l'Académie tout court* (THE *Académie*). The equivalent of the Royal Academy of Music in Britain is *le Conservatoire national supérieur de musique*, and of the Royal Academy of Dramatic Art, *le Conservatoire national d'art dramatique*.

Because of an unwritten agreement, *un accord tacite*, that a *Maréchal de France* will be elected without opposition, the unopposed election to the *Académie Française* of a writer who is considered to be on the point of death is known as *une élection de Maréchal*. This happened to François Mauriac in 1933, soon after he had been operated upon for cancer of the vocal cords. He proceeded to live for almost another forty years and to be the only member of the *Académie Française* to take an active part in *la Résistance*.

See also ACADÉMIE in IV.

accessoires, n.m.p. – in the theatre, the props and costumes.

achever, v. – not to achieve, which is *réaliser (ses ambitions), atteindre (ses fins), arriver (à son but),* but either to finish – *Je viens d'achever mon roman,* I've just finished my novel – or to finish off (also *donner le coup de grâce à quelqu'un).* Likewise, *achèvement* is completion, as in *l'achèvement des travaux a été retardé par le mauvais temps, une série de grèves,* the completion of the work has been held up by bad weather, a series of strikes, while an achievement can be frequently translated by *une réalisation* (see RÉALISER in II).

admirer, v. – (sometimes) to be amazed, as well as to admire. As in *J'admire qu'il soit venu si tard,* I'm amazed he's come so late.

agréable, adj. – as in English, except that 'I'm quite agreeable' is *je suis parfaitement d'accord.*

amateur, n.m. – in addition to its use in a sporting context (*un cycliste amateur, professionnel),* this word is used more frequently than in English to indicate an enthusiastic admirer, as in *amateur de jazz, amateur de beaux livres.* It has no hint of the lack of expertise* which English 'amateur' sometimes implies.

arrière-pensée, n.f. – not second thoughts (to have second thoughts is *réviser ses idées, changer d'avis)* but an ulterior motive. See ULTÉRIEUR in V.

audience, n.f. – occasionally used nowadays in the English sense of audience, especially when discussing *l'audience d'un livre,* the number of people likely to read and be influenced by a book, or *l'audience d'un homme politique.* Of a theatre or concert-hall, however, one says *l'auditoire* or *le public,* and Jean-Paul Sartre made a nice distinction when he complained on p. 270 of *Qu'est-ce que la littérature?* (1947) that the contemporary middle-class writer has *des lecteurs mais pas de public. Audience* is more properly used in the sense of an audience given by a monarch or the Pope, or in that of a legal hearing. See AUDITEUR in I.

audio-visuel, adj., n.m. – unlike its English equivalent, this word is used in French as a noun as well as an adjective, and has a wider meaning: it encompasses not only modern teaching aids but is also the generic term for radio and television. Thus the 1982 Act reorganizing the French radio and television service is called *la Loi sur l'Audio-visuel.*

The successive reforms of this service (the last one had been in 1974), and the widespread dismissal, *les licenciements,* of station managers and journalists that follow any major political upheaval – May 1968, the Socialist victory of May/June 1981 – show how politically sensitive and controversial the problem of the media is in France. The State has *un monopole de diffusion*, a broadcasting monopoly. The notion of broadcasting as *un sevice public* has in France always been interpreted in the narrow sense of service to the régime – and even to the government currently in power. This state of affairs may be seen as symptomatic of *une certaine méfiance instinctive d'autrui*, a certain instinctive mistrust of others which characterizes French society (see SUSPICIOUS in V, ALSACIEN in IX) as well as revealing the absence of the kind of *consensus national* which finds expression in British radio and television.

The 1982 Act had as one of its declared aims to ensure freedom of broadcasting from government control, by the appointment of *une Haute Autorité* of nine members, *inamovibles** (who cannot be removed) during their *mandat** (term of office), and responsible for appointing the heads of the different networks and for overall policy. However, the majority of the members of the new *Haute Autorité*, established in September 1982, representing the different interest groups involved, have well-known left-wing sympathies. There is at present no independent commercial television network in France, and advertising on the State channels is very strictly controlled, permitted only at specific times of the day, and never in the middle of programmes. Although the recent Act has legalized local *radios libres*, representing minority views and interests, each one has to be authorized, and they are not allowed to derive any income from commercial advertising.

There are three *chaînes** *de télévision*, television channels, in France: *la première chaîne*, TF1; *la deuxième chaîne*, Antenne 2 (aerial 2); and *la troisième chaîne*, FR3. The last of these carries a certain number of regional programmes. Each *chaîne* is independent of the others and competes with them for viewers, and there is no co-ordination in programming. According to a recent *sondage*, public opinion poll, the vast majority of French *téléspectateurs*, television viewers, are very unhappy about the quality of what they see on their sets, *leurs téléviseurs, leurs postes de télévision, le petit écran, la petite lucarne* (literally, the little screen, the little skylight), and this view is shared by some foreign observers. The first thing that strikes the Anglo-Saxon viewer is that the evening's entertainment is normally centred around a major programme, starting about 8.30. This may also say something about the eating patterns of the average French family. As for the actual programmes, in addition to the large number of Westerns and imported serials (*Dallas, Starsky and Hutch, The Forsyte Saga, I Claudius*), one is struck by the poor quality of the children's programmes and the relative absence of comedy shows and 'sitcom'; there is no indigenous equivalent of *The Last of the Summer Wine*, *M*A*S*H*, *Dad's Army* or *Cheers*, and especially not of *Coronation Street*. The more memorable programmes include nature documentaries, programmes of *haute vulgarisation scientifique et littéraire* (see below, VULGARISATION, HAUTE), intellectual games, productions of plays and grand opera.

There are three main State radio networks: *France-Musique* and *France-Culture* clearly belong to the same country as Lulli and Debussy or Montaigne and Renan (although for some years the Right has accused *France-Culture* of being run by dangerous left-wing intellectuals). *France-Inter*, the French radio station most easily obtainable outside France, at least in Western Europe, provides a staple diet of pop music (both American and French), interviews with entertainers, asinine phone-ins and sports news. The extended news magazines are also interrupted by jingles and accompanied by unscripted discussions and phone-ins on current affairs, interviews such as Jacques Chancel's former long-running series of *Radioscopies* (available on cassettes), and weekly historical and arts programmes. The British listener, at least, is struck by the absence from French radio of good middle-brow culture, especially as presented to British listeners on BBC Radio 4. One might be tempted to apply to French radio Jean-François Revel's comment on de Gaulle (*En France*, 1965, p. 42): *Le général de Gaulle a parfaitement raison de penser qu'il incarne la France, il a tort de croire que cela soit flatteur pour lui.* (General de Gaulle is quite right to believe that he is the incarnation of France, he is wrong to think that this is flattering for him.)

Many French listeners, especially of the younger generation, choose one of the commercial *postes périphériques* (Europe 1, Radio Luxembourg, Radio Monte-Carlo). Although broadcasting from outside France, they aim at French audiences, and the French government is a majority shareholder. Games, phone-ins and pop music are prevalent, there are frequent interruptions for advertisements, *des spots publicitaires*, but the news bulletins and political commentaries are less *hexagonaux* (see HEXAGONE in II).

Radio-France Internationale does not have, at least outside *la Francophonie*, the French-speaking world, the impact and standing of its American and British equivalents, the insomniacs' friends: the Voice of America and the BBC World Service.

ballade, n.f. – has taken on the English meaning of a long narrative poem. In 1952 Albert Camus wrote a preface to Wilde's *La Ballade de la Geôle de Reading* entitled *L'Artiste en prison*. The word, however, still retains the associations of a shorter poem written to a strict rhyming scheme, as in Villon's *Ballade des Pendus*.

bande, n.f. – not a band but a gang, as in the expression *faire bande à part*, to go off in a gang, form a separate group. A military band is *la musique d'un régiment, une musique militaire*; a village (brass) band is *une fanfare*. A jazz band is *un orchestre populaire*, but a pop group is, inevitably, *un groupe*. *Une bande dessinée*, frequently shortened to B.D., is a strip cartoon/US comic strip celebrating the exploits of characters as different from one another as the indomitable Astérix and the anguished intellectuals in Claire Brétecher's *Les Frustrés*. The B.D. has been a major vogue in France for the last twenty years, and has even given rise to *Une histoire de France en bandes dessinées* (Larousse), a comic-strip history of France.

bleu, adj. – *un conte bleu* is a sentimental story, not a blue one, *une plaisanterie un peu leste, une anecdote grivoise*. In the Army, *un bleu* is a raw recruit.

caméra, n.f. – a ciné-camera rather than a camera, *un appareil photo*.

caractère, n.m. – not a character in a novel or play, *un personnage*, but the non-physical attributes of a person, or a person with certain set characteristics. Thus La Bruyère presents us in *Les Caractères* (1688–94) with particular types of individual who are described under names of Greek derivation. See also CARACTÉRISÉ in I.

carnation, n.f. – flesh tints, in a painting, or the colour of a person's skin. A carnation, *un œillet*, as in *il portait un œillet à la boutonnière* (buttonhole).

comédien, n.m. – an actor, but not necessarily a comic one, except when deliberately contrasted to *tragédien*: *Je l'aime mieux tragédien que comédien*, I think he is better in tragic roles than in comic ones. Thus, *c'est une excellente comédienne* means 'she's a very good actress', but 'Marilyn Monroe was a very good comedienne' is *M.M. était très bien dans les rôles comiques*. They put on tragedies as well as comedies at *La Comédie française. Il est un peu comédien*, he's a bit of a play actor, he puts it on a bit. A ham actor, *un cabotin*. For *comique* see also below, OPÉRA.

composer, v. – to compose, as in *composer des vers*, to write poetry, or *composer une symphonie*, but also in the sense of to be ready to compromise, e.g. *Les Bordelais sont des gens tranquilles et qui composent*, People from Bordeaux don't cause trouble and are always ready to compromise. Also to dial a telephone number, to set up a text for printing, and, intransitively, to sit an examination.

concert, n.m. – in addition to its normal musical meaning, is still used sometimes in a diplomatic context, as in *le concert européen*, the interrelationship of European powers; this used to be known as the concert of Europe.

correct, adj. – not only correct, in the sense of *une phrase grammaticalement correcte*, a grammatically correct sentence, and in that of observing the rules of formal politeness (*au Casino de Monte-Carlo, une tenue correcte est de rigueur*, you have to wear a jacket at the Casino in Monte Carlo; *pendant les premiers jours de l'Occupation, les Allemands se sont montrés très corrects*, in the summer of 1940 German soldiers stood up to give their seats to old ladies in the Métro), but in that of adequate, or satisfactory. Thus the reviewer of *The Four Seasons* in *L'Humanité* for 9 October 1981 wrote that *Le film est correctement mis en scène, bien interprété en moyenne*, the film is adequately directed, generally well acted. It is often used in the sense of 'right' or appropriate, as when Edith Cresson, the Minister for Agriculture at the time, wrote in *Le Figaro* for 8 December 1981 that *Garantir un revenu* suffisant aux agriculteurs, c'est d'abord garantir des prix corrects aux produits agricoles*. (If you are going to guarantee an adequate income for farmers, you must start by guaranteeing suitable prices for agricultural produce.)

creative – creative literature, as in novels, plays, poems, as opposed to literary criticism, *la critique littéraire*, or scholarship, *l'érudition*, is perhaps best rendered by *la littérature proprement dite* or *les œuvres d'imagination*. The French talk about *la critique créatrice* when discussing the tendency of modern literary criticism to become an art form in its own right with little apparent connection with the work of art ostensibly under discussion.

créer, v. – to create, but also to perform a play, a musical work or a dramatic role for the first time: *en 1943, Monelle Valentin créa le rôle d'Antigone, dans la pièce d'Anouilh*. The noun *la création* is similarly used in the theatre and concert hall for the first performance.

difficile, adj. – generally as in English, but see below, FASTIDIEUX.

directeur, n.m. – the manager, the head of a firm, *d'une entreprise**, or the chief editor of a newspaper or review, but not the director in the cinema, theatre and television, who is *le metteur en scène*, whereas the producer is *le réalisateur*. A radio programme producer is also *un réalisateur*. See also DIRECTEUR in III.

distribution, n.f. – note the meaning of cast, in a play, and of prize-giving, *la distribution des prix*. *Le générique*, the credit titles, the list of everyone who has taken part (*collaboré*) in making a film or a television programme. See COLLABORATEUR in II.

éditer, v. – to publish, rather than to edit, though one does speak of *l'édition Lafuma des Pensées de Pascal*, the one which classifies them according to his own manuscript, as opposed to *l'édition Brunschvicg*, which groups them according to subject matter. *L'édition* is publishing, as in *l'histoire fait les beaux jours de l'édition*, publishers are making a good profit from history books. The editor of a newspaper is *le rédacteur en chef* or *le directeur*, but an editorial is *un éditorial*. The word is still considered as something of an Anglicism, especially since it is so difficult to fit in with terms such as *rédacteur*.

A publishing house is *une maison d'édition*, and if you are *édité chez Gallimard, chez Grasset,* or indeed anywhere, you may well find yourself being looked after by one of the authors regularly published by that house, and not by someone who might otherwise be an academic or a civil servant. Thus from 1944 to his death in 1960, Albert Camus had a regular job with Gallimard, *où il avait son fixe*, where he drew a salary in addition to his royalties, *ses droits d'auteur*. In this way he avoided having to publish books simply to earn money.

emphase, n.f. – not emphasis, which is *l'accent mis sur*, but an exaggerated, rhetorical mode of expression, as when *Le Monde* observed on 29 October 1981 of the fashionable Jean-Edern Hallier's style of expression, *L'emphase et les inflexions de voix passent pour être belles et envoûtantes, mais attestent qu'on ne se fie pas toujours à la pure signification de la parole, lot des peuples civilisés* – Rhetorical and verbal effects are considered splendid and spell-binding, but betray only occasional reliance on the pure meaning of words, which characterizes civilized peoples. Cf. La Bruyère (1645–96): *Les plus grandes choses n'ont besoin que d'être dites simplement. Elles se gâtent par l'emphase,* The greatest things need to be said simply. They are spoiled by rhetoric. Thus *emphatique* is rhetorical, bombastic, not emphatic, *d'un ton décidé, avec insistance*. He was very emphatic about it, *Il a beaucoup insisté là-dessus*.

encore, adv. – in order to invite a performer to play another piece of music, one shouts *Bis! bis! Encore* is an adverb meaning still or again, and can also be used ironically in the sense of 'even then'. A French teacher was once asked to explain how he used the traditional system of marking pupils' work out of twenty. He replied: *Vingt, c'est le Bon Dieu. Dix-neuf, c'est moi. Dix-sept, c'est le collègue – et encore.* He then added: *Et les élèves, le maximum c'est quinze* – Twenty is God. Nineteen is for me. Never more than seventeen – at most – for a colleague . . . And no pupil ever gets more than fifteen.

exposition, n.f. – note that one says *une exposition de tableaux, de peinture*, not *une exhibition*, which has the slightly derogatory sense of 'showing off'.

fastidieux, adj. – tiresome, annoying, boring; not fastidious, hard to please, which is *difficile*.

fluent – oddly enough, no exact equivalent. He was very fluent about it, *Il en a parlé avec beaucoup d'aisance, d'éloquence.* He speaks English very fluently, *Il parle très bien l'anglais, Il parle l'anglais avec beaucoup d'aisance, Il parle l'anglais couramment.*

général, n.m., adj. – as in English, except that Boillot warns us to translate 'I get the general idea' as *Je le comprends plus ou moins*, and argues that *les idées générales* are abstract ideas. See below, RÉPÉTI-TION.

générique, adj. – generic, but note *le générique*, the credit titles for a film or a television programme.

geste, n.m., n.f. – distinguish between *un geste*, a gesture, and *une geste*, a legend or a collection of epic poems, as in *La Geste du Saint Graal*.

honnête, adj. – not only morally honest and civilized, as in the seventeenth-century *honnête homme*, but also polite, courteous, decent. *Le Petit Robert* defines *leste*, which means slightly salacious, as *qui dépasse la réserve prescrite par l'honnêteté du langage*, going beyond the normal modesty of polite language. See also HONNÊTE in V.

humeur, n.f., **humour,** n.m. – the word *humeur*, when used abso-lutely, means bad temper. Even the strong-willed and rationalistic Madame de Merteuil is guilty of it in Laclos's *Les Liaisons dangereuses* (1782), recognizing in letter 131 that it might become *un piège*, a trap, but finally allowing it to determine her conduct. The tendency of the French to refer to their own *sens du comique* but to the English *sens de* *l'humour* is perhaps linked to the fact that the books of funny authors such as Marcel Aymé or Georges Courteline have a biting edge lacking in *Three Men in a Boat, The Diary of a Nobody* or *The Heart of a Goof.* The *Anthologie de l'humour noir* which the Surrealist André Breton published in 1939 predated the English (though not the American) concept of black humour by several years.

idiome, n.m. – a language, especially one peculiar to a particular group, as *l'idiome des gens de mer, des robins* – nautical, legal language. An idiom in the sense of an idiomatic expression is *un idiotisme*.

ignorer, v. – although occasionally used in the English sense as in *il est plus commode d'ignorer ce qui gêne*, it is more convenient to ignore anything awkward, its more usual meaning of 'not to know' comes out clearly in the slogan on which Jules Romains's Dr Knock builds his fortune: *Tout homme bien portant est un malade qui s'ignore,* Every healthy person is ill without knowing it (*Knock ou le triomphe de la médecine,* 1923); and in the eminently sensible comment in *Le Figaro Magazine* of 30 April 1982, *la plus belle pédagogie du monde ne permet pas d'enseigner ce que l'on ignore,* the finest teaching method in the world will not enable you to teach what you don't know.

improve – *améliorer,* except that the French encourage one to translate 'I've come here to improve my French' as *Je suis venu ici pour perfectionner mon français.* However well you succeed, they will always say: *Vous parlez très bien le français, mais avec un léger accent belge.* See below, PRATIQUER, and LAISSER-FAIRE in III.

incohérent, adj. – not incoherent, *incapable de trouver ses mots, de parler correctement,* but lacking in consistency. Thus *des propos incohérents* are self-contradictory statements. *La cohérence d'un argument** suggests the way in which all the different aspects of it fit together.

inconvénient, n.m. – is not an adjective in French, but a noun, meaning a drawback or disadvantage (often used to avoid the ambiguity between *désavantage* and *des avantages*). Inconvenient is *mal commode, mal choisi* or *inopportun,* according to the context. *Inconvenant,* adj. is improper, unseemly: *de temps en temps, à Lourdes, l'Eglise rabroue des initiatives par trop inconvenantes* (*Le Monde,* 13 August 1983), from time to time, at Lourdes, the Church rebuffs initiatives that are much too unseemly.

index, n.m. – an index to a book, and the *Index librorum prohibitorum,* as in *toute l'œuvre de Sartre est à l'Index depuis 1948.* Also the index finger, as when Louis Pauwels spoke with scorn, in *Le Figaro Magazine* for 16 January 1982, of the slowness with which certain intellectuals came out in support of Hayek's views, and commented: *quand ils lèvent l'index, c'est seulement pour prendre le vent*, when they lift their index finger, it is only to see which way the wind is blowing. Note *l'annulaire*, ring finger, *le majeur*, middle finger. See also INDEX in III.

intelligence, n.f. – intelligence, animal, human and military, but also understanding, as when Claude Roy commented, in *Le Nouvel Observateur* for 9 January 1982, that Virginia Woolf's literary criticism was *écrite avec cette intelligence de l'art qui n'appartient qu'a ceux capables de le maîtriser, parce que la seule critique créatrice est celle des créateurs* (written with that understanding of art which is the monopoly of those who can master art themselves, since the only creative criticism is the one produced by creative writers) (see above, CREATIVE). *Etre d'intelligence avec l'ennemi* means to be in league with the enemy, as when in Act III, Scene 5 of Racine's *Phèdre* (1677), Thésée asks: *Mon fils, mon propre fils/Est-il d'intelligence avec mes ennemis?*

intervalle, n.m. – a gap in space or time, as in *un étroit intervalle entre deux murs* and *à intervalles réguliers*, at regular intervals. An interval at the theatre is *un entracte*.

long-winded – *interminable*. Not the same as *un ouvrage de longue haleine*, a work which took a lot of time and perseverance to complete.

méchant, adj. – not only wicked, as in the line from Racine's *Athalie* which Françoise used to quote after the departure of Eulalie in Proust's *Du côté de chez Swann* (1913), *Le bonheur des méchants comme un torrent s'écoule*, the prosperity of the wicked is carried away by the rapids, but also fierce as in *Chien méchant* (Beware of the Dog), and worthless. Thus *un méchant livre* is not a wicked book but simply a bad one, and *une méchante cravate* a cheap, threadbare tie, not a villainous-looking one.

misérable, adj. – either, as in Hugo's *Les Misérables* (1862), very poor, suffering from *la misère*, poverty, or wretched, accursed, deserving of pity. This is a miserable place, *Quel endroit sinistre* (see below, SINISTRE). He's a miserable character, *Il est bien lugubre*. He had a miserable journey, *Il a fait un voyage bien pénible, bien difficile*.

nature morte, n.f. – still life (in painting).

nègre, n.m. – in addition to the ethnic meaning, is also used for the poorly-paid hacks whom some distinguished writers have from time to time been accused of employing to write their works for them.

notation, n.f. – in addition to the musical meaning as in English, is also used for the system of marks awarded annually to French civil servants and on which their promotion depends. See AVANCEMENT in I.

opéra-comique, n.m. – not primarily a comic opera. The French are still not happy about *le mélange des genres*, the mingling of tragic and comic elements firmly condemned by the aestheticians of the seventeenth century. A consequence of this in the musical sphere, *dans le domaine de la musique*, is that any opera containing spoken dialogue has traditionally had to be performed at the *Opéra-Comique* and not at the *Opéra*. Georges Bizet's *Carmen* (1875), for example, was performed at the *Opéra-Comique*, which is merely a *théâtre lyrique subventionné*, and not at the *Opéra*, whose official title is *L'Académie nationale de musique*. Nowadays, however, spectacular productions (*à grand spectacle*) even of operas with some spoken dialogue are given at the *Opéra*. The terms *théâtre lyrique* and *œuvres lyriques* are generic terms for opera.

organe, n.m. – a physiological organ, but not a church one. This is generally *les orgues* (in the feminine) or *un orgue*, as in *les grandes orgues de Notre-Dame de Paris* and *un orgue de Barbarie*, a barrel organ. *Il a un bel organe*, he has a good voice (no erotic overtones; these are evoked, as in English, by *un membre* – Henry de Montherlant once said that *le fusil est le deuxième membre viril de l'homme*, the gun is man's second virile member). Also used for the press, in phrases such as *La Croix, organe de la pensée chrétienne progressiste*. See also ORGANE in I.

ouvreuse, n.f. – an usherette. You must remember to tip her for showing you to your seat, under pain of an embarrassing incident such as the one which – some years ago, admittedly – spoilt the pleasure of one man attending an old-fashioned detective play, *un drame policier*. On realizing that she was to receive no tip, the *ouvreuse* hissed to him: *C'est le Général, l'assassin.*

pamphlet, n.m. – a short piece of writing attacking a person or an institution, e.g. *les pamphlets de Voltaire*. A (commercial) pamphlet is *une brochure, un dépliant publicitaire*.

pantomime, n.f. – a mime show, sometimes illustrating a spoken text, but not a pantomime, for which the French have (*Dieu merci*) no equivalent.

partition, n.f. – a musical score, not a partition in a building, which is *une cloison*, as in *la valse des cloisons*, the expensive game played by all administrations when they reorganize themselves.

pétulant, adj. – lively. Petulant is *boudeur, maussade.* Perhaps a *faux ami* which helps to explain why Petula Clark has been so much more successful in France than in the English-speaking world.

phrase, n.f. – a sentence, not (except in music) a phrase, which is *une expression* or *une locution. Il appartient à la catégorie la plus insupportable des casse-pieds* (bores): *il termine toujours ses phrases* – he always completes his sentences.

plaisant, adj. – can mean agreeable, but note also *vous êtes plaisant,* you're being ridiculous.

plastique, adj. – in *les arts plastiques*, the visual arts. Note that plastic is *de la matière plastique*, not to be confused with *le plastic*, an explosive substance much used in terrorist outrages in France during the Algerian war and since.

pourpre, adj. – crimson, whereas purple is *violet*.

pratiquer, v. – to practise charity or medicine, or to take part in a sporting activity, as in *pratiquer la pêche*, but not to practise, either one's French or one's backhand in tennis, *son revers.* Then, one uses *exercer*, or *s'exercer*, as in *Je suis venu à Paris afin d'exercer mon français, mais je n'y trouve que des étrangers.* Note that *depuis que je pratique Proust* means 'since I've started reading Proust regularly'. See above, IM-PROVE.

prétendre, v. – to claim, not to pretend, *faire semblant. Il prétend tout savoir, mais il est obligé de faire semblant lorsqu'on lui demande de lire un formulaire*. En fait, c'est un analphabète* – He claims he knows everything, but he has to pretend when you ask him to read a form. In fact, he's illiterate (also *illettré*).

puzzle, n.m. – a jigsaw puzzle.

redondant, adj. – used like the English redundant for style and language, but not in the context of staff reduction, *la compression de* *personnel*; here the French say *licencié pour causes économiques**, and call someone who has been made redundant *un licencié économique.*

répétition, n.f. – note the meaning of rehearsal. *La répétition générale,* sometimes just *la générale,* is the final dress rehearsal.

réplique, n.f. – in addition to replica, means retort, reply, especially a reply made during a stage dialogue.

résumer, v. – not to resume, *reprendre, recommencer,* but to summarize. *Un résumé* is a summary, whereas *un sommaire* is usually a table of contents of a book (also called *une table des matières*) or a list of articles in a review or magazine.

rogue, adj. – not roguish, *espiègle,* but scornful, arrogant, *plein de morgue.* He's a rogue, *c'est un escroc, un filou, un méchant garçon.*

roman, adj. – when talking about ancient Rome, as in Roman architecture, the French use *romain,* as in *l'architecture romaine. L'architecture romane, l'art roman,* pre-Gothic medieval art or architecture, as in the nave at Vézelay. When the same rounded arches are in an English cathedral, we call it Norman or Romanesque. *Romanesque,* however, either means romantic, as in *c'est un personnage très romanesque,* or appertaining to the novel. Thus *la technique romanesque* is narrative technique. *Les langues romanes,* the Romance languages.

sensible, adj. – sensitive, not sensible, *sage, raisonnable.* French children are told to be *sages,* and 'Do be sensible' is *Soyez raisonnable. La sensibilité* nevertheless has the same meaning as in *Sense and Sensibility,* and had in the seventeenth century the very strong meaning of able to feel emotion, and especially love – cf. Phèdre's lament in Act IV, Scene 5, *Hippolyte est sensible et ne sent rien pour moi.*

sentence, n.f. – not a grammatical sentence, *une phrase,* but either a penal one (also called *la peine,* as in the death sentence, *la peine de mort*) or a sententious saying.

séquelle, n.f. – not a sequel, *une suite,* but the consequence, result of an action.

série, n.f. – not a series like *Dallas* or *Tintin,* which is *un feuilleton.* Gallimard's famous *Série Noire,* with appetizing titles such as *Pas d'orchidées pour Miss Blandish, Y a pas de Bon Dieu, Et ta sœur, Des machabées à la pelle* (Stiffs by the shovelful), is a collection of crime novels, originally translated from the American but later produced at home, *de fabrication française, des produits du pays. Une série noire* is a succession of disasters, and *des marchandises fabriquées en série* are mass-produced goods, as opposed to *de fabrication artisanale* (see ARTISAN in II). Also a break in billiards, or in snooker (not a game widely played in France). *Une tête de série* is a seeded player in tennis. See also BACHELIER in IV.

sinistre, adj. – not only sinister, but also gloomy, as in the Goncourts' famous description of the always meticulously dressed Baudelaire as *correctement sinistre*, impeccably gloomy. *Un sinistre* means an accident for which you make a claim on your insurance, and a disaster or natural calamity. Sartre stressed the continuity of his cosmic pessimism when he remarked, in April 1964, *Nous sommes des animaux sinistrés* (struck with disaster), *l'univers reste noir*. In the same way, areas that suffer severe flooding, drought, etc., may be declared *des zones sinistrées* and receive assistance from public funds under favourable terms and accelerated procedures. See also SINISTRE in III.

solution, n.f. – no difference with the English in phrases such as Couve de Murville's famous *Pour chaque solution, nous avons un problème*, but note *une solution de continuité*, a gap, as in Le Clézio's comment in *Le Monde*, 22 January 1982: *Chez Sartre, il n'y a pas de solution de continuité entre le romancier, le dramaturge et le philosophe*, In Sartre there is no gap between the novelist, the playwright and the philosopher.

sommaire, n.m., adj. – as a noun, not a summary (*un résumé*) but a list of contents as of a book. As an adjective, note its frequent use meaning perfunctory, unthinking: *en 1974 Giscard d'Estaing ne reprend pas à son compte les campagnes anticommunistes sommaires, auxquelles les Gaullistes de l'UDR ont recours* (Serge Sur, *La Vie politique en France sous la Ve République*, 1982, p. 477), in 1974 Giscard d'Estaing did not indulge in the unthinking anticommunist campaigns to which the Gaullists of the UDR had recourse.

speaker, n.m., **speakerine,** n.f. – radio, television announcer. Hi-Fi speakers are *des baffles*.

susceptible, adj. – not only touchy, *hypersensible*, but also capable of or likely to, as in *Emportez un livre susceptible de vous intéresser*.

sympathique, adj. – pleasant, agreeable (often shortened to *sympa* by French adolescents). *Encre sympathique*, invisible ink. Sympathetic, *compatissant*.

timing – perhaps one of the most difficult words to translate into French, both in a sporting and in a literary context. Even George Orwell's remark in his essay on Swift that 'good writing is very much a question of timing' has to be rendered by a paraphrase. *La capacité d'employer le mot juste au moment voulu* is one possibility, another is *manier l'à-propos à la perfection*. Boileau (1633–1711) was nevertheless talking about the same thing when he said that Malherbe (1555–1628) *D'un mot mis à sa place enseigna le pouvoir*, taught how powerful a correctly placed word could be.

'He timed his speech to perfection', *Il a admirablement choisi le moment et la durée de son discours.*

Top of the Pops – *le tube numéro un* is the record selling most copies at the moment. The actual programme is called *le hit parade* or occasionally, to placate the purists, *le palmarès de la chanson*. There is no term for Golden Oldie, Revived Forty-Five or Rave from the Grave, but the French did invent the term *la mode Rétro* – cult of the thirties (*les années trente*), forties, fifties, sixties, seventies, or any other decade (*une décennie* – see DÉCADE in II) which is currently being resurrected to the delight both of young and old. In a linguistic field that is as colourful as it is ephemeral, the latter are (or have been) charmingly referred to by the former as *des Son et Lumière, des croulants* (about to collapse), *rayon des Argus* (in the second-hand car list), *des PCA (pas cotés à l'Argus*, too old and decrepit to appear in the second-hand car list), *des PPH (passeront pas l'hiver*, won't survive winter) or even *PPN (passeront pas la nuit*, won't last till morning).

transmetteur, n.m. – not a (radio) transmitter (*un émetteur*) but a relay-station. A (radio) receiver is *un récepteur.*

truculent, adj. – earthy, realistic, as in *la prose truculente de Rabelais*, or *un personnage truculent*, a colourful character. In one of the episodes in Claire Brétecher's *Les Frustrés*, her left-wing intellectuals are gloomily sitting around lamenting the decline of *le sens de la fête* in modern life, and contrasting it with *la truculence* of Rubens's paintings. It turns out that they are having *une fête*, a party. *Truculent* also means fierce-looking, but a truculent character would be *quelqu'un d'agressif, de féroce*, or *un mauvais coucheur.*

usuels, n.m.p. – in a French public or university library (*une bibliothèque municipale ou universitaire*), the reference books, dictionaries, etc., which are available for consultation in the Reading Room. Open access (*rayons ouverts au public*) is rare in French libraries, one exception being the library of the *Centre Pompidou* in Paris.

utilités, n.f.p. – small parts in the theatre, as in *jouer les utilités*, to be a bit-part player. The word *figurant* is also used with this meaning. Note that a project can be *déclaré d'utilité publique*, thus authorizing the compulsory purchase of the necessary private land. Public utilities are *les services publics, les équipements* collectifs**, or sometimes *les viabilités* (see VIABLE in III).

verbe, n.m. – not just a verb but words in general. See *L'Evangile selon Saint Jean: Au commencement le Verbe était et le Verbe était avec Dieu et le Verbe était Dieu*. Cf. Henri Amouroux's remark in a broadcast on *Les Français sous l'Occupation: La guerre des radios sous l'occupation allemande a fourni une occasion* (see OPPORTUNITÉ in II) *unique à ceux qui savaient manier le verbe*. (Radio warfare during the German occupation provided a unique opportunity for anyone who could use language.)

vers, n.m. – although *une tragédie en vers* is a tragedy in verse, *un vers* is not a verse (*une strophe*) but a line of poetry. A verse in the Bible is *un verset*.

version, n.f. – one's own account of what happened, *votre version des événements*, but also a translation from a foreign language into your own (see also THÈME in IV). The first version of the EEC text for *un règlement (obligatoire dans tous ses éléments et directement applicable dans tout état membre)* – regulation – or *une directive (laisse à l'état membre le choix des moyens propres à atteindre le but défini)* – directive – could well be *la première rédaction*, or *l'avant-projet*. *A Bruxelles, la plupart des documents sont rédigés* (composed) *en français*. See also *un film en version originale**, with the original soundtrack, *sous-titré en francais*, with French subtitles. A dubbed film is *un film doublé*.

vulgarisation, haute, n.f. – although *vulgaire* has the same meaning as in English – in September 1958, at a meeting held to protest against the policy of *L'Algérie Française* and the return to power of General de Gaulle, Jean-Paul Sartre remarked *Je ne crois pas que de Gaulle approuve la torture. Il doit trouver cela vulgaire* – the attempt to make specialist findings understandable to the general public is considered quite respectable, and is called *la haute vulgarisation*. In a characteristic pun, however, the neo-Freudian structuralist Jacques Lacan (1901–81) referred to *la haute vulgarisation* as *la poubellication* (a blend of *la publication* and *la poubelle*, rubbish bin).

Selective Reading List

'FALSE FRIENDS'

In 1928, Maxime Kœssler and Jules Derocquigny published *Les Faux Amis ou Les Trahisons du vocabulaire anglais* (Vuibert). This work was the subject of two review articles, with supplementary lists, by Félix Boillot in the December 1928 and September 1929 issues of *French Quarterly*. These articles, with a full list, were subsequently incorporated by Boillot in his *Le Vrai Ami du traducteur anglais–français et français–anglais* (Presses Universitaires de France, 1930), a work that was followed in 1956 by the same author's *Le second Vrai Ami du traducteur* (Editions J. Oliven). A revised, augmented version of Kœssler's and Derocquigny's book was published in 1975 by Maxime Kœssler under the title *Les Faux Amis des vocabulaires anglais et américain* (Vuibert), and in 1981 there appeared an English-language equivalent, C.W.E. Kirk-Greene's *French False Friends* (Routledge & Kegan Paul).

Among other works devoted to the difficulties encountered in translating from French into English, mention should be made of J.G. Anderson, *Le Mot Juste, a dictionary of French and English homonyms*, revised by L.C. Harmer (Dent, 1938), and Frederick Fuller, *A Handbook for Translators (with special reference to International Conference Translation)* (Gerrards Cross: Smythe, 1973).

DICTIONARIES

As is mentioned in the Introduction, we have not attempted to give all the meanings of the words discussed, and readers wishing to discover other meanings will need to refer to a good dictionary. In recent years several excellent and (subject to the rapid changes taking place in the English and French languages) up-to-date dictionaries have appeared. Among the bilingual general dictionaries we particularly recommend:

Collins-Robert French–English English–French Dictionary (Société du Nouveau Littré, Collins) or *Harrap's New Shorter French and English Dictionary* (Harrap).

Obviously, it is often necessary to supplement use of a bilingual dictionary by consulting a monolingual French dictionary, and for general use we suggest:

Dictionnaire alphabétique et analogique de la langue française (Le Petit Robert) (Société du Nouveau Littré) or *Larousse de la langue française – Lexis* (Larousse).

Anyone interested in the contacts between the English and French languages should consult:

J. Rey-Debove and G. Gagnon, *Dictionnaire des anglicismes – les mots anglais et américains en français* (Robert).

For readers wishing to familiarize themselves with the registers of French and English slang, we recommend:

G.A. Marks and C.B. Johnson, *Harrap's Slang Dictionary: English–French/French–English*, revised and edited by Jane Pratt (Harrap, 1984), and R.J. Hérail and E.A. Lovatt, *Dictionary of Modern Colloquial French* (Routledge & Kegan Paul, 1984).

Readers with a special interest in administrative, commercial and legal French might need to consult more specialized dictionaries, and we should mention (in alphabetical order):

Camille, Claude and Dehaine, Michel, *Harrap's French and English Dictionary of Data Processing* (Harrap).

Chaudesaigues-Deysine, A.E. and Dreuilhe, A.E., *Dictionnaire anglais–français et lexique français–anglais des termes politiques, juridiques et économiques* (Flammarion).

Collin, Françoise, Pratt, Jane, Collin, Peter, *Harrap's French and English Business Dictionary* (Harrap).

Coveney, James and Moore, Sheila J., *Glossary of French and English Management Terms. Lexique de termes anglais de gestion* (Longman).

Doucet, Michel, *Dictionnaire juridique et économique: français–anglais, anglais–français* (La Maison du Dictionnaire).

Glomot, Sylvain and Salen, Henry, *Dictionnaire de la publicité et du marketing: anglais–français, français–anglais* (La Maison du Dictionnaire).

Quemner, Thomas A., *Dictionnaire juridique français–anglais: droit, finances, commerce, douanes, assurance, administration* (Editions de Navarre).

For all dictionaries the most recent edition is recommended.

CONTEMPORARY FRENCH SOCIETY AND INSTITUTIONS

Here, one has *l'embarras du choix,* and we can do no more than mention a few *recent* books that might serve as starting points for students of modern languages and non-specialist readers wishing to pursue major topics discussed in this book. Most of these works contain bibliographies that will permit in-depth study.

On France from the French Revolution to the beginning of the second half of the twentieth century:

Cahm, Eric, *Politics and Society in Contemporary France (1789–1970), a documentary history* (Harrap, 1972).

Zeldin, Theodore, *France, 1848–1945* (2 vols, Clarendon Press, 1973–7).

On Vichy and the Occupation:

Paxton, Robert O., *Vichy France: old guard and new order, 1940–1944* (Columbia University Press, 1982).

On post-war France:

Hanley, D.L., Kerr, A.P. and Waites, N.H., *Contemporary France: politics and society since 1945* (Routledge & Kegan Paul, 1979).

Hantrais, Linda, *Contemporary French Society* (Macmillan, 1982).

Wright, Vincent, *The Government and Politics of France* (Hutchinson, 1979).

On the French economy:

Holmes, Graeme M. and Fawcett, Peter D., *The Contemporary French Economy* (Macmillan, 1983).

On French intellectuals in the 1930s and 1940s:

Lottman, Herbert R., *The Left Bank: writers in Paris from Popular Front to Cold War* (Heinemann, 1982).

On Gaullism:

Charlot, Jean, *The Gaullist Phenomenon* (Allen & Unwin, 1971).

Touchard, Jean, *Le Gaullisme, 1940–1969* (Seuil, 1978).

On the French Left:

Johnson, R.W., *The Long March of the French Left* (Macmillan, 1981).

Touchard, Jean, *La Gauche en France depuis 1900* (Seuil, 1977).

On the French Right:

Rémond, René, *Les Droites en France* (Aubier Montaigne, 1982) (supersedes the same author's earlier *La Droite en France, de la Première Restauration à la Cinquième République*).

On French society and politics in the 1980s:
Ardagh, John, *France in the 1980s, the definitive book* (Penguin Books, 1982).

Pickles, Dorothy, *Problems of Contemporary French Politics* (Methuen, 1982).

Zeldin, Theodore, *The French* (Collins, 1983).

On the French 'élites':
Birnbaum, Pierre, *Les Sommets de l'Etat, essai sur l'élite du pouvoir en France* (Seuil, 1977).

Suleiman, Ezra N., *Politics, Power and Bureaucracy in France* (Princeton University Press, 1974).

Suleiman, Ezra N., *Elites in French Society: the politics of survival* (Princeton University Press, 1978).

On the influence of the media:
Debray, Régis, *Le Pouvoir intellectuel en France* (Editions Ramsay, 1979).

On French education:
Halls, W.D., *Education, Culture and Politics in Modern France* (Pergamon, 1976).

On the decentralization debate and local and regional government:
Gontcharoff, Georges and Milano, Serge, *La Décentralisation, nouveaux pouvoirs, nouveaux enjeux* (Syros, 1983).

Gourevitch, Alexis, *The Politics of Local Government Reform in France* (University of California Press, 1980).

Lagroye, Jacques and Wright, Vincent, *Local Government in Britain and France, problems and prospects* (Allen & Unwin, 1979).

Machin, Howard, *The Prefect in French Public Administration* (Croom Helm, 1977).

Peyrefitte, Alain, *Le Mal français* (Plon, 1976).

On French law, as it affects the average French citizen:
Berthoin, M.H. and Durand, H., *Vous et la Loi, guide pratique de vos droits et vos responsabilités* (Sélection du Reader's Digest, 1979).

Finally, the annual *Quid* (Robert Laffont) is a wide-ranging compilation of information concerning all things French.

Index of Head-Words